STUDY AND REVISE

AS/A2 Level

Sociology

Tables and data have been adapted from original data in *Social Trends* and other sources. Answers to AEB exam questions are purely the work of the author and carry no endorsement from the AEB. Every attempt has been made to contact copyright holders and gain permission prior to publication.

First published 2000
exclusively for WHSmith by

Hodder and Stoughton Educational
338 Euston Road
LONDON NW1 3BH

Text © David Abbott 2000

All rights reserved. No part of this publication may be reproduced or transmitted in any form or by any means, electronic or mechanical, including photocopying, recording or any information storage and retrieval system, without permission in writing from the publisher.

A CIP record for this book is available from the British Library

Text: David Abbott with Tony Buzan
Mind Maps: The Buzan Centres

ISBN 0-340-74332-8

```
        10 9 8 7 6 5
Year    2005  2004
```

Typeset by Wearset, Boldon, Tyne and Wear

Printed and bound in Great Britain for Hodder & Stoughton Educational by The Bath Press, Bath

CONTENTS

Revision for A Level success — v
by Tony Buzan

Revision made easy — viii

Chapter 1 Families and households — 1
- Definitions and theories of families and households — 1
- The family and industrialisation — 3
- How families and households are changing — 5
- Changes in gender roles and power relationships — 7
- Childhood and the social construction of age — 8

Chapter 2 Culture and identity — 11
- Definitions of culture and identity — 11
- Different theories of culture and identity — 12
- The production and consumption of culture — 13
- Youth subcultures — 15
- Class and culture — 16
- Gender, ethnicity and culture — 17

Chapter 3 Education and training — 21
- Sociological perspectives on education — 21
- Explaining differences in educational attainment — 24
- Explaining gender and ethnic differences in attainment — 26
- Education and training policies — 28

Chapter 4 Wealth, poverty and welfare — 31
- Sociological explanations of the distribution of wealth — 31
- Sociological explanations of poverty — 32
- Defining and measuring poverty — 34
- Welfare, poverty and social policy — 36
- Sociological explanations of the role of the welfare state — 37

Chapter 5 The mass media — 41
- Theories of the mass media — 41
- Ownership and control — 42
- The selection and presentation of media content — 44
- The influence of mass media — 45
- Media effects and violence — 47
- The representation of class, gender, ethnicity and age in the media — 48

Chapter 6 Work and leisure — 52
- Definitions and theories of work — 52
- Different theories of the management and organisation of work — 54
- Conflict and co-operation in the workplace — 55
- The effects of technical change on work satisfaction — 56
- Explanations of unemployment — 57
- The relationship between work and leisure — 58

Chapter 7 Power and politics — 61
- Definitions of power — 61
- Sociological theories of power — 62
- Politics and political systems — 63
- Power and the role of the state — 63
- Decision-making and the political process — 64
- Sociological explanations of voting behaviour — 66
- The influence of the mass media on politics and voting behaviour — 67

Chapter 8 Religion — 70
- Definitions and theories of religion — 70
- Religious organisations — 72
- Religion and social change — 73
- Explanations for the growth of new religious movements — 74
- The secularisation debate — 75

Chapter 9 World sociology — 79
- Definitions and theories of development and underdevelopment — 79
- Aid and strategies for development — 81
- Industrialisation and urbanisation in developing countries — 83
- Aspects of development — 84

Chapter 10 Crime and deviance — 88
- Defining crime and deviance — 88
- Explanations of crime and deviance — 89
- Official statistics and the measurement of crime — 91
- More recent theories of crime — 92
- Gender and crime — 92
- Ethnicity and crime — 93
- Social reactions to crime and deviance – the role of the mass media — 94

Chapter 11 Health — 97
- Definitions of health and illness — 97

Contents

	Theoretical approaches to health and illness	98
	Social differences in health	101
	Sociological explanations of health differences	101
	Healthcare services	102
	Mental health	103

Chapter 12 Stratification and differentiation 106
- Theories and definitions of stratification and differentiation 106
- How sociologists measure social class 108
- Gender, ethnicity, employment and lifechances 109
- Changes in the class structure 110
- Social mobility 113

Chapter 13 Theory and methods 116
- Key sociological perspectives 116
- The relationship between theory and methods 118
- Sources of data and research methods 118
- Practical and ethical issues and their influence on research 120
- Is sociology a science? 121
- Science, values and social policy 122

Solutions to crosswords and wordhunts 125

Index 127

Study and Revise for A Level success — INTRODUCTION

You are now in the most important educational stage of your life and are soon to take exams that may have a major impact on your future career and goals. As one A Level student put it: 'It's crunch time!'

At this crucial stage of your life, the thing you need even more than subject knowledge is the knowledge of **how** to remember, **how** to read faster, **how** to comprehend, **how** to study, **how** to take notes and **how** to organise your thoughts. You need to know how to **think**; you need a basic introduction on how to use that super computer inside your head – your brain.

The next few pages contain a goldmine of information on how you can achieve success, both at school and in your A Level exams, as well as in your professional or university career. These pages will give you information on memory, thinking skills, speed reading and study that will enable you to be successful in all your academic pursuits. You will learn:

1. How to remember more *while* you are learning.
2. How to remember more *after* you have finished a class or a study period.
3. How to use special techniques to improve your memory.
4. How to use a revolutionary note-taking technique called Mind Maps that will double your memory and help you to write essays and answer exam questions.
5. How to read everything faster, while at the same time improving comprehension and concentration.
6. How to zap your revision.

How to understand, improve and master your memory

Your memory really is like a muscle. Don't exercise it and it will grow weaker; do exercise it and it will grow incredibly more powerful. There are really only four main things you need to understand about your memory in order to increase its power dramatically:

1 Recall during learning – you must take breaks!

When you are studying, your memory can concentrate, understand and remember well for between 20 and 45 minutes at a time. Then it needs a break. If you carry on for longer than this without one, your memory starts to break down. If you study for hours non-stop, you will remember only a fraction of what you have been trying to learn and you will have wasted valuable revision time.

So, ideally, *study for less than an hour*, then take a five- to ten-minute break. During this break, listen to music, go for a walk, do some exercise or just daydream. (Daydreaming is a necessary brainpower booster – geniuses do it regularly.)

During the break your brain will be sorting out what it has been learning and you will go back to your study with the new information safely stored and organised in your memory banks.

Make sure you take breaks at regular intervals as you work through your *Study and Revise AS and A2 Level* book.

2 Recall after learning – surfing the waves of your memory

What do you think begins to happen to your memory straight after you have finished learning something? Does it immediately start forgetting? No! Your brain actually *increases* its power and carries on remembering. For a short time after your study session, your brain integrates the information making a more complete picture of everything it has just learnt. Only then does the rapid decline in memory begin, and as much as 80% of what you have learnt can be forgotten in a day.

However, if you catch the top of the wave of your memory, and briefly review back what you have been revising at the correct time, the memory is stamped in far more strongly and stays at the crest of the wave for much longer. To maximise your brain's power to remember, take a few minutes and use a Mind Map to review what you have learnt at the end of a day. Then review it at the end of a week, again at the end of a month and, finally, a week before the exams. That way you'll surf-ride your memory wave all the way to your exam, success, and beyond!

3 The memory principle of association

The muscle of your memory becomes stronger when it can **associate** – when it can link things together.

Think about your best friend and all the things your mind automatically links with that person. Think about your favourite hobby and all the associations your mind has when you think about (remember) that hobby.

When you are studying, use this memory principle to make associations between the elements in your subjects and to thus improve both your memory and your chances of success.

4 The memory principle of imagination

The muscle of your memory will improve significantly if you can produce big **images** in your mind. Rather than just memorising the name of an historical character, **imagine** that character as if you were a video producer filming that person's life.

In *all* your subjects, use the **imagination** memory principle.

Study and Revise for A level success

Your new success formula: Mind Maps®

You have noticed that when people go on holidays or travels they take maps. Why? To give them a general picture of where they are going, to help them locate places of special interest and importance, to help them find things more easily and to help them remember distances, locations and so on.

It is exactly the same with your mind and with study.

If you have a 'map of the territory' of what you have to learn, then everything is easier. In learning and study, the Mind Map is that special tool.

As well as helping you with all areas of study, the Mind Map actually *mirrors the way your brain works*. Your Mind Maps can be used for taking notes from your study books, taking notes in class, preparing your homework, presenting your homework, reviewing your tests, checking your and your friends' knowledge in any subject, and for *helping you understand anything you learn.*

As you will see, Mind Maps use, throughout, Imagination and Association. As such, they automatically strengthen your memory muscle every time you use them. Throughout this *Revise AS and A Level* book you will find Mind Maps that summarise the most important areas of the subject you are studying. Study them, add some colour, personalise them, and then have a go at drawing your own – you will remember them far better! Put them on your walls and in your files for a quick and easy review of the topic.

Using Mind Maps

Mind Maps are a versatile tool – use them for taking notes in class or from books, for solving problems, for brainstorming with friends, and for reviewing and revising for exams – their uses are infinite! You will find them invaluable for planning essays for coursework and exams. Number your main branches in the order in which you want to use them and off you go – the main headings for your essay are done *and* all your ideas are logically organised.

Super speed reading and study

What happens to your comprehension as your reading speed rises? 'It goes down.' Wrong! It seems incredible, but it has been proved that the faster you read, the more you comprehend and remember.

So here are some tips to help you to practise reading faster – you'll cover the ground much more quickly, remember more *and* have more time for revision and leisure activities.

How to make study easy for your brain

When you are going somewhere, is it easier to know beforehand where you are going, or not? Obviously it is easier if you do know. It is the same for your brain and a book. When you get a new book, there are seven things you can do to help your brain get to 'know the territory' faster.

1. Scan through the whole book in less than 20 minutes, as you would do if you were in a shop thinking whether or not to buy it. This gives your brain control.

2. Think about what you already know about the subject. You'll often find out it's a lot more than you thought. A good way of doing this is to draw a quick Mind Map on everything you know after you have skimmed through it.

How to draw a Mind Map

1. Start in the middle of the page with the paper turned sideways. This gives your brain more radiant freedom for its thoughts.

2. Always start by drawing a picture or symbol. Why? Because **a picture is worth a thousand words to your brain**. Try to use at least three colours, as colour helps your memory even more.

3. Let your thoughts flow, and write or draw your ideas on coloured branching lines connected to your central image. These key symbols and words are the headings for your topic.

4. Next, add facts and ideas by drawing more, smaller, branches on to the appropriate main branches, just like a tree.

5. Always print each word clearly on its line. Use only one word per line.

6. To link ideas and thoughts on different branches, use arrows, colours, underlining and boxes.

How to read a Mind Map

1. Begin in the centre, the focus of your topic.
2. The words/images attached to the centre are like chapter headings; read them next.
3. Always read out from the centre, in every direction (even on the left-hand side, where you will have to read from right to left; instead of the usual left to right).

Study and Revise for A level success

3. Ask who, what, why, where, when and how questions about what is in the book. Questions help your brain 'fish' the knowledge out.
4. Ask your friends what they know about the subject. This helps them review the knowledge in their own brains and helps your brain get new knowledge about what you are studying.
5. Have another quick speed through the book, this time looking for any diagrams, pictures and illustrations, and also at the beginnings and ends of chapters. Most information is contained in the beginnings and ends.
6. Build up a Mind Map as you study the book. This helps your brain organise and hold (remember) information as you study.
7. If you come across any difficult parts in your book, mark them and move on. Your brain *will* be able to solve the problems when you come back to them a little bit later, much like saving the difficult bits of a jigsaw puzzle for later. When you have finished the book, quickly review it one more time and then discuss it with friends. This will lodge it permanently in your memory banks.

Super speed reading

1. First read the whole text (whether it's a lengthy book or an exam paper) very quickly, to give your brain an overall idea of what's ahead and get it working. (It's like sending out a scout to look at the territory you have to cover – it's much easier when you know what to expect.) Then read the text again for more detailed information.
2. Have the text a reasonable distance away from your eyes. In this way your eye/brain system will be able to see more at a glance and will naturally begin to read faster.
3. Take in groups of words at a time. Rather than reading 'slowly and carefully', read faster, more enthusiastically. Your comprehension will rocket!
4. Take in phrases rather than single words while you read.
5. Use a guide. Your eyes are designed to follow movement, so a thin pencil underneath the lines you are reading, moved smoothly along, will 'pull' your eyes to faster speeds.

Helpful hints for exam revision

To avoid exam panic, cram at the start of your course, not the end. It takes the same amount of time, so you may as well use it where it is best placed!

Use Mind Maps throughout your course and build a Master Mind Map for each subject – a giant Mind Map that summarises everything you know about the subject.

Use memory techniques, such as mnemonics (verses or systems for remembering things like dates and events or lists).

Get together with one or two friends to revise, compare Mind Maps and discuss topics.

And finally...

- *Have fun while you learn* – studies show that those people who enjoy what they are doing understand and remember it more and generally do better.
- *Use your teachers* as resource centres. Ask them for help with specific topics and with more general advice on how you can improve your all-round performance.
- *Personalise your* **Study and Revise AS and A2 Level** *book* by underlining and highlighting, by adding notes and pictures. Allow your brain to have a conversation with it!

Your amazing brain and its amazing cells

Your brain is like a super computer. The world's best computers have only a few thousand or hundred thousand computer chips. Your brain has 'computer chips' too; they are called brain cells. Unlike the computer, you do not have only a few thousand computer chips – the number of brain cells in your head is a *million million*! This means you are a genius just waiting to discover yourself! All you have to do is learn how to get those brain cells working together, and you'll not only become more smart, you'll have more free time to pursue your other fun activities.

The more you understand your amazing brain, the more it will repay and amaze you!

Study and Revise AS and A2 Level Sociology

Revision made easy

This book is not intended to replace your textbooks, which will contain much more detail and information than is possible in a book of this size and nature. As exams approach however, the very bulk of your textbook, which was perhaps once a comfort, may become more intimidating as you realise how much there is to learn. The aim of this book is to enable you to identify and evaluate the key concepts and theories used in AS/A Level Sociology and provide you with a brief overview which will enable you to structure your revision effectively.

The structure and ideas behind this book

It is recommended that you read Tony Buzan's introduction very carefully, as this will give you a good understanding of how mind mapping can help you revise, and it will also enable you to put his techniques into practice as you work through the book during your revision programme.

Study and Revise AS and A2 Level Sociology focuses on the key concepts and ideas needed for success at AS/A Level. It also shows how you can apply your knowledge, how concepts and findings can be interpreted, and how to evaluate sociological theories so as to be able to construct a sound argument. Using Tony Buzan's Mind Map's, which are based on sound psychological research into the way our brain and memory function, *Study and Revise AS and A2 Level Sociology* will enable you to:

- improve your understanding of key concepts
- see the connections between the different topics on your syllabus
- make your revision more active, and therefore more effective.

All of this will make your revision more successful and more fun!

There are several points which you need to be aware of before commencing your revision:

1. There are three key sections in AS Sociology: Families and Households, Education, and Sociological Methods. However, there may be slight variations depending on which Examining Board's syllabus you are using, or which options your teacher has prepared you for. For the A2 examination there are further options, but you will find all the topics are covered by this guide.

2. Clearly you will want to concentrate on the topics you have learnt with your teacher and are preparing for the exams. Do note, however, that Theory and Method is a key topic and the concepts and theories involved should be applied to all the topics you study. Equally, Stratification and Differentiation is a key topic with relevance throughout sociology syllabuses. Culture and Identity is another topic which should be applied across the subject. Your teacher will give you guidance on the key concepts and theories which you need to be aware of in these important topics.

3. AS/A2 Sociology is not just about memorising key facts, concepts and studies. The examiners will be concerned to see you demonstrate your understanding and your ability to apply sociological concepts and findings, rather than just show that you have learnt by heart a mass of material. Since sociology is, above all, characterised by debate and competing theories, it is important for you to demonstrate your ability to evaluate competing theories.

Starting your revision

As Tony Buzan implies, it is important not to leave your revision until the very end of your course. You are much better advised to try and integrate your revision into your regular homework timetable. Short revision sessions can easily be added into a regular homework routine, or you can even use some of your otherwise 'dead' travelling time. Mind mapping allows you to condense the material you need to remember, and so you can make effective use of even short periods of time.

You will need to ensure that you spend your study time wisely. For sociology that must involve reading your class notes and your textbook *selectively*, and ensuring that you develop your understanding of the main concepts and theories. You also need to become familiar with the sort of questions which you will face in the exam. Your teacher may provide you with past papers, but if this is not possible, contact your exam board yourself and obtain copies. Whilst there are some changes being made to the syllabuses with the introduction of the AS/A2 system, the exams will continue to use data response questions and longer essay questions. This guide provides many examples of both types of question, as well as answers to the data response questions and sample essays. Answers to the data response questions will enable you to check your ability to interpret data. The sample and outline essays will provide you with a guide as to how to structure longer answers, as well as give you an indication of the sort of material which can be included.

The main points Tony Buzan makes, and the implications for revising, can be briefly summarised as follows:

Revision made easy

1. Our brains work most effectively when we harness their ability to associate. Therefore, use as many senses as possible to make the material you are working on both interesting and relevant to other things, e.g. use colour, mnemonics, and images.

2. Short, sharp and focused learning sessions are more effective than long, unfocused sessions, since the optimum concentration span is between 20 and 45 minutes. Equally, since your memory of learnt material will quickly fade if you do not use it, make sure that you review regularly.

3. Mind Maps allow you to apply these principles to your revision. A Mind Map will enable you to summarise material briefly and memorably in a way which reflects your own understanding of the material you have learnt – so you can personalise your learning. It will also help you to fit your learning into bite size chunks and, thus, you should be able to use your time much more effectively.

4. Mind mapping applies particularly well to sociology, since it provides an effective way of showing that all the topics studied are interrelated. It can, thus, aid and improve your understanding. For instance, we cannot really gain a full understanding of education unless we know something about stratification, sociological theory, and research methods. Mind mapping will enable you to draw out these connections.

Using this book

Each chapter starts with a data response item. These questions test your interpretation skills, but they also raise important theoretical and empirical points about the topic concerned. Key theories and concepts are reviewed and explained, and critical and evaluative points have been highlighted using the **Checklist** feature. **Factfiles** include key data which you can use in evaluating theoretical debates, or reiterate key conceptual, theoretical, or methodological points. Each chapter ends with a **sample question** and **answer**, and the answers provided are either in full or are brief outlines of suggested arguments and material. Sample answers should not be seen as 'model' answers in the sense that they represent a correct, or the best, or the only possible answer to a question. The answers aim only to demonstrate the skills which need to be shown in a good answer. Since sociology is a subject where there are always opposing arguments, it would be quite possible to find two (or even more) entirely different answers to the same question, which would both be deserving of an A grade! The sample answers and answer advice given in this book are entirely the work of the author and are intended solely as examples. They should not be interpreted as 'correct solutions', and all questions could be answered adequately or very well, in many different ways. Answers and advice are the responsibilty of the author and have not been endorsed by any examining board.

You should be able to read through a chapter of this guide in about an hour, and this could form a basic element of your revision programme. You will, however, also need to spend time examining past papers, completing practice answers, planning exam answers, and reading through your notes and handouts. You will also, of course, spend time drawing Mind Maps in order to help you organise and remember all the necessary material.

Lastly, remember that Mind Maps can be used in various ways:

- to make essay plans
- to highlight particular parts of topics
- to show relationships between different topics or theories
- to summarise whole topics, theories, or even the whole subject.

Families and households — CHAPTER 1

PREVIEW

You need to know:
- definitions and theories of families and households
- industrialisation and the family
- how families and households are changing
- changes in gender roles and power relationships
- the family and social policy.

Definitions and theories of families and households

Definitions

The family

American researcher George Murdock provided the following definition of the family:

> The family is a social group characterised by common residence, economic co-operation and reproduction. It includes adults of both sexes, at least two of whom maintain a socially approved sexual relationship, and one or more children, own or adopted, of the sexually cohabiting adults.

While Murdock was aware of the range of living arrangements which exist, he saw the nuclear family as a basic unit and claimed that this unit was universal (existed everywhere). Other sociologists prefer to use simpler definitions of the family, and would draw attention to several key family forms:

- **The nuclear family** – consists of no more than two generations (parents and children).
- **The extended family** – consists of more than two generations. They may live in the same household; this is referred to as the classic extended family. Litwak refers to the modified extended family; the members of our extended family whom we may see and keep in touch with periodically, but who live in different households.
- **The reconstituted family** – the reconstituted family is formed by adults who have been married previously and who bring children from their previous marriage to a new marriage, forming a new family unit.

The household

Sociologists frequently refer to the household rather than the family, and use it as a unit of study. A household is simply a group of people who live in the same house and share living accommodation or eat meals together. While most families live in

TEST YOURSELF

Households by size

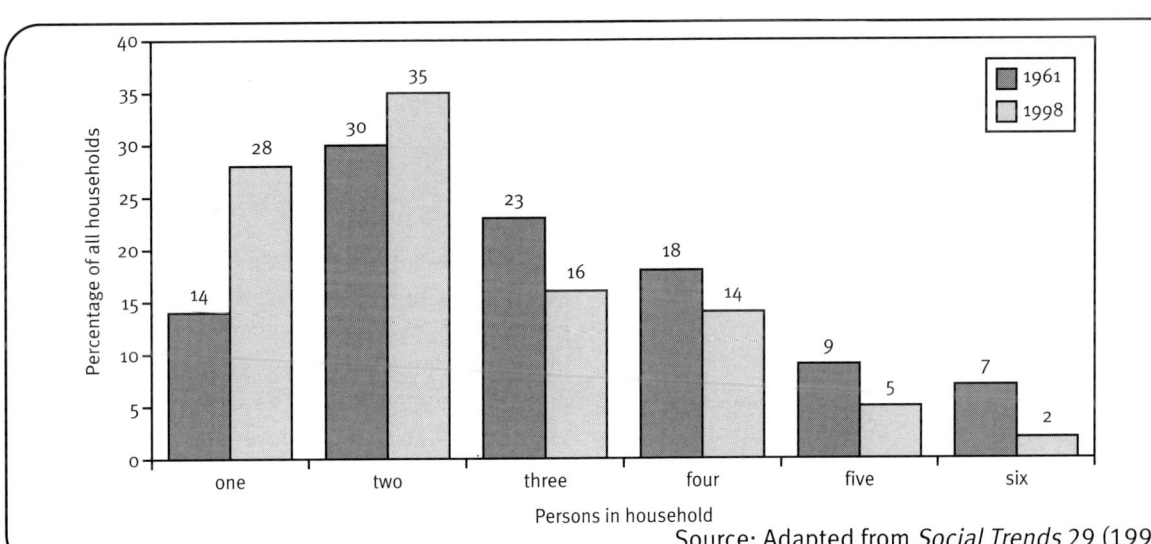

Source: Adapted from *Social Trends* 29 (1999)

1. Describe the trend in household size between 1961 and 1998 from the data in the graph above.
2. What percentage of households in 1998 consist of between three and four people?
3. What conclusions may be drawn about the nature of the typical family in Britain in 1998 from this data?

Study and Revise AS and A2 Level Sociology

Families and households

> **Answers**
>
> 1 The data in the table shows that there has been a significant rise in the number of one- and two-person households, and the numbers of households with more than two people has decreased. This could be interpreted as evidence for an increasing tendency to live in nuclear families, but conclusions should not be too hasty, since one- or two-person households are not nuclear families, though they may have been previously, or may become so in time.
> 2 30% (16+14)
> 3 No conclusions may be drawn about the nature of the typical family, since this data reflects the compositions of *households*. Sociologists and social researchers frequently use the household as a unit of measurement, due to the difficulties in defining the family, and because frequently it is more relevant to the questions they are investigating.

households, not all households correspond to a family unit. Distinguishing between families and households enables sociologists to acknowledge the fact that many nuclear families have relations with a wider set of extended family members.

Is the family universal?

George Murdock argued that the nuclear family was a universal social institution. There are several objections to this view.

- Cross-cultural evidence suggests that alternatives to the nuclear family certainly exist, or have existed.
- There is other evidence of family diversity, e.g. Kibbutzim (Israeli communes), ethnic diversity of family types within the UK, and increasing numbers of single parent families.
- What counts as a family varies in different societies and at different times in history. What is meant by the term 'family' is, therefore, not universal (the same), all the time, and in all places.

Theories of the family

Functionalism

Functionalist sociologists see the nuclear family as a functional necessity in modern society. The nuclear family carries out essential functions for society, and the decline of the nuclear family would have dysfunctional consequences for the social system.

George Murdock argued that the family carries out universal functions for society; these are functions which must be carried out in all societies. Murdock refers to sexual and reproductive functions, economic functions, and the educative role of the family.

In terms of sexuality and reproduction, Murdock sees the family as a regulatory mechanism. The family provides an institution which is able to stabilise sexual desire and permit reproduction within a protective and beneficial environment. The family also provides a basic economic support system, as well as a means of educating, or socialising the young, into a set of shared norms and values.

Talcott Parsons' view of the family complements that of Murdock. Parsons places particular emphasis on what he sees as the two key roles of the nuclear family; the stabilisation of adult personalities, and the primary socialisation of children. Parsons argues that the family performs a vital role in providing a refuge from the outside world for adults. In the family, adults are able to gain unconditional love and to escape from the constraints and stresses of their public roles, e.g. those encountered in the workplace. By doing this, the family may function as a 'safety-valve', harmlessly releasing frustrations generated in the workplace.

Parsons claims that the family also provides the essential foundation of primary socialisation through which children learn the shared norms and values of their culture. Indeed, the culture is 'internalised' and becomes an integral part of personality, structuring the personality of the child.

Parsons argues that the nuclear family best fits the needs of modern industrial society. This is because the nuclear family enables people to be geographically and socially mobile, allowing individuals to move around and find the job which best suits their abilities, and allowing employers to recruit from a national labour market. Parsons sees the nuclear family as supporting a meritocratic society.

Marxism

Marx's colleague, Friedrich Engels, argued that the family came into existence with the invention of private property. Engels argues that, prior to the invention of private property, people existed in what he termed a 'promiscuous horde', and the parentage of an individual could be uncertain. If a system of private property and the inheritance of property was to work effectively, some way of guaranteeing the parentage of individuals had to be devised. Engels suggests that the family and marriage were the solutions to this problem.

Marxist views of the role of the family concentrate on the part which it plays in reproducing capitalist society. The family is seen primarily as a means of social control. Marxist views emphasise the way that the family can be seen as an institution which carries out important functions for capitalism, such as reproducing labour power, and producing ideological justifications for capitalism.

Zaretsky argues that families, and particularly women, provide the domestic labour necessary for capitalist society to be maintained. Without a mass of women working to maintain families, through cleaning, cooking, and so on, capitalist society would need to find some other way of maintaining a workforce. The family reproduces labour power.

Zaretsky also claims that the family has become a unit of consumption. Adults use their earnings to buy more than just the necessities of life, and indeed work extra hours in order to be able to buy more goods for their families. This can be seen as a form of social control, since workers are locked into a system whereby they feel obliged to work hard and for long hours in order to provide the non-essential, luxury goods which come to be regarded as essential in capitalist society. This helps reproduce capitalist society.

Whereas functionalists see the family as socialising the young into shared norms and values, Marxists may argue that the family can be a very authoritarian institution which indoctrinates the young into an acceptance of capitalist ideology. The young learn how to accept authority and hierarchy, rather than how to challenge it.

Feminism

There are three main versions of feminist thought; liberal, radical, and Marxist feminism. All varieties of feminist thought have made an important contribution to sociological understanding of the family, and have offered an alternative to 'malestream' perspectives on the family.

Feminists have argued that patriarchy is a key concept for a full understanding of the role of the family. The concept of patriarchy refers to male dominance. Feminists argue that the family reinforces patriarchy and oppresses women. The family primarily serves the needs of men.

Delphy and Leonard claim that, while men may help with household tasks, they rarely take responsibility for housework and childcare, seeing these tasks as the responsibility of their wives. Women's key role is seen to lie in looking after the household and supporting their husbands.

Marxist-Feminists, such as Ansley, have revised the functionalist view that the family fulfils the role of a safety valve, dissolving men's tensions and frustrations. Ansley agrees that this is exactly what the family does, but argues that it is women who have to absorb their partners' frustrations. Other feminists have demonstrated how this may even involve domestic violence.

Interactionist views

Marxism and Functionalism are structural theories, and many feminists are also influenced by structural theories. However, interactionist theories can also be applied to the study of the family, providing a contrasting view which takes more account of the meanings which individuals attach to the family, and the actions they may take to create their own family relationships.

Interactionist theory reminds us that roles are negotiated and that many social institutions, which we take for granted, are socially constructed. Backett has studied the ways in which the role of parent is socially constructed and learnt through an examination of parents' relationship with their children.

David Clark has developed a typology of marriage relationships, identifying several key types of marriage. 'Drifting marriage' refers to couples who have not made long-term plans, 'surfacing marriages', refer to couples containing at least one person who was married previously, and 'established marriages' refers to couples who have planned out a future to some extent.

Critical views and the radical psychiatrists

Another set of views that focus on the interactions within families, comes from a mixed group of academics who offer some insights into the darker side of family life. Psychiatrist Ronald Laing, writing in the 1960s, argued that schizophrenia could be seen as at least partly caused by poor relationships between family members. Laing claimed that, in some families, a process which can be broadly compared to negative labelling and scapegoating, could produce a schizophrenic identity. Psychiatrist David Cooper points out that family relationships can be suffocating and can constrain individual personal development. Other researchers have, in recent years, directed the attention of sociologists to the existence of physical, mental, and sexual abuse in families.

Families and households

CHECKLIST

The theoretical perspectives on the family all have to be used critically. The following are some of the key points which should be noted:

- ✓ Both Marxist and Functionalist analyses tend to assume that the nuclear family is the dominant form of family structure, and thus neglect diversity. They also tend to assume that the family does fulfil the functions that each theory attributes to it.
- ✓ Marxist approaches are often criticised for explaining the family solely in terms of its economic functions for society. Marxism is, thus, said to be economically reductionist.
- ✓ Functionalism tends to give a highly optimistic view of the family, and neglects conflict within the family and the dysfunctional aspects of the family.
- ✓ Both structural approaches to the family tend to be deterministic, and this can make analysis of the family based on these theories rather inaccurate and over-generalised. Feminists, the radical psychiatrists and interactionists have been helpful in rectifying these weaknesses. Postmodernism has helpfully emphasised diversity, although it can be argued that, in rejecting the possibility of generalising, it becomes contradictory and untenable as a general sociological theory.

Postmodernist views

Postmodernist theory suggests that we live in a society where culture, identity, and lifestyle are less fixed and much more open to choice. For some sociologists this means that we must revise our view of the family. The family is now a matter of lifestyle and choice. For these sociologists, the family is not universal, and we should discard concepts which claim that one family form is universal. Such thinking reflects modernist attempts to give preference to a certain form of family, usually the nuclear family.

Sociologists should acknowledge the diversity of family forms, and examine the family more as a process than as a structure. David Morgan has argued, such is the diversity and fluidity of family forms, that it would be more helpful for sociologists to replace the concept of the family with the term 'family practices'.

The family and industrialisation

Industrialisation and the family

There has been a longstanding debate as to the relationship between industrialisation and the nuclear family. There are two sides to this debate:

1. Functionalists argue that it was industrialisation which led to the creation of the nuclear family, and that the nuclear family best fits the needs of industrial society.

2. Other researchers argue that the nuclear family was common before industrialisation, and that it was the nuclear family which caused industrialisation, not the other way around.

Structural differentiation of the family

Families and households

Industrialisation created the nuclear family

Young and Willmott claim that:

- The pre-industrial family worked as a unit of production, with all family members co-operatively working together to earn a living. Many households would have consisted of extended families.
- Industrial society saw the separation of home and work, the exclusion of women and children from the workplace, and the creation of the male breadwinner.
- The family became a unit of consumption, centred around the nuclear family. Relations with the extended family declined, and it became more common for family members to live further apart and see each other less frequently.

Talcott Parsons argued that modern industrial society requires:

- a geographically mobile workforce
- a meritocracy – the best jobs must go to those best qualified to do them.

This also means that industrial society requires nuclear families, since it is this family form which is best able to meet these two requirements. This is because a nuclear family can move around according to where work is (geographically mobile), and fits better with the idea of meritocracy, since people from a nuclear family background are less restricted by family ties.

The nuclear family was not created by industrialisation

Social historian Peter Laslett argues that:

- The nuclear family was common before industrialisation.
- According to his research on family size (using parish records), only 10% of families lived in groups larger than the nuclear family before the Industrial Revolution.
- It was, therefore, the existence of the nuclear family which enabled industrialisation to occur.

Historian Michael Anderson produces another view, arguing that his research on Preston in the mid-nineteenth century indicates that extended families were actually more typical in industrialising society than they had been previously. Anderson argues that it was the extended family which best fitted the needs of industrialising society, offering a network of support for those moving into the industrialising towns and seeking work.

How families and households are changing

Is there a typical family?

There has been some disagreement between sociologists as to whether there is any one form of the family which can be seen as typical.

Robert Chester has been a strong supporter of the idea that the nuclear family, or what he terms the neo-conventional family, is the typical family form. Chester sees the typical family as consisting of a married couple and their children. Males are still the key breadwinner, although Chester concedes that increasingly women work too. However, Chester argues that most women work part-time, and their work is seen as secondary to their key role in the family. Chester concludes that, since most adults marry and have children, it is safe to conclude that the typical family is the neo-conventional family.

Other sociologists have been less convinced. It can be pointed out that in 1998 only 23% of households consisted of a couple and their dependent children. Whilst it may be right that the neo-conventional family is common, other sociologists prefer to emphasise the complexity and diversity of family and household structures. This is particularly important because the neo-conventional or nuclear family can be used ideologically, held up as a role model to which all should aspire, and against which alternative living arrangements are negatively compared or defined as deviant.

Class and diversity

Eversley and Bonnerjea's study of family structure identifies the way in which family structure varies in different regions, and this in turn can be linked to class. Eversley and Bonnerjea claim to correlate different family structures with six different geographical areas, including the prosperous south and south-east, and inner cities. Family structure in the south and south-east for instance is argued to contain a high proportion of two-parent families with dependent children, while inner city areas are associated with higher rates of social deprivation, and larger proportions of single-parent families, young single people, and ethnic minorities. Other class differences in family and household structure include average age at marriage and the pattern of conjugal roles.

Single-parent families

Single-parent families and households are an increasingly important social phenomenon. In 1998 single-parent households comprised 7% of all households, but more importantly perhaps, they represented 20% of all households *with dependent children*. The British Household Panel Survey (sponsored by the government) found that between 1991 and 1997 around 12% of single parents remarried or formed a new partnership each year. Thus, there is a steady rate of new families or reconstituted families being formed. In 1996, 42% of all marriages were remarriages.

Government statistics in 1998 showed that 35.8% of births occurred out of wedlock, and that between 1993 and 1996 the proportion of cohabiting couples living together at the time their child was born had fallen from 75% to 58%. Martyn Denscombe has argued that this may reflect a radical shift in attitudes towards the traditional family, with an increasing number of parents purposely choosing the option of bringing up their child alone.

Ethnicity and diversity

Family and household structures amongst ethnic minorities reflect another aspect of diversity, with non-white ethnic minority groups constituting some 6% of the UK population according to the 1991 Census. Westwood and Bhachu claim that extended family structures are common amongst Sikh and East African Asians, with some 21% of households consisting of extended families.

As Westwood and Bhachu point out however, this is not a majority, and the trend amongst these groups is towards nuclear families. 'Asian' households tend to be larger than in other ethnic groups, and family kinship networks play an important role. Ballard has argued that amongst South Asian families there is a tendency to preserve traditions, and this includes distinctive gender roles for husband and wife. Care should be taken not to stereotype non-white ethnic minority families as inevitably consisting of extended family networks.

FACTFILE

- **The average household now consists of 2.4 people. The average household size has, therefore, decreased since the beginning of the twentieth century, when the average household consisted of around four people.**
- ***Social Trends* in 1997 reported that over a quarter of households were one-person households and that this could be expected to increase in forthcoming years.**

Divorce trends and explanations of divorce

In 1994, the UK had the highest divorce rate in the European Union, and approximately 40% of current marriages will end in divorce. Sociologists identify several key factors which may influence the divorce rate:

- Changes in the law have changed the grounds for divorce, and have provided the financial aid needed to pay legal costs.
- People may have increased (and perhaps unrealistic) expectations of marriage.
- Women are increasingly independent, and changes in their social status and position make divorce a viable proposition.
- There have been big changes in social values – in an increasingly secular (non-religious) society there is less stigma attached to divorce.
- Demographic changes have also played a part in change – people are living longer and spending more time together as partners in marriage, and having fewer children than previous generations. This may mean that marriages are put under more stress as couples are together longer, and having less children means that women can be free of childcare duties relatively early in life.

Using theories to explain divorce

The factors listed above may only offer a partial explanation of why divorce rates have increased; some of the factors simply show that people have more opportunity to divorce. In order to provide a more complete explanation, theoretical perspectives can be applied. The following are just two examples.

Giddens

Giddens's comments on marriage and family life (see below) suggest that divorce may be explained in terms of women's dissatisfaction with marriage and a desire for more equal relationships. It may also reflect men and women's search for the 'pure relationship' – that is a relationship based purely on personal satisfaction rather than on economic needs.

Marxism and Marxist-Feminism

Marxists and Marxist-Feminists, such as Nicky Hart, explain the increase by pointing to women's contradictory situation due to capitalism. Women are expected to care for the family as well as seek paid employment. The strains which result from this double burden may lead to conflict between partners. Functionalists could also provide a similar explanation, though they would use the concept of 'role conflict'.

It is also important to note that increased divorce rates can be interpreted in different ways. As Giddens points out, some have argued that higher divorce rates mean that the family is in decline. An alternative view is that, since many people remarry, people now have much higher expectations of marriage, and that, if they do not succeed at first, they are keen to try again with a new partner.

> **FACTFILE**
> - Ken Plummer (1997) reports that in the late 1990s sociologists and researchers have estimated that as many as 40% of marriages will end in divorce.

Changes in gender roles and power relationships

Sociologists have been interested in the social relationships within the family, and particularly in gender roles and power. One particular focus has been on conjugal roles – or the roles of the partners in marriage. These interests raise the issue of who benefits most from the family, but for sociologists they also raise difficult issues of how to study and measure power.

The conjugal roles debate

Two of the key studies in this area were those of Elizabeth Bott, and Young and Willmott. Bott identified two main forms of conjugal roles, segregated and joint. Segregated roles involved distinctive roles in the marriage and socially, whereas partners with a joint conjugal role were more likely to share roles and activities, both socially and in the marriage. Bott related this to the type of social networks in the community – close knit networks providing more structured and traditionally organised support for families and loose knit networks providing less support and forcing the partners to help each other.

Young and Willmott's research on family and kinship systems investigated the issue of whether there were trends towards increasing equality in marriage roles. In *The Symmetrical Family* (1975), Young and Willmott argued that conjugal roles had become more equal, with many families demonstrating joint conjugal roles, sharing leisure time, decision-making, and, they reported, some 72% of husbands in their sample (consisting of 1928 respondents) helping with housework at least once a week. However, these optimistic findings have been strongly criticised on methodological grounds by several researchers, and other research findings contradict those of Young and Willmott.

Oakley and Boulton are amongst those critical of the use of survey methodology on this issue. They point out that the questions used by researchers lack depth and do not provide a valid picture of conjugal roles. Oakley points out that helping once a week is hardly sufficient evidence (it is a weak indicator) on which to claim an equality of roles. Boulton agrees that surveys lack depth, and argues that a key issue is which partner is seen as having the main responsibility for certain household and childcare tasks.

Stephen Edgell presents the view that power and equality in conjugal relations can be measured more adequately by examining the process of decision-making. This approach suggests that the concept being studied – power in conjugal relations – can be operationalised in a different way to the previous studies which focused on household tasks. Edgell's study of middle-class families found that women did have power in the family, but it was in areas which were seen as less important. The power to make decisions about what were seen as the most important issues was monopolised by men.

Lydia Morris studied conjugal roles in families in the north-east of England. She was particularly interested to see if high rates of male unemployment led to changes in conjugal roles in the family, believing that men with no paid work might be willing to help with domestic work to relieve the tedium. On the contrary, Morris found men in the north-east unwilling to resort to what they saw as 'women's work'. Morris explained this as the result of a strong patriarchal and masculine ideology which rigidly segregated male and female roles.

Conclusions from this, and other research, require careful evaluation. While there is some evidence of changes in conjugal roles, many sociologists would urge caution before concluding that a state of equality has been reached.

Changing gender relations

On the changing nature of gender relations it is worth noting two recent studies.

Anthony Giddens – *The Transformation of Intimacy*

Giddens has recently argued that family life is becoming increasingly democratised. Giddens claims that there has been a transformation in family life. Nowadays, family life is less about tradition and living

Families and households

one's life as fate, and much more about achieving emotional satisfaction and personal development. He argues that women are now more independent and able to voice and act upon their demands for equality in marriage. This has created problems for men and contemporary notions of masculinity and the male role in marriage are having to be re-thought.

Duncombe and Marsden – *Emotion Work*

Jean Duncombe and Denis Marsden have examined family relationships in the light of American sociologist Arlie Hochschild's concept of emotion work. They argue that men are less capable of dealing with emotions and emotional issues, and that men, who leave these to their wives, avoid the emotional aspects of family life.

Whereas Ann Oakley wrote of women's double burden, referring to the need to have paid employment and be responsible for housework and childcare, Duncombe and Marsden suggest that women now have a triple burden. Not only are contemporary women holding down jobs and looking after their families, they are also having to do the 'emotion work' involved in running a family; listening to the problems of others, and providing emotional comfort and support to children and adults.

> **FACTFILE**
> - It is important to discuss the concepts of validity and operationalisation in questions on conjugal roles, gender and power.

Childhood and the social construction of age

Hockey and James provide examples of cross-cultural studies which demonstrate how childhood is constructed in other cultures. For the Hausa and Chisunga peoples in Africa, for instance, childhood ends when a child reaches puberty. This may vary between individuals, so childhood is not determined by age in years. In Britain by contrast, young people are classed as minors for most purposes until the age of 18, regardless of individual differences. From a similar perspective, the studies of anthropologist Margaret Mead demonstrated how some cultures in the pacific islands did not have taboos concerning children's sexuality as we do in western society.

Hockey and James argue that it was industrialisation which created our current notions of childhood. In contemporary culture, childhood is socially constructed in such a way as to make children dependent upon adults. Children and childhood are romanticised and idealised, and children's sexuality is denied.

Eisenstadt takes the view that the development of youth cultures in the years following the Second World War was a functional response to the prolonged period of education young people faced before gaining employment and full adult status. Youth cultures provided young people with a different status and role, and enabled the young and society generally to manage the transition to adulthood. In effect, this extended the period of youth, thus indicating the fact that age is socially constructed.

The family and social policy

Sociologist Janet Finch suggests that governments of all political parties encourage and promote the nuclear family as normal and natural, and as the best form of family. Veronica Beechey argues that social policies reflect a familial ideology, that is a set of beliefs which represent the nuclear family as the preferred norm. Social policies, therefore, reinforce and support the nuclear family.

The National Insurance scheme devised by Sir William Beveridge in 1943, aimed to provide financial aid and benefits to the old, the sick, and the unemployed. However, married women were not eligible for most benefits, and the Beveridge Plan was based around the assumption that the natural role for women would be to act as carers and mothers. This legislation, thus, had the effect of making married women financially dependent upon their husbands.

In 1993, the Child Support Agency (CSA) was established, with the aim of forcing absent fathers to provide for the maintenance of their children. Sociologists have observed that this legislation helps to reduce state expenditure on family benefit and income support. The legislation, therefore, reinforces the idea that the nuclear family is the ideal family form, as well as the idea that individuals should be dependent upon their family rather than the state.

The ability of gay and lesbian couples to be legally married, to adopt children, or in the case of lesbian couples, to receive artificial insemination has been limited. Gay and lesbian couples are not universally accepted as legitimate or as deserving of equal treatment.

> **FACTFILE**
> - Governments of all political parties have constructed social policies which tend to support and promote the nuclear family as the ideal family structure.

Families and households

Sample question and answer

Discuss the extent to which sociologists support the idea that the modern family is symmetrical. (Adapted from AEB, 1995).

Young and Willmott's research in the 1960s and 70s coined the term 'the symmetrical family' and since then, whilst much has changed in family and gender issues, the debate has continued. The media in recent years has provoked a great deal of speculation about gender and family issues, and it was the media which created the term 'new man'. Sociological studies enable these speculative ideas to be thoroughly tested.

In *The Symmetrical Family*, Young and Willmott published the results of their extensive research into family life in Greater London involving interviews with 1928 individuals. Young and Willmott argued that conjugal roles were becoming increasingly symmetrical. Although women still did most housework and childrearing and took responsibility for these tasks, more men were helping with housework, and husbands and wives were tending to share decision-making much more than previous studies had indicated. Young and Willmott found that 72% of men helped with housework (not including washing up) at least once a week. On this basis, Young and Willmott felt justified in arguing that the family was increasingly based on symmetrical conjugal roles, hence the title of their book. Young and Willmott (Y&W) do not imply that men and women do the same household tasks, but they do imply that a much greater degree of equality is entering into gender relationships in the family.

These findings have been subjected to considerable criticisms by numerous sociologists. Feminist Ann Oakley (author of *The Sociology of Housework*) argues that Y&W's methodology is unsatisfactory, since they appear to base their claim on one fixed response question, asking whether husbands helped with a household task at least once a week. This method provides no means for further probing and, thus, no way of gauging the regularity and quality of this extra 'help' (as it appeared to be). Oakley's criticisms point up the lack of validity which can be associated with questionnaire methodology. Mary Boulton has taken this criticism further and argued that the key issue which Y&W's methodology failed to explore was whose responsibility childcare and housework was seen to be. Boulton suggests that only qualitative methodology can provide a satisfactory picture of the nature of gender relations in the family, and argues that questionnaire methods will probably always over-estimate the amount of work that men do in the household and childcare.

Other criticisms have centred on the representativeness of Y&W's research since, despite their large sample, they concentrate on working-class families (the sample also had a slightly skewed age distribution). Oakley's own research on housework found marked differences between middle and working-class families, with the middle class appearing to have more equal conjugal roles than the working class, though still not to such an extent that they could be termed equal. Edgell's study also supports these findings, but a problem with both is that they are based on small samples. Two large-scale surveys based on more recent research, The British Social Attitudes Survey of 1991 and the survey completed by the Lancaster Regionalism Group in 1988, both show limited signs of greater sharing of housework. On this basis it seems that there has been no radical change in conjugal roles.

Yet further criticisms have come from those who suggest that much research in this area operationalises conjugal roles in a very limited and unimaginative way. Edgell suggests that a key issue to examine is decision-making in the family; however, again his results indicate that men take the most important decisions, e.g. (moving house or buying a car). Interestingly, women do have power in the home, but as feminists would point out, women's power is usually restricted to the private sphere; to the family and home.

In the 1970s, the results of this sort of research led Oakely to refer to women's double burden; not only did women have to be housewives and mothers, increasingly they also had to work in paid employment to supplement family income. Research in the 1990s by Duncombe and Marsden, also operationalises conjugal roles in a wider sense, and examines what they call emotion work. Not only are women holding down jobs and looking after their families, they are also the ones in the family who 'play the happy families game', working to keep husband and children happy and secure, through organising social activities, for example. Men in contrast, can be emotionally distant in the family.

Giddens in *The Transformation of Intimacy*, suggests that we are now living through an age of the democratisation of the family and witnessing a growth in the importance of the 'pure relationship'. Giddens claims that women are more insistent in their demands for equality, and men are being forced to adjust to considerable changes in their roles in the family and in society. Giddens's views, though, are not entirely supported by empirical research. As Lydia Morris's research in the early 1990s in north-east England showed, even high rates of employment did not lead men to change 'macho' attitudes and play a greater role in housework; that continued to be seen as 'women's work'.

In conclusion, it appears that however conjugal roles are operationalised for the purposes of empirical research, considerable inequalities and differences in roles seem to remain, despite some signs of change. Postmodernists argue that choice and diversity are now with us, but in the family it seems that this is not entirely true.

Families and households

TEST YOURSELF

Across
2 Common type of family (7)
6 Robert Chester uses this term to describe dual-career families (3,12)
9 Some argue that Young and Willmott's study lacks this (8)
11 Absent fathers have been critical of it (3)
12 Historian who studies families in Preston (8)
14 This sociologist believes that families are becoming more democratic (7)
15 According to Murdock the nuclear family is ... (9)
18 Female sociologist critical of Young and Willmott (6)
19 Live together, but may not be a family (9)
20 System of marriage with more than one partner (8)

Down
1 Radical psychiatrist critical of the family (5)
3 Historian who researched pre-industrial family (7)
4 This theory is critical of malestream theories (8)
5 One of the key functions of the family according to Parsons (13)
7 Duncombe and Marsden argue that men cannot do this sort of work (7, 4)
8 Sociologist who devised the concept of structural differentiation (7)
10 System of male dominance (10)
13 Israeli commune (7)
16 Family beyond two generations (8)
17 Feminist who discusses familial ideology (7)

Solution on page 125

Summary

1 Sociologists have not always agreed on how to define the family, and this has meant that they have reached different conclusions on issues such as whether there is a typical family and whether the family is universal. Many sociologists now distinguish between the family and the household in an attempt to avoid some of these problems of definition.

2 It can be argued that there is now a diversity of family forms in British society, although the nuclear family is still common. In answering questions about typicality, diversity and universality, students should refer frequently to concepts such as validity and representativeness, as well as discussing definitions of the family.

3 Issues such as conjugal roles and divorce can be seen in the context of changing gender relations and changing attitudes to sexuality in contemporary society. Again, students will do well to evaluate issues of empircal evidence with care. Central to questions on conjugal roles for example, are the concepts of validity, representativeness, and operationalisation. Equally though, divorce statistics may be interpreted in various ways, and students will be rewarded for demonstrating this.

4 Despite considerable social change and family diversity, social policies still reinforce the idea that a nuclear family is the best form of family. Social policy can be seen as a form of social control, providing a range of sanctions to promote the nuclear family and discourage dependency on the state.

Culture and identity — Chapter 2

PREVIEW

You need to know:
- definitions of culture and identity
- different theories of culture and identity
- the production and consumption of cultural products
- the relationship of culture to class, gender, age, and ethnicity.

TEST YOURSELF

Households in the UK with consumer durables, 1995–1996

Durable	Percentage of households
Colour television	97
Black and white television only	2
Telephone	93
Washing machine	90
Deep freezer	89
Video recorder	79
Microwave	70
Compact disc player	52
Tumble drier	51
Home computer	25
Dishwasher	20

Source: Adapted from *Social Trends* 27 (1997)

1. How many households contained a colour television in 1995–96?
2. How many households contained a home computer in 1995–96?
3. Does the data in the table provide any evidence that we now live in a consumer culture?

Answers

1. 97%
2. 25%
3. It would be very hard to reach any firm conclusions simply on the basis of this data. The data does demonstrate the very high levels of relative affluence in the UK, and to this extent it can be seen as giving some evidence that we now live in a consumer society. Postmodernist claims that structures such as class are fragmenting, and that cultural barriers are becoming blurred, are highly debatable, but at least this limited empirical data does give some indication of the sort of social changes which have occurred and which have influenced the postmodernist approach.

Definitions of culture and identity

What is culture?

Sociologists define culture in several ways:

- Culture can be seen simply as the way of life of a society. In this sense, culture refers to the norms and values of a society, or more broadly, the belief systems of a society. Within this definition, reference can also be made to the material culture, that is, the objects and artefacts (or products) used and created by a culture, such as guns, CD players, and cars.

- Another way of defining culture is to say that it refers to symbols and symbolic behaviour, such as language. However, symbolism is present in many aspects of social life, such as our clothes and jewellery for instance. Material culture may be used symbolically by members of society, e.g. to indicate status.

Also important to sociologists are cultural products such as the mass media, music, and even food. These cultural products vary in nature and form between different societies and different social groups, and may be used symbolically. The study of cultural products and symbols, the way they are used, and their relationship to identity has become an important area of sociological study in recent years.

What is identity?

Identity refers to the way we see our selves, or the sense of 'self' which develops throughout our life. Sociologists see the process of developing an identity as occurring within a culture. The process by which we learn the norms and values of our culture is termed socialisation. A person's identity, thus, reflects the culture in which they have been brought up.

Types of culture

In addition to the basic definitions of culture given above, sociologists may refer to a range of different types of culture.

High culture

High culture is the culture of elite groups within society. Discussion of high culture often focuses on particular cultural products and art forms, and the way that elite groups may use these to distinguish themselves from the lower classes.

Low culture

Low culture is the opposite of high culture, and refers to the culture of the lower social classes. Some

Culture and identity

sociologists prefer to use the term popular culture rather than low culture.

Popular culture

As indicated above, popular culture refers to cultural products and forms that have a wide-ranging appeal to the bulk of the population.

Mass culture

The idea of mass culture is related to the concept of mass society. Modern urban society is seen as producing a society where social differences are reduced, producing an undifferentiated culture. For many commentators, this also produces cultural norms and cultural products that are reduced to the lowest common factor, thus leading to a society which is morally decadent, and whose cultural products lack distinction and value. In a mass culture, cultural products are produced for a mass market. The terms low, popular and mass culture, thus refer to basically similar things, but indicate different approaches to them.

Folk culture

Folk culture refers to the way of life common in 'simple' societies, typically tribal societies or pre-industrial societies, where there are fewer social differences and society is based on tradition. Such societies are seen as being more integrated and homogeneous. Status is ascribed, and geographical and social mobility is more limited. This produces a culture that is seen by some sociologists as less impersonal, and more 'authentic' or more real.

Subcultures

Many sociologists argue that some social groups adapt the norms and values, and lifestyles of society to their own particular circumstances. Thus, while they share many of the norms and values of the wider (or host) society, subcultures also differ in significant ways. Subcultural groups may even make a point of highlighting their differences in order to signify their opposition to mainstream norms and values. Examples of subcultures would be criminal subcultures, pupil subcultures, occupational subcultural groups, as well as subcultures based on differences of age, ethnicity, gender, class, or religious belief.

> **FACTFILE**
> - Culture can be defined as a general 'way of life' consisting of the shared norms and values which bind a society together.
> - An alternative view of culture is to see it as a set of shared symbols which carry meanings and significance within particular cultures. In this sense, culture can be seen as rather like a code. Once we can understand the symbols (code), they reveal a great deal about the values and rules which govern behaviour in a particular society.

Different theories of culture and identity

There are a range of sociological approaches to culture and identity.

Sociobiology

Sociobiologists such as E.O. Wilson, argue that human behaviour is best explained in terms of evolutionary theory and biological functions, rather than culture.

Functionalism

Functionalists, such as Durkheim, saw culture as fulfilling an essential role for a society in creating a set of shared norms and values which integrated the society, creating the order and stability necessary for a successful society.

Both Durkheim and Parsons saw socialisation into culture as essential for a stable sense of identity. Durkheim however, did see identity in industrial society as becoming increasingly individualistic, a trend which he felt would have negative consequences since it would erode collective solidarity and break down social integration.

Functionalists see modern society as creating a mass culture, whereby all social groups basically share the same norms and values. Some functionalists have argued that subcultural groups may form in particular situations, broadly sharing the norms and values of the wider society, but adapting to the demands and needs of their own situation.

Marxism

Marxism refers, not to a common culture, but to a dominant culture. This is because Marxists believe capitalist society is best seen in terms of the

Culture and identity

base/superstructure model of society. Capitalist society is dominated by the ruling classes (the owners of capital) and ruling class ideology. Capitalist culture is, thus, a reflection of ruling class ideology. Self-identity in such a society is the result of indoctrination rather than socialisation.

Identity in capitalist society is determined in terms of one's class position. This dominates all conceptions of self-identity, and unsurprisingly, Marxist thought pessimistically characterises individual identity in capitalist society in terms of alienation.

Capitalism produces a mass culture, but it is enforced rather than shared. Mass culture encourages cultural production to become defined in terms of, and dominated by the need to make, profit. Culture becomes commodified. Subcultures may develop in capitalist mass culture, and they are usually representative of an attempt to reject the dominant ideology and dominant mass culture.

Social action theory

Social action or interpretive theories provide a contrast to structural theories such as Marxism and Functionalism. Culture is seen as something that is created by skilled social actors, and is the outcome of social process and negotiation. Identity is the result of interaction. It may thus be negotiated, or it may be the result of a labelling process. It is possible to have a stigmatised identity as a result of negative labelling. Through the processes of interaction, negotiation and labelling, certain social groups may form subcultures whose norms and values differ to some extent from those of the wider society

Feminism

There are a variety of feminist approaches, but all would see culture in contemporary society as a patriarchal culture. By this, feminists mean that the culture is one where men dominate in most areas of social life. The patriarchal nature of contemporary culture is seen as the key aspect of culture.

Feminists argue that identity in patriarchal society is gendered; thus the most important determinant of individual identity is gender, since how an individual is regarded, and the roles which are considered to be open to them, will largely depend on their gender.

Postmodernism

Postmodernists argue that contemporary society has undergone radical change, including cultural change. Culture in industrial capitalist society was a mass culture. This culture could be seen as reflecting the class structure or the institutional framework needed by industrial society, depending upon your perspective. Culture in contemporary society is fragmenting.

Since society is now increasingly affluent, consumption – how we spend our money – is now far more important than focusing on an individual's place in the production process (e.g. their position in the class or occupational structure).

Self-identity is much more fluid, and individuals can create their own identity through the purchasing of cultural products and choice of lifestyle. The differences between various cultural products and styles are now increasingly blurred. It is possible to pick and mix different styles and tastes, regardless of whether you are working or middle class, white or black, male or female, young or old. The boundaries between high and popular culture are also being blurred and are becoming increasingly irrelevant. In postmodern society, culture is fragmenting.

FACTFILE

- **Sociological theories do not agree about the role of culture in contemporary society.**
- **Sociological theories also have different views about what culture is; Marxists for instance see it as a form of social control or ideology, while functionalists see it as shared norms and values which integrate society. In this sense what culture is and what it does in a society is *contested*.**

The production and consumption of culture

In recent years, sociological debate has focused on the processes of cultural production, the ways in which culture is 'consumed', and the implications this has both for self-identity and for the nature of culture in contemporary society.

In this context, the term cultural production refers to the process of creating cultural objects and artefacts, and sociological study has tended to focus on products such as music, clothes, leisure (e.g. football), and men's toiletries, to mention just a few examples.

Cultural production

Marxist views

Marxists taking a political-economy approach argue that cultural artefacts (like all products in capitalist

Culture and identity

> **CHECKLIST**
>
> Many evaluative points can be made on the way sociological theories explain culture. However, a few key points can be identified as follows:
>
> ✓ The functionalist view that culture works as a sort of 'social glue', integrating members of society into shared norms and values, must be considered critically. Surely there are many examples within society where competing cultural values lead to conflict rather than consensus, e.g. religion?
>
> ✓ Marxist analyses of culture and identity can be criticised as economically reductionist and overly structural. The first point leads Marxists to assume that culture can always be explained in terms of economic functions, and the second refers to the tendency in Marxism to have a limited view of the power of human actors and their ability to think reflectively.
>
> ✓ Interactionist accounts of culture and identity have been criticised for being trivial and descriptive. It has been argued that they fail to explain precisely social phenomena because they neglect structural factors.
>
> ✓ Certainly, postmodernist accounts of culture and identity have been extremely fashionable in recent years. However, critics argue that they exaggerate the scale of social change and that cultural differences are not as blurred as postmodernists imply. Moreover, postmodernism can appear extremely voluntaristic – implying that individuals can adopt any identity they please seems to suggest that structural factors do not constrain behaviour (e.g. can everyone afford to buy the goods to reflect their desired identity?).

society) become seen purely as commodities to be bought and sold at the highest possible price. In the case of cultural products such as music, television programmes, films, theatrical productions, or other works of art, exactly the same rules apply. Moreover, the restricted ownership of the means of production of cultural goods means that, far from all members of the public getting the culture which they desire, capitalist owners produce what they believe the public wants.

Marxists can argue that this means cultural production is reduced to the lowest common factor, with the result that the sort of mass culture that is produced by these structures, is of low quality. This is the view taken by the Frankfurt School. Marxists, thus, take the view that cultural production in capitalist society is commodified, and is aimed at supplying a mass market. This produces a dehumanising mass culture.

In general terms, Marxist theory sees culture, not as something which individuals can create, but as something that is structurally determined. Many sociologists (including Marxists) would see this as a weakness. Other strands of thought in Marxism (influenced by Gramsci) would suggest that the production of culture does not simply reflect economic structures. The so-called culturalist view argues that culture and the cultural tastes of social groups may have some degree of autonomy from the economic base of society. The economic base of society does not determine every aspect of the superstructure.

Pluralist views

Pluralists argue that there will be many different social groups involved in cultural production, and the various cultural products they make will have to compete for a limited amount of attention from the public. The success or failure of various cultural products will generally reflect the real preferences and tastes of the public, since they will not consume products they dislike. Producers will keep trying out new products until they successfully satisfy public demands.

Postmodernist views

Postmodernists see cultural production as something that is aided mainly by the power of the mass media in contemporary society. The philosopher Jean Baudrillard, argues that we now live in a society which is media saturated. The media and the hyperreal images that it produces have become the key source of our culture.

Postmodernists argue that contemporary society is no longer organised on the basis of production (as Marxists would argue), but is organised instead on the basis of consumption. What is now important in cultural production is the symbolic value of cultural products.

Culture and identity

Cultural consumption

Sociologists explain the social significance of consumption in a variety of ways.

Veblen

The Norwegian-American sociologist Thorstein Veblen was one of the pioneers of the study of consumption. He coined the term 'conspicuous consumption' to describe the behaviour of subordinate social groups aiming to improve their status and social standing. Veblen's work, thus, demonstrated the importance of consumption and its relationship to status.

The Affluent Worker Study

Goldthorpe and Lockwood's seminal study of the British working class argued that the consumerism of the workers studied reflected a straightforward desire to lead as comfortable a lifestyle as possible. The authors rather pointedly argued that the workers did not see buying a washing machine as a form of social mobility, but merely as a way of having cleaner clothes with less effort. The study suggests that sociologists should make the same interpretation of the behaviour as the workers had.

Marxist views

Marxist thought provides several interpretations of the significance of consumption.

The Frankfurt School Marxists argue that capitalism and the consumerism that it promotes has negative effects. It produces a mass culture which promotes false needs and works as an ideology. Mass culture leads to 'commodity fetishism' — the craving to possess the cheap cultural products of capitalism — which is a false need and distorts human nature. Mass culture, thus, distracts attention from the true nature of capitalist society, and acts as a form of social control.

The individual identity produced by this consumerist, mass culture is one that is alienated from its true potential. Marcuse wrote of 'one-dimensional man', implying that identity in mass culture was lacking in depth. Marxists influenced by Gramsci argue that some forms of popular culture that the working classes consume (for instance pop music) can in fact provide the basis for a resistance to capitalism. The work of the Centre for Contemporary Cultural Studies (CCCS) at Birmingham University provides many examples of this sort of approach, arguing that youth subcultural styles, such as Mods and Skinheads, represented a working-class resistance to capitalism.

Postmodernist views

The differences between high and popular culture are now becoming blurred, and regardless of class, gender, or ethnic background, individuals will consume a variety of cultural products and mix different styles. This means that individual identity is now constructed from many influences and there is an endless plurality of cultures to choose from. Individuals are now able to create their own lifestyle through their consumption choices, and are unconstrained by structural factors (e.g. class). Saunders argues that consumption differences, e.g. home-ownership, are more important than position in the class structure.

Studies by Mort and Nixon suggest that cultural definitions of masculinity have become much more flexible, and that men are able to create their own masculine identity through the adoption of different styles of clothing and fashion accessories.

An increasing number of people may be disregarding what were previously boundaries between high and popular culture. Those who support the postmodernist view may cite as evidence the increasing popularity of opera (high culture), including its use to promote football (popular culture).

A criticism of postmodernism is that, as yet, postmodernists appear to have relatively little empirical data to support their position.

FACTFILE

- **Social Trends (1999) provides data on the percentages of the population attending various cultural events during 1996–97. 54% of the population attended a cinema, but only 24% went to a play, and 12% to a classical music concert. Only 7% went to ballet or the opera.**
- **Social Trends does not provide information on the class background of those attending the events, but it provides some evidence with which to evaluate postmodernist claims of the blurring of cultural boundaries. So, there may be some blurring of boundaries occurring, but arguably only on a very small scale at the present time.**

Youth subcultures

Sociological interest in youth subculture focuses on three main issues:

Culture and identity

1. the function which youth subcultures have in society
2. whether there is one youth culture which expresses the norms and values of all young people
3. how youth subcultures are changing.

Functionalist views

Functionalists such as Eisenstadt argue that youth cultures emerged in industrial society to help ease the transition to adult status. Industrialisation saw adolescent status continue for a longer period of time than in previous ages, as the time spent in education increased. This resulted in an ambiguous status for young people, leading to status frustration. Eisenstadt and other functionalists, such as Parsons, saw this as creating a common youth culture, shared by all young people, and providing a means of reducing status frustration.

Marxist views

A basic Marxist approach could see youth culture as yet another example of commodification. The development of youth cultures in Britain and the USA after the Second World War, reflected increasing affluence, and was a market which was heavily developed by capitalist industrialists and businessmen. Young people, both then and now, represent a highly lucrative market, since they have a relatively high disposable income.

In Britain the neo-Marxist approach of the CCCS has been highly influential. Members of the CCCS such as Clarke, Hebdige, Jefferson and Hall, conducted studies into working-class youth cultures and argued that they were best understood as forms of protest and resistance to the oppression of capitalist society.

Marxists though would be critical of the functionalist term 'youth culture'. They would argue that this assumes all youth have the same culture, and therefore neglects class differences.

Feminist views

Feminists, such as Angela McRobbie point out that the CCCS also had their own biases, and were blind to the important differences of gender. McRobbie argued that girls' teenage subculture is different to that of boys'. McRobbie refers to a 'bedroom culture', which provides girls with their own cultural space and identity.

McRobbie's work can be understood in the context of other feminist work which identifies the primary role of women in contemporary patriarchal culture in the private sphere, as well as earlier feminist work, such as that by Oakley, which demonstrates the differential socialisation experienced by girls.

Postmodernist views

Postmodernists argue that culture is fragmenting, and this view is applied to youth culture. Baudrillard argues that in postmodern culture images and styles are taken out of their original context and turned into commodities. This has the effect of stripping away the original meaning and intention lying behind the style or image, so that it becomes purely a fashion accessory.

Postmodern culture is, therefore, characterised by endless pastiche – a mixing of styles, as well as parody and irony, since none of the styles or images can be taken seriously. This reflects the postmodernist's view that truth is always relative.

Postmodernists would, thus, argue that there is no longer a definitive youth culture, but rather an endless plurality of cultures and styles, many of which simply use and mix elements of previous youth cultures. The sociologist Paul Willis adopts a position very similar to this in his book *Common Culture*.

Recent studies

Steve Redhead's 1993 research into rave culture gives some grounds for arguing that rave culture in the 1980s did become something of an oppositional culture. However, Redhead took the view that the culture was understood by the participants in so many different ways, that it could not be seen as a form of opposition.

Sarah Thornton's 1995 study, *Club Cultures*, applied the concept of cultural capital to clubbing and rave culture. Thornton found that clubbers did make distinctions between themselves and between various types of music and different clubs. The effect of these distinctions was to create a status hierarchy. This view would, therefore, contradict a postmodern view of youth culture, since postmodernists argue that the mix of styles does not involve a hierarchy.

Class and culture

Sociologists are interested in the way class and culture interrelate, and in particular in the following issues:

- Do different classes have different subcultures?
- Is class now a less important influence on identity than culture?

Culture and identity

- What are the functions of culture and how do classes use culture?

Socialisation and class cultures

Some sociologists would argue that different classes do have different subcultural norms and values and that individuals are socialised into these from an early age. In the 1960s, John and Elizabeth Newsom found marked class differences in child-rearing practices. Working-class parents tended to be more authoritarian than middle-class parents.

Basil Bernstein found that working-class children and families used a 'restricted language code' more frequently than they used 'elaborated code'. This disadvantaged working-class children's chances of educational success.

Herbert Hyman and Barry Sugarman, writing in the late 1960s and early 1970s, argued that working-class children had different norms and values, which made educational success more difficult. Working-class culture emphasised values of immediate gratification, fatalism, present-time orientation, and collectivism. In contrast, the middle classes had values which promoted the idea of deferred gratification, were optimistic and future oriented (planning for the future), and stressed the importance of individualism. Different cultures had different values, and lead to very different identities, with class being the key determinant of identity.

Marxists and Functionalists would agree that, while all classes will share a common or dominant culture, subcultural variations will develop due to differences in the social situation of particular social groups. Marxists and Functionalists explain subcultures in different ways, however, with Marxists seeing them as class based, while functionalists refer more to differences in status, which may not be tied to class.

More recently, some sociologists have argued that class is no longer an important aspect of identity, and that class cultures have fragmented. This view is mainly identified with postmodernist thought. Pakulski and Waters for instance, argue that survey evidence supports the view that class is not considered by many people to be an important source of their identity. Lash and Urry also take the view that the links between class and identity are being eroded in postmodern society.

This view is also supported by Peter Saunders, a sociologist sometimes associated with the New Right. Saunders argues that the key divisions in contemporary society are in terms of consumption patterns, rather than class differences, and it is consumption patterns which are becoming a key source of identity.

In contrast, Gordon Marshall argues that class differences in lifechances have not diminished in recent years, and in a survey conducted in the late 1980s Marshall found that most respondents were able and willing to identify their social class location.

Pierre Bourdieu provides a view which argues for the continuing importance of class and culture. Bourdieu claims that class remains important, but that different social classes have varying degrees of what he calls 'cultural capital'. Bourdieu argues that parents of the higher social classes are able to provide their children with cultural capital, which consists of a range of linguistic and other cultural competences or practices. These can include a whole range of cultural tastes and lifestyles. Possession of the valued cultural tastes, e.g. a familiarity with classical music, an upper class accent or an appreciation of the arts, will confer high status upon an individual.

Gender, ethnicity and culture

Gender and culture

Sociologists have concentrated their interests on two broad questions regarding the role of gender in contemporary culture:

1. Is gender an important influence upon identity?
2. Are gender identities changing?

Feminists such as Sylvia Walby argue that contemporary culture is a patriarchal (male-dominated) culture. This culture led to the creation of two spheres of activity, the public sphere and the private sphere. Women's primary roles and power are seen to lie in the private sphere; that is, in the home and in family life. Patriarchal culture has, thus, created both gendered roles and a gendered identity for women. Women's identity is mainly defined by their role in the family and in reproduction. This has not prevented women from challenging patriarchal culture and gaining more independence, but it has not made it easy for women either.

Studies by Sue Lees, Michelle Stanworth, Sue Sharpe, and Ann Oakley, have demonstrated the way that women's identity has been shaped through socialisation and differential treatment in the education system.

More recently, sociologists studying masculinity, such as Morgan, Hearn, and Mac an Ghaill, have pointed out that men's identities have also been shaped by patriarchal culture. Male identity most commonly develops in contrast or opposition to female identity,

Culture and identity

males being encouraged to adopt values of independence, and mental and physical toughness. Importantly, men are encouraged to pursue success in the public sphere, with work and career becoming of primary importance in men's lives.

Sociologists influenced by postmodernist theory have argued that cultural models of masculinity and femininity have changed in recent years. Connell, for instance, argues that it is more helpful to examine masculinities, rather than simply masculinity, since there are now a wide range of alternative male identities which men can adopt. Studies by Mort and Nixon have identified and debated whether masculinity has not become feminised to some degree.

Ethnicity and culture

- Is there a homogeneous British culture, or are ethnic minorities preserving their distinct ethnic identities?
- How are ethnicity and nationalism related, and how do they influence identity?

In recent years sociologists have devoted considerable attention to re-examining the concepts of race and ethnicity. Some sociologists prefer not to use the concept of race, arguing that it is not a valid scientific concept. Genetic scientists Steven Rose and Steve Jones argue strongly for this viewpoint. Ethnicity can be used as an alternative to race. All people, regardless of colour, have an ethnic origin. Ethnicity refers to the cultural group a person originates from.

Sociologist Tariq Modood points out that ethnicity is often confused with skin colour. Furthermore, he observes the category 'Asian', commonly used in Britain, is in fact very vague, since it labels as one group a variety of groups of people who can be divided by religion, nationality, and language.

Ethnicity, however, may be closely related to the nation-state. Anderson argues that nation-states are 'imagined communities'. Dominant cultural groups define the nation in such a way as to reflect their own interests and culture. National cultures invent a set of symbols, traditions, and heroes, which function so as to integrate members of the culture (or citizens of the nation-state). However, they also define citizens or members by contrasting them with 'outsiders', or foreigners, who are excluded and whose identity may be seen as stigmatised.

Some sociologists (e.g. Gilroy and Barker) have argued that racism in British society has taken on a new form, and refer to the 'new cultural racism'. These commentators argue that racism now consists of a subtle cultural denigration of minority ethnic cultures and an insistence that ethnic minorities should conform to mainstream 'British' cultural values.

In the light of these theoretical perspectives, sociologists have been interested to see whether ethnic minorities are maintaining their own cultures, or whether they are becoming integrated into British culture. Studies by Gardner and Shakur, Modood and Hides seem to indicate that ethnic minorities in Britain are maintaining their own cultural norms, values, beliefs, and way of life.

Other studies, such as those by Butler, Drury and Song, seem to offer support for the idea that ethnic minority cultures gradually change and adapt to the demands of having to live in a nation-state with a different national culture to their own.

Sociologist Stuart Hall concludes that there is some evidence to support the idea that there is an increasing 'hybridity' of culture in Britain, meaning a mixing of cultures. This view reflects a postmodernist approach to ethnicity and culture. However, it may be considered by some that the empirical evidence supporting such a view is limited.

The theory of the globalisation of culture suggests that two, apparently contradictory processes may be occurring simultaneously. Globalisation theory suggests that powerful forces may be acting against ethnic diversity. The social and cultural dominance of western industrialised societies (especially American society), may be leading to a homogeneous global culture, that is a world culture which is the same everywhere. At the same time, such a process will lead to resistance from national or local cultures, which want to maintain a distinctive way of life.

FACTFILE

- **Research by Cumberbatch (1990) on the portrayal of women in advertising indicates that strong stereotypes still predominate.**
- **There are still more men in adverts than women, and men are more likely to be shown participating in paid employment than women; 30% of men were shown working, while only 16% of female roles in adverts were of this nature.**
- **While only 7% of women in adverts are shown in the role of a housewife, they are still twice as likely as men to be engaged in a domestic task.**
  Source: Jones and Jones, *Mass Media* (1999).

Culture and identity

Sample question and answer advice

Critically discuss the view that capitalism produces a mass culture.

(AEB 1998)

This question is centrally involved with the concept of mass culture, which is commonly associated with the views of the Frankfurt School Marxists. Answers could usefully start with an explanation of the term mass culture, which can be contrasted to folk culture, and popular culture. A detailed discussion of the Frankfurt School's concept of mass culture is essential. In this view, capitalist society creates false needs which are satisfied by mass culture. Mass culture is seen by the Frankfurt School sociologists to be debasing, and it operates as a form of social control; the masses are pacified and made passive by the cheap mass culture of Hollywood and the media, and the pop music business. The Frankfurt School also use the terms commodification and 'commodity fetishism', describing the process by which culture is reduced to a product, and the masses are turned into uncritical puppets, desperate for their next dose of cheap, cultural distractions.

This view can be evaluated by consideration of several other studies and theories. Pluralists would argue that mass culture is highly differentiated, with different levels and different types of cultural product for different social groups. Neo-Marxists would be critical of the elitism of the Frankfurt School, yet Marxist influenced political economists, such as Golding and Murdock, might wish to support the idea that culture in capitalist society is mass culture and it is commodified. The work of the CCCS is an example of Marxist based sociology which sees popular culture as a form of resistance to the dominant ideology and culture of the bourgeoisie. Studies by Redhead, Thornton, Willis, McRobbie, and Mort and Nixon, could all be used to argue that people use popular culture creatively and often to make a critique of dominant culture and cultural forms. Moreover these studies could also reinforce the point that while capitalism creates cultural products on a large scale and turns them into commodities, that does not mean that the consumers of culture can accurately be seen as a mass or as an undifferentiated whole.

TEST YOURSELF

X	Q	W	N	O	I	T	A	S	I	L	A	B	O	L	G
C	A	E	Y	N	X	O	G	P	J	Q	V	Z	L	V	B
U	P	F	R	A	N	K	F	U	R	T	L	E	A	Q	D
L	V	C	S	C	H	O	O	L	Z	U	F	L	B	S	P
T	X	A	Q	P	L	J	M	B	V	T	U	W	E	S	F
U	H	Y	B	R	I	D	I	T	Y	N	R	K	L	A	O
R	Y	I	M	V	B	A	H	C	J	B	K	I	L	U	B
A	Z	I	P	W	X	N	C	D	M	S	L	Y	I	M	O
L	N	U	L	D	O	Q	P	R	O	C	L	V	N	M	L
D	G	O	B	X	N	W	I	K	R	U	A	L	G	G	A
E	N	D	I	Y	R	T	R	B	T	R	H	S	B	A	T
P	B	N	Q	T	I	Y	J	V	G	O	X	M	V	K	I
R	C	I	M	K	A	F	M	Q	J	C	C	C	S	Y	P
I	X	V	T	J	P	C	S	A	K	L	W	N	R	P	A
V	W	C	D	E	G	X	I	Z	G	Y	K	W	Y	H	C
A	Q	F	R	C	D	Z	R	F	B	X	I	A	T	P	L
T	M	V	A	X	K	V	E	X	I	M	M	G	O	V	A
I	S	B	L	V	L	R	M	F	R	D	Z	F	P	L	R
O	I	I	L	O	O	P	U	Y	I	E	O	H	Q	H	U
N	H	P	I	M	F	K	S	P	P	Z	C	M	A	A	T
X	S	U	R	B	N	L	N	L	A	B	V	P	M	D	L
F	I	O	D	A	Q	O	O	E	Q	G	R	U	Y	O	U
H	T	Q	U	W	A	G	C	D	S	F	W	Y	T	N	C
I	E	R	A	X	A	T	Y	K	M	V	E	T	H	C	E
V	F	B	B	Y	E	R	U	T	L	U	C	B	U	S	Q

Solution on page 126

Study and Revise AS and A2 Level Sociology

Culture and identity

> **Summary**
>
> 1. Sociologists do not agree on how culture is best defined, nor do they agree in their explanations of the role of culture in contemporary society. Many exam questions will provide students with opportunities to evaluate the way in which culture is a contested concept.
>
> 2. When discussing the debates on the production and consumption of culture, it is worth noting that many sociological perspectives are very speculative and do not always offer much empirical evidence in support of their position. The postmodernist view that consumption is now a more important determinant of identity than social class can be usefully evaluated by referring to current debates about class, and in particular the issue of whether class is dead (Chapter 12).
>
> 3. Studies of femininity and masculinity in contemporary culture, influenced by postmodernism, have stressed the way that the differences between the two have become blurred, and moreover that there are many different cultural versions or forms of masculinity and femininity. Put another way, there are many masculine and feminine identities available to individuals in contemporary society. This view can usefully be applied to other topics.
>
> 4. The concept of globalisation, although difficult to evaluate, has become increasingly important in sociology, and can be applied to many other topics. Arguably the most useful conclusion regarding debates about globalisation is the view that it leads simultaneously to a homogenisation of culture, and also to many local resistances to a globalised culture.

Education and training — Chapter 3

PREVIEW

You need to know:
- how different sociological perspectives explain the role of education
- the main patterns of educational attainment of social class, gender, and ethnic groups and sociological explanations of the differences in attainment between these groups
- sociological analysis of school organisation, including teacher–pupil relationships, pupil subcultures, the hidden curriculum, and the organisation of the curriculum
- education and training policy, including vocationalism and training, lifelong learning, and the National Curriculum

TEST YOURSELF

Participation rates in higher education by social class in the UK

Social class	Percentage of pupils in final year of compulsory schooling	
	1991–92	1997–98
Professional	55	80
Intermediate	36	49
Skilled non manual	22	32
Skilled manual	11	19
Partly skilled	12	18
Unskilled	6	14
All social classes	23	34

Source: Adapted from *Social Trends* 29 (1999)

1 By how much has the participation rate in higher education for those from the Professional class increased between 1991–92 and 1997–98?
2 By how much has the participation rate in higher education for those from the unskilled manual class increased between 1991–92 and 1997–98?
3 Briefly describe the general trend of the data in the table.

Answers

1 25%
2 8%
3 The table shows a clear and marked increase in participation in higher education across all classes. However, it also shows that there are significant differences, thus indicating the persistence of class advantage in educational attainment.

Sociological perspectives on education

The main sociological perspectives analysing the role of education are the Functionalist, Marxist and Interactionist approaches.

Functionalism

Functionalist sociologists examine how education fits into the overall structure of society and the functions it fulfils. Durkheim saw education as having a vital role to play in integrating industrial society and creating social solidarity. The education system of a society could create social solidarity through teaching common norms and values. This is a function that Durkheim believed only schools could carry out, since they provided a link between the individual and society. In an industrial society, where individuals would eventually have a particular job in a specialised division of labour, integration into a shared set of norms and values is essential if society is to function effectively.

For Parsons the education system was a key means of socialising the young, forming a bridging point between the particular values of the family and the universal (common) values of the wider society. Parsons saw such a process as necessary if a society was to maintain value consensus. Particularly important was the transmission of two key values:

1 a focus on individual achievement (striving to achieve one's best in all activities)
2 belief in equality of opportunity.

American Functionalists Davis and Moore suggest that the education system performs the function of what they term 'role allocation', in other words grading and selecting young people in terms of their skills and abilities and on the basis of this grading, allocating them to particular roles, or jobs. According to Davis and Moore, occupations in a specialised industrial society will have varying requirements in terms of skill and intellectual ability. The education system will ensure that the most able and determined people gain the best qualifications and are most highly rewarded.

Davis and Moore argue that the education system carries out these functions meritocratically, that is, fairly and without bias. Bias would be dysfunctional, resulting in a society which did not function properly since the most able did not necessarily get allocated to the functionally most important roles.

Education and training

Marxism

Marxism, like Functionalism, is a structural theory, and is thus concerned to examine the role which education plays in society. However, Marxism is a conflict theory, and it therefore reaches very different conclusions about the role of the education system to Functionalist theories.

Althusser refers to the education system in capitalist society as an Ideological State Apparatus (ISA). The role of the education system is to reproduce the two key groups or classes in society, and to do so in such a way that the division of society into these two groups will seem fair (legitimate).

The education system, therefore, is an institution devoted to social control. It helps to create an ideology, which suggests that the ruling classes deserve their privileges and that the working class get what they deserve.

Bowles and Gintis are two American sociologists whose work developed the Marxist explanation of the role of the education system. This theory is often referred to as a 'correspondence theory', since it suggests that education corresponds to capitalism's need for a workforce. Like Althusser, Bowles and Gintis see the education system as being involved mainly with the reproduction of labour power, and with legitimating the class differences arising from that process. They argue that education tends to reward conformity to dominant values rather than foster a truly critical and questioning outlook.

Students are frequently motivated by 'external rewards'. In other words, students do not follow their own interests, nor necessarily learn useful skills. They work to gain paper qualifications that will improve their job prospects (sometimes referred to as credentialism). The hidden curriculum teaches students to accept hierarchy and authority.

The education system creates the illusion of equality, but in reality rewards tend to be distributed according to social background. Bowles and Gintis argue that the higher IQ scores of American graduates is not the cause of their educational success; it is simply the effect of the longer period of time they have spent in higher education compared to non-graduates of the same age.

Interactionism

Marxism and Functionalism are both structural theories and explain social institutions in terms of how they maintain a social system. Interactionism, in contrast, examines education in terms of the processes which occur within schools. Interactionist theories are, thus, said to focus on the 'micro level', whereas structural theories concentrate on the 'macro level'.

Labelling and the self-fulfilling prophecy

Interactionist theory has suggested that teachers do not always treat pupils equally. The idea of 'typing' or labelling suggests that teachers may make judgements as to the likely behaviour and ability of individual pupils or classes. These judgements then have an influence upon the formation of the pupil's self-concept. As interactionist theory in general suggests, the way individuals behave is largely influenced by the way others act towards them.

A study by Hargreaves, Hester and Mellor, found that teachers typing of pupils occurred in three stages; speculation, elaboration, and stabilisation. In early meetings, teachers made judgements about the pupil's potential, not so much through objective educational evidence, but on the basis of more subjective evidence such as appearance, personality, and enthusiasm.

Rosenthal and Jacobsen's classic study of the self-fulfilling prophecy demonstrated the power, which such judgements might have. Pupils entering a primary school were tested for intelligence. The teachers were falsely told that certain pupils were of particularly high ability. When Rosenthal and Jacobsen tested the children's intelligence again at the end of the year, they found that those falsely identified as being of high ability had in fact made much greater improvements than other children who had not been identified as specially able.

Rosenthal and Jacobsen argued that teachers had in some way communicated their higher expectations to the specially selected children, and they concluded from this that teachers' predictions become self-fulfilling prophecies; tell children that they will succeed or fail, and this is what happens.

Banding and class

Research by other sociologists has shown that the effects of teachers' typing and labelling of pupils' abilities, influence the way that schools treat pupils according to their membership of social groups, i.e. on the basis of their class, ethnicity, or gender.

Stephen Ball's research in the 1970s demonstrated that there was a strong relationship between a pupil's social class and the 'band' in which the school placed them. Students from the higher social classes had a much better chance of getting into the higher bands than those from manual backgrounds. In addition, children in the higher bands generally had higher rates of educational attainment and a larger proportion stayed on for A levels than children in the lower bands.

Ball argues that these patterns were influenced by teachers' judgements and behaviour, pupils in the lower bands being 'cooled down' (teachers had lower expectations and did not encourage them to stay on, gain further qualifications, etc.) and pupils in the higher bands being 'warmed up' or encouraged.

School subcultures

Whereas the Marxist and Functionalist perspectives tend to assume that the education system is successful in role allocation or the reproduction of a passive labour force, Interactionist theory has noted the way that many pupils reject the values of the school and create their own deviant subcultures.

Hargreaves' study, *Social Relations in a Secondary School*, showed how the processes of labelling leads to the creation of pro- and anti-school subcultures. Pupils who were seen as failures or who were negatively labelled by the school, would attempt to gain status by rebelling against the values of the school.

Peter Woods has argued that Hargreaves' division of pupils into two subcultural groups is too simplistic. Woods adapts Merton's categories of subcultural response and argues for a variety of adaptations to the values of the school.

Other sociologists, such as Martin Hammersley, have argued that it is mistaken to assume that a school will have a consensus about its values and aims; this is a functionalist view. It is quite possible that teachers will disagree about aims, values, and policies of the school and will therefore, act differently and even enforce rules in very different ways. This means pupils' actions may vary a lot depending on the situation. Thus, it may be difficult to identify clear subcultural values and groups.

Other theories

Feminism

Feminists have mainly focused on the patterns of gender inequality that the education system has often reproduced. Feminist research has indicated the gender bias evident in the hidden curriculum and the patriarchal assumptions which are integrated into the design of the curriculum, as well as the way teachers may label on the basis of gender. As society and education have changed, feminist sociologists have examined how gender identities are shaped within schools.

CHECKLIST

✓ The functionalist belief in the meritocratic nature of the education system is strongly challenged by other perspectives and by empirical evidence. However, the debate must be carefully evaluated, so students answering questions on this issue should be sure to include some points in favour of the meritocracy thesis (e.g. the majority of students in the UK attend state schools, free state education for all).

✓ Marxist approaches to education meet the familiar criticism of economic reductionism. Students can draw usefully on the work of Willis to provide a more sophisticated evaluation of the Marxist perspective. Willis' study seems to contradict the assertion of Bowles and Gintis, that schools create the 'passive and obedient workforce required by capitalism'. Although education is still seen as a way of reproducing labour power, it is seen as the outcome of a more complex process and one in which people actively help to create social structures.

✓ Interactionist studies of education can be seen as offering some valuable empirical evidence to what can be a rather theoretical debate. Arguably though, sociologists need to synthesise both structural and action theories to gain a more complete understanding of education.

Social democratic views

Social democracy is a set of political ideas and a viewpoint rather than a sociological perspective. However, it is important to mention it in this context, since many education policies applied by governments have been influenced by social democratic ideas.

Social democrats acknowledge the severity of social inequalities, and see the education system as one area where governments can intervene in social life and make improvements. Social democrats believe that putting a greater quantity of funds and resources into the education system, as well as more egalitarian policies, such as comprehensive schooling and mixed ability teaching, will create a fairer and more equal society. The role of the state is to act rather like a referee, preventing cheating, and ensuring fair play for all.

Education and training

The New Right

The New Right perspective is again more of a political view than a sociological perspective, though there are some sociologists who are linked to the New Right. Again, the New Right's approach to education is important for the light it sheds on education policy, particularly in the 1980s and 1990s.

New Right thinkers and politicians wanted to see state involvement in education reduced, and parental freedom of choice increased. They also wished to see a traditional curriculum, emphasising the basics. The New Right favoured streaming and selection, since they believed that pupils had very different abilities, which required differential treatment. They also supported private education, and were critical of multicultural education.

Postmodernism

Postmodernist views can be applied to the analysis of education. Postmodernists have been amongst those who argue that the division of labour in western societies has shifted from Fordism to post-Fordism. A post-Fordist division of labour requires flexible workers, who are multi-skilled and able to work in a variety of different roles.

Postmodernists argue that these needs are changing education. In higher education particularly, differences between subject boundaries are less important, and a whole range of different courses have been developed, including distance learning and part-time courses.

There is also an emphasis on lifelong learning, increasing stress upon education as a form of self improvement, and encouragement for students to take more self-responsibility for their personal development. This reflects the postmodernist view that class is increasingly less important, and that identity is more influenced by cultural factors and consumption. It also seems worth noting in this respect, that governments increasingly encourage students to see themselves as customers rather than students.

Explaining differences in educational attainment

One of the key areas of interest to sociologists is to explain the patterns of attainment indicated above. This is also an issue, which many exam questions address. The variety of explanations can usefully be divided into two sets of factors: input factors and school factors.

CHECKLIST

✓ Other theories can be usefully applied to offer criticisms of the main theoretical perspectives.

✓ In some cases, they may provide an opportunity to update older theories, or can be used to put educational change and policies into political context.

✓ Postmodernists' focus on the impact of the changing division of labour offers some useful insights into education, but whether aspects of social structure, such as class, ethnicity, and gender, can be ruled out of sociological analysis is a matter of considerable debate.

Those favouring input factors tend to see social structures, such as class, ethnicity, and gender, as the key determinants of success. These are characteristics, which pupils bring into school with them, and it may be argued that schools can do relatively little to change the social inequalities related to them.

Those who concentrate on school factors take a more optimistic view, and argue that it is the processes occurring inside the school which explain the different outcomes.

Input factors

IQ

Psychologists such as Eysenck, Jensen, Burt and more recently, American sociologists Charles Murray and Richard Herrnstein, have argued that the key determinant of educational success is intelligence. Moreover, most of these writers claim that intelligence is innate and, therefore, fixed.

Jensen, Murray and Herrnstein have made the controversial claim that there are significant differences in intelligence between different ethnic minority groups (or 'races'). They claimed that their research (in the USA) demonstrated that blacks were less intelligent than whites. Arguments critical of this body of research focus on the methodological problems of untangling heredity and environmental (nature and nurture) factors and the difficulty of finding a culture free test.

Class

Many sociologists have seen class as a key determinant of educational success. However, there have been two key strands in this tradition of research. Some sociologists see the economic (or material) advantages associated with higher socio-economic groups as being the most important factor, whereas others have argued that different classes have different value systems, and it is this that leads to differences in attainment.

Material explanations

Some sociologists have found evidence that the key factors are material or economic, rather than cultural. A study by Halsey, Heath and Ridge (1980), *Origins and Destinations*, used survey material from the Nuffield Mobility Study, based on some 8500 individual men. Halsey *et al*.'s, study found that around 75% of working-class men left school on reaching the required school leaving age, while in the service class 75% continued to study beyond the compulsory minimum.

The main reason given for leaving was financial; working-class families could not afford to keep their children at school. The authors of this study also point out that, when working-class boys did stay on to continue their studies, there was no marked difference in attainment levels when compared to other classes. The study, therefore, seems to suggest that as causes of working-class underachievement (at least as far as boys were concerned, and in the period studied), cultural factors were not as significant as economic factors.

Research by J.W.B. Douglas, though frequently seen as providing evidence of the significance of cultural deprivation, also gives evidence that poor living standards have an adverse affect on educational attainment. Douglas' evidence showed that children living in conditions rated as 'unsatisfactory' scored below children living in 'satisfactory' conditions.

Cultural explanations

Cultural deprivation theorists, such as Hyman, Sugarman, and Douglas, explain the educational attainment of working-class pupils as being the result of a different set of values (e.g. instant gratification, present orientation).

Douglas argued that working-class parents are less inclined to encourage their children to strive for academic success. This conclusion was based on extensive research in schools, and on interviews with parents, staff, and children.

Bernstein has argued that cultural differences in language put working-class children at a disadvantage. Bernstein's research suggested that working-class children's speech tended to be confined to what he termed a 'restricted code', whereas middle-class children were adept at using 'elaborated code'. The 'elaborated code' is the language of the school, thus middle-class children will have an advantage over working-class children.

Criticisms of cultural explanations focus upon the methodology used (often questionnaires or interviews), which may exaggerate the extent of subcultural differences in values between classes, and the value-judgements made by sociologists.

Douglas' assumption that working-class parents are less interested and committed to educational success than middle-class parents can be questioned. Douglas bases this conclusion on evidence gained from primary school teachers about which parents are most frequent attenders of parent evenings. He neglects to consider a range of material (economic) factors that could make it harder for working-class parents to attend these meetings. The data can, thus, be interpreted in different ways.

School factors

It has been argued that input factors alone do not determine pupils' chances of educational success. Other sociologists have suggested that the following factors, some already discussed in considering the interactionist perspective, are equally, if not more, important:

Type and quality of the school

Michael Rutter argued that, despite structural factors such as class, a well-organised school could still enable its pupils to succeed. Thus, the quality of school organisation and the type of school, e.g. comprehensive, grammar, secondary, could indeed make a difference. More recently, Peter Mortimore has suggested that the quality of a school can account for about 10% of the variations in exam performance between different schools.

Teacher–pupil relations

As discussed (page 22), labelling theory and closely associated concepts such as the self-fulfilling prophecy, suggest that students' success is dependent upon the way teachers label them.

Streaming and banding

Ball's study (page 22), demonstrates how labelling may be used to create streams or banding in secondary schools.

Education and training

Curriculum organisation and the hidden curriculum

The formal curriculum consists of all the courses which are taught and tested, including non-examined courses such as PSE. The hidden curriculum refers to attitudes and values which are not formally taught or tested.

It may be argued, by feminists for instance, that the hidden curriculum transmits sexism and sexist values. This could occur through curriculum organisation, if for example boys and girls are not always allowed to study the same subjects or options, as used to happen in many schools. The concept of the hidden curriculum is associated with Marxist sociologists Bowles and Gintis (see page 22).

FACTFILE

- In 1994 about 7% of the school population consisted of pupils in private schools. Egerton and Halsey (1993) found that, despite the expansion in higher education in the late 1980s and early 1990s, the advantages of the service class in gaining access to university were not diminished. Students from service-class origins were more likely to gain places at the more prestigious universities. It seems likely that such educational advantages will lead to advantages in gaining employment.

Michael Young and Nell Keddie point out that there is a hierarchy of knowledge, with academic knowledge having the highest status, and more practical and vocationally-oriented knowledge having low status. As Keddie's study demonstrated, teachers' organisation of the curriculum can mean that students receive different treatment, according to the teachers' assessment of students' abilities. As has been indicated above, this assessment may be based on labelling rather than objective assessments of student ability.

Summary

1. Sociologists may explain differences in attainment in terms of either input factors or school factors.
2. Many would agree that neither set of factors is sufficient to explain attainment differences.
3. Differences in educational attainment are the result of a combination of input factors (e.g. class, gender, ethnicity) and school factors, such as labelling. The two sets of factors interact; labelling for instance often occurs on the basis of a pupil's class, gender, or ethnicity.

Explaining gender and ethnic differences in attainment

Gender and ethnic differences in educational attainment can be explained in terms of the concepts and theories discussed above.

Gender

The nature of gender differences in educational attainment changed in the mid-1990s, with girls achieving better than boys in all subjects at GCSE, and in most A Level subjects. However, there are still important differences in choice of subjects with girls being less likely to study A Levels and degrees in science subjects. There are also still

Explaining educational success

Education and training

notable differences in career opportunities for women.

Girls' previous underachievement and current educational subject choices are usually explained in terms of the factors set out below.

Input factors

Sociologists such as Goldstein have found limited evidence of innate differences in aptitude, but the significance of such findings is open to interpretation. Feminists argue that patriarchal attitudes prevalent in society effect the expectations and wishes of parents and, indeed, of female students themselves.

School factors

A range of studies, including those by Sharpe, Lees, and Stanworth, document the labelling and stereotypical treatment of female students. Kelly's study of girls and science education demonstrated how this influenced the girls' chances of success in science. Other studies indicate that the curriculum is permeated with sexist assumptions and that the hidden curriculum also acts to reinforce patriarchy.

The improved performance by girls in recent years could be explained in terms of the following factors:

- The National Curriculum – this ensures that all students have to study the same, compulsory subjects.
- Affirmative action on the part of schools and teachers – more single-sex classes, projects such as Girls into Science and Technology (Alison Kelly).
- An increase in the expectations of girls – more women are working now, and deciding to have a career and a family.
- An increase in the service sector – there are more professional and non-professional opportunities in service sector jobs, as traditional industrial manual work declines. This has provided opportunities for women in the labour market.

Although girls' educational attainment has improved, sociologists would be swift to point out that there are still inequalities in attainment in higher education, and gender differences in subject choices remain marked.

> **FACTFILE**
> - Girls have performed better than boys at A Level since 1988–89.

Ethnicity

Input factors

Sociologists such as Murray and Herrnstein, and psychologists Eysenck and Jensen, have argued that ethnic differences in educational attainment are the result of innate differences in intelligence. Many sociologists, though, are highly critical of the validity of IQ tests. Attainment differences can also be explained in terms of cultural differences, language differences, or in terms of cultural deprivation. Others would argue that educational differences reflect economic differences and that ethnic disadvantage is the result of economic disadvantage, rather than racism. It could be argued, though, that economic and cultural disadvantage are interrelated, and that it is pointless trying to separate them analytically.

School factors

The usual range of school factors can be applied to the explanation of ethnic attainment differences. Studies of labelling and, more recently, of school exclusions of disruptive pupils have led some sociologists to argue that schools are 'institutionally racist'. Such studies would emphasise the role of school factors in explaining ethnic minority educational attainment.

Input factors or school factors?

There is debate as to the relative importance and explanatory value of these sets of factors. Pilkington points to the considerable differences which exist between different ethnic minority groups. Some Asian groups, for instance, achieve much the same level as white ethnic groups, while others have fallen some way behind. One interpretation of this sort of explanation is that it is input factors (perhaps income or class position) which are more important in explaining ethnic minority educational attainment.

Other researchers, such as Cecille Wright and David Gillborn, have argued that the education system can be institutionally racist. This is a complex concept requiring sophisticated evaluation. However, in essence it implies that, while individual teachers may not act intentionally in a racist manner, the effects of their beliefs and the way they treat students can have racist consequences. This explanation tends to focus on the role of school factors, such as labelling and institutionalised racism.

Education and training

> **FACTFILE**
> - Data on ethnicity and educational attainment has to be interpreted carefully. Such data frequently does not distinguish between different ethnic minority groups, nor does it differentiate between class, gender, and ethnicity. For instance, data may indicate how many 'Asians' gain A Levels, but it fails to distinguish between different Asian groups, fails to examine how those 'Asians' from different social classes compare, and fails to examine whether there are differences in attainment between males and females in the ethnic category.

> **Summary**
> 1. In the case of gender and ethnicity, it can be suggested that both input and school factors are needed to explain educational attainment.
> 2. Sexism and racism exist in the wider society, as well as within educational institutions. Schools often reflect the inequalities and prejudices of the wider society.
> 3. Gender and ethnic differences in attainment can be explained by reference to economic and to cultural factors.

Education and training policies

The 1944 Education Act

The 1944 Education Act created a system of free, compulsory education for all up to the age of 15. The so-called tripartite system consisted of grammar, technical, and secondary schools, which were said to have 'parity of esteem', but which offered respectively, academic, technical, and 'practical' education. Entry to the elite grammar school was through the 11-plus examination. The system was widely perceived as rigid and unfair. The tripartite system perpetuated class inequalities in the education system, and forced pupils into specialist academic or vocational routes at an early age.

Comprehensive Education

The Labour Government in 1965 required all local education authorities to make plans to scrap the tripartite organisation of schools and create comprehensive schools which would take students of all abilities. The aim of comprehensive schooling was to reduce inequalities of educational opportunity and outcome. How successful comprehensives were in achieving this is widely debated, since some have argued that streaming and setting continued in comprehensives and that residential segregation led to reinforcement of class differences.

The New Vocationalism

The New Vocationalism is the term given to a range of education and training policies which emerged in the 1970s and 1980s. Rising youth unemployment lead to a concern that many school leavers were unable to gain employment due to a lack of qualifications.

This led to a range of government initiatives, including new qualifications and new training courses, all aimed at providing non-academic school leavers with useful vocational qualifications or training. The courses included the Youth Training Scheme (YTS), which subsequently became Youth Training, and the Certificate in Pre-Vocational Education (CPVE).

Government organisation also reflected the perceived link between education and employment, with courses such as YTS funded by the Department of Employment (through the agency known as the Manpower Services Commission). In 1997, New Labour further developed this relationship by combining the education and employment departments, forming the DfEE (Department for Education and Employment).

Sociologists have made various criticisms of new vocationalist policies. Dan Finn's study argues that the policies asssumed that school leavers were unemployable, when the key problem was simply structural unemployment. Phil Cohen argues that many of the policies led to poor quality training courses which failed to give trainees any substantial skills.

1988 Education Reform Act (ERA) and The National Curriculum

The 1988 ERA brought about radical change to the education system. For the first time ever, English and Welsh schools had a national curriculum and national testing was imposed by the government. The act also encouraged diversity of educational provision, with the role of local education authorities reduced and the establishment of grant maintained schools and city technology colleges. League tables have been another important outcome of the act. The publication of school examination results was intended to enable parents to make considered choices and to force schools to compete.

Education and training

1997 and 'New Labour'

'New Labour' has instigated a number of policies aimed at raising standards in education. Labour has been keen to emphasise the importance of high educational standards in creating a competitive economy. Ministers also refer to the importance of global competition by their use of the term 'world class education'.

Labour has created a number of Education Action Zones – EAZs. Extra funds and powers will be given to some 25 Local Education Authorities, although two of the EAZs will be run by private sector companies. EAZs aim to raise standards in deprived areas. The policy can usefully be compared with the Educational Priority Areas of the 1960s, and the Headstart project in the USA.

New Labour has also introduced compulsory a literacy hour in the primary curriculum, voluntary Home–School contracts, and the reform of A Levels in the secondary sector.

Labour has also set about creating a University for Industry, aimed at providing a range of courses for those who have completed compulsory education. This is a key plank in government plans for 'Lifelong Learning', along with the proposal to create 'individual learning accounts', whereby government and employers will pledge to provide funding for training for all adults. These policies can be seen as creating a labour force that fits the needs of a post-Fordist division of labour.

FACTFILE

- **Government statistics in 1997 show that the number of exclusions from schools had increased, with some 15% of the school population being excluded. Those most likely to be excluded were boys, and boys with special educational needs, and Afro-Caribbean boys, were disproportionately likely to be excluded.**
  Source: *Sociology Update* (1999).

TEST YOURSELF

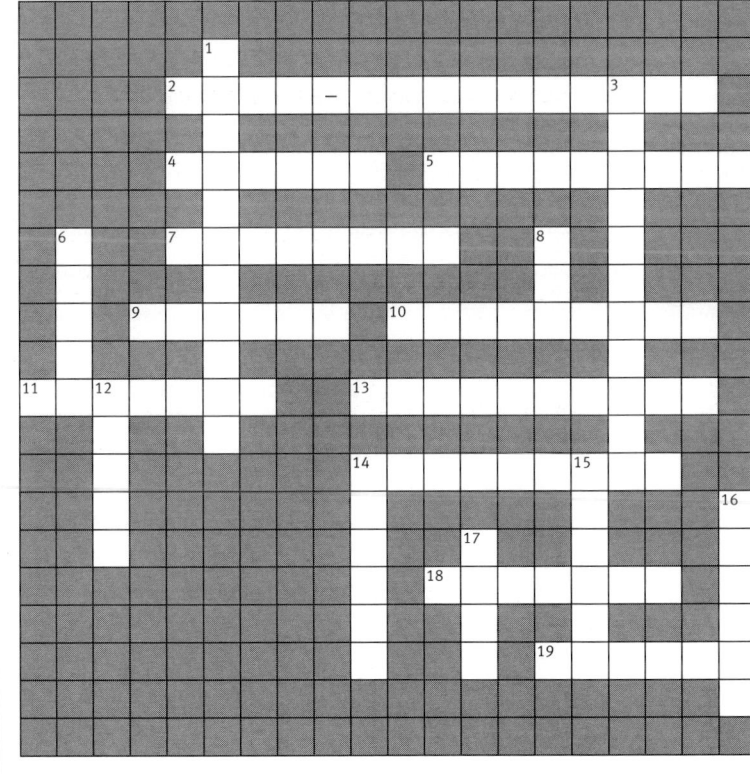

Across
2 Rosenthal and Jacobsen believed that labelling could lead to a type of prophecy (4, 10)
4 He studies why working-class kids get working-class jobs (6)
5 A sociologist interested in language codes (9)
7 The inventor or cultural capital (8)
9 The New Right wanted education to be run on the principles of this ... (6)
10 Policy in USA which aimed to alleviate cultural deprivation (9)
11 Mr IQ (7)
13 The system associated with the 1944 Education Act (10)
14 What Hargreaves says teachers do to students (9)
18 A sort of theory demonstrated by Bowles and Gintis (7)
19 The author of *Just Like a Girl* (6)

Down
1 According to functionalists, the education system creates this (11)
3 Functionalists believe that education provides this (11)
6 She researched on girls and science education (5)
8 Form of management introduced by the 1988 Education Reform Act (3)
12 A report on education and ethnicity (5)
14 Marxists say that education reproduces this sort of power (6)
15 The author of deschooling society (6)
16 The opposite of the formal curriculum (6)
17 A sociologist who studies Beachside Comprehensive (4)

Solution on page 125

Study and Revise AS and A2 Level Sociology

Education and training

Sample question and answer

Outline and assess the contribution of interactionist approaches to an understanding of the unequal distribution of educational achievement.

(Adapted from AEB 1998)

While structural theories explain differences in educational attainment in terms of input factors, such as the class, ethnicity, or gender of students, or in the case of functionalists the differences in ability, interactionists seek the main cause of differential attainment in processes occurring within the school. In this way, structural and interactionist theories reflect different approaches to the structure/action debate in sociological theory.

Interactionist theories have seen differential attainment mainly as the result of labelling or typing by teachers, and have also examined concepts such as that of the self-fulfilling prophecy, and anti-school subcultures. Interactionist theory argues that an individual's self-concept is the result of how others respond to the individual, and this frequently involves labelling. Becker for instance found that American high school teachers had a common image of the 'ideal pupil', such pupils tended to reflect the social characteristics and attitudes of the teachers, and thus tended to come from higher socio-economic classes. Hargreaves, Hestor and Mellor, found that teachers 'type' students through a three stage process of speculation, elaboration, and stabilisation. Rosenthal and Jacobsen's research indicated that teachers' judgements could create a powerful effect; the self-fulfilling prophecy, whereby students could respond strongly to teachers' labelling. Research from various studies by Ball, and Hargreaves for instance, shows how teachers and schools generally tend to label students on the basis of social class. Ball, for instance, found very strong correlations between social class and academic banding in his study on 'Beachside Comprehensive'. Wright and Gillborn have demonstrated that labelling also occurs on the basis of ethnicity, while Spender and Stanworth for example, demonstrate that girls too are labelled in various ways (usually with negative consequences) by teachers.

Several key criticisms have been made of these contributions, generally from a structural position. Structural theorists often argue that interactionism does not provide any explanation of power. While the interactionist studies mentioned above do reflect the fact that some social groups are treated unequally within schools, structural theorists can argue that interactionism can only describe this process. It cannot, though, explain why working-class students, female students, and 'black' students are negatively labelled, unless that is, interactionists resort to structural theories, such as Marxism or conflict theory, for example.

Secondly, while structural theories are often said to be deterministic, portraying actors as automatically responding to social forces, a similar criticism can, ironically, be aimed at interactionism. Interactionists often seem to imply, despite their emphasis on the fact that labels are negotiable, that labelling is a one-way process; an individual is negatively labelled and the label sticks. Structuralists might complain that it is hard to know why labelling works in some instances and not in others. To conclude evaluation of these criticisms, structural theorists may sum up interactionism as descriptive rather than explanatory, and may argue that the interactionist study of the 'meanings of actors' in interaction does not, on its own, provide much of a sociological explanation of educational attainment.

In their defence, interactionists may draw on several points. Firstly, they could argue that their research is highly practical and empirical. It provides detailed evidence and findings of the processes which occur in real schools. Interactionists may also argue that, while structures are important, people are not inanimate objects, nor are they without consciousness. People think and reflect and act as they do for reasons. Structural research often rules out the investigation of actors' reasons and motivations and, therefore, interactionist research is needed to complement it. Interactionist research can provide a greater degree of validity than is offered by structural explanations. Interactionists such as Ken Plummer would argue that the key aim of interactionism was to reveal precisely the way that schools treat those without power. Lastly, interactionists could point to the practical usefulness of their research. Schools and teachers have the possibility of changing their practices and promoting policies which can make the education system fairer.

In conclusion, it can be argued that, while interactionist theory undoubtedly does have weaknesses (particularly explaining power), it has not been an approach to the sociology of education without value. What the criticisms from structural and interactionist approaches perhaps show most clearly, is that sociological explanations of differential attainment require both school and input factors to be addressed. Neither on their own are sufficient. The same can be said for sociological theories generally; sociology needs to examine structure and action, though of course, how this is done is the subject of further debate.

Summary

1. When evaluating differences in educational attainment, it is useful to plan answers in terms of input factors and school factors. Arguably, both sets of factors are important, and neither one on its own is sufficient to explain the patterning of educational attainment found.

2. Other debates which need to be treated carefully are those which examine differential attainment in terms of either economic factors or cultural factors. It can be argued that both sets of factors are important here, although perhaps the evidence of Halsey, Heath and Ridge might be seen to suggest that the key difference is not cultural, but economic.

3. Questions focusing on ethnicity or gender differences can be explained by applying general sociological theories. While some reference to particularly relevant studies is vital, general theoretical explanations can be applied, e.g. input factors and school factors, economic and cultural explanations.

4. Remember too that sociologists are now more sensitive to differences between different ethnic minorities and that masculinity and femininity are also now seen as rather broader categories.

Wealth, poverty and welfare — CHAPTER 4

PREVIEW

What you need to know:

- sociological explanations of the distribution of wealth
- definitions and explanations of poverty
- problems involved in the measurement of poverty
- welfare, poverty and social policy
- key debates about the role of the welfare state.

Sociological explanations of the distribution of wealth

Definitions of wealth and income

There is no one definition of wealth accepted by all sociologists. A basic definition could be that wealth is the total value of resources and material possessions owned by a person, after any debts have been deducted.

However, John Scott (Fulcher and Scott, 1999) argues that wealth is best defined in relative terms:

The wealthy have resources that allow them to enjoy benefits and advantages that are not available to others in their society.

This definition has the benefit of highlighting the relationship between wealth and poverty, which is important, since some sociologists argue that both wealth and poverty have the same causes. Moreover, both wealth and poverty can be defined in relative terms, that is, in terms of some perceived 'norm' or average which is expected within a society.

Some sociological studies examine a particular type of wealth – income, but this is only one form of wealth. Income can be defined as money which is received regularly, such as a wage.

FACTFILE

- There is no agreed definition of wealth. Wealth and poverty can be defined in relative terms and have the same causes.

Explanations of the distribution of wealth

Functionalist views

Functionalists would see the unequal distribution of wealth throughout the population as inevitable and

TEST YOURSELF

Adults holding selected forms of wealth in the UK by ethnic group, percentage,[1] 1996–97						
Type of account	White	Black	Indian	Pakistani/ Bangladeshi	Other groups[2]	All ethnic groups
Current account	80	63	70	45	71	79
Building society account[3]	54	37	39	19	39	53
Premium bonds	19	4	8	2	7	19
Stocks and shares	16	8	16	3	12	15
TESSA	10	3	12	1	7	10
PEPs	8	2	5	1	6	8
Any	89	78	82	57	80	89

[1] Age standardised percentage in each ethnic group holding each form of wealth.
[2] Includes those of mixed origin.
[3] Excluding current accounts and TESSAs.
Source: Adapted from *Social Trends* 29 (1999)

1. Which ethnic group owned the highest percentage of stocks and shares in 1996–97?
2. What percentage of the population had a current account in 1996–97?
3. Why is it important to consider aspects of stratification other than class in this topic?

Wealth, poverty and welfare

> **Answers**
>
> 1 'White' and 'Indian'.
>
> 2 79%
>
> 3 There are several reasons why the different aspects of stratification need to be considered. Firstly, it is important for students to apply their knowledge from different topics and to identify the links between different topics. Wealth, welfare and poverty cannot be fully understood without some reference to stratification. It is also important because, increasingly, sociologists are becoming aware of the need to study the way in which the different elements of stratification are interrelated. The sociologist Harriet Bradley is one who has argued this case strongly. These points seem to be born out by the findings in this area; namely that women, the old, and certain ethnic minority groups, as well as those in lower socio-economic classes, are disproportionately likely to be amongst the poor.

functionally necessary. Wealth is a reward to the most able individuals who perform the most important roles in society. The wealth these individuals accumulate acts as an incentive and encourages the most talented members in society to strive for highly rewarded positions. The wealthy are also able to contribute to the community, for instance by providing employment opportunities, so the distribution of wealth is also seen in functionalism as legitimate (fair).

Marxist views

Marxists see the unequal distribution of wealth as the inevitable consequence of capitalism, which is based on the exploitation of one class by another.

Weberian views

Weberian views argue that the distribution of wealth in capitalist societies is partly the result of the supply and demand for various skills in the job market. Those with skills which are scarce and highly regarded receive the highest incomes and may stand, therefore, to accumulate high levels of wealth, while those whose skills are less scarce (or just easier to obtain), and not so highly regarded, will have lower income and less wealth.

Weberians, thus, refer to primary and secondary labour markets, those workers in the former having preferential incomes and conditions to those in the latter. Weber argued that workers or professional groups who could control access to their professions would be more likely to gain higher rewards. However, status and political power are also important factors in determining income and wealth, and these may have little to do with supply and demand, or skill.

Weberian views tend to overlap with social democratic thought on inequalities in wealth and income; both views would see a role for the state in intervening to limit the range of inequality, for instance by imposing minimum wage levels and taxation.

New Right views

New Right thinkers, like functionalists, see inequalities in income and wealth as inevitable, necessary and highly beneficial to the maintenance of a flourishing society. Without inequality, New Right thinkers argue, there would be a lower standard of living for all, since there would be no incentives to encourage individual initiative and enterprise. Market forces create inequalities in income and wealth, but for those who agree with the views of the New Right, it is not possible to have wealth without having a division between rich and poor.

The difference between the New Right and functionalist thought is that, for the New Right, the state is a mechanism which hampers the most efficient operation of market forces and which, therefore, ought to be reduced to the bare minimum necessary for orderly society. Functionalists of course, see the state as expressing and generating value-consensus.

Feminist views

Feminists can contribute something to theoretical explanation of inequalities in income and wealth, since they can point to the invariably male bias of much research into income and wealth.

Many sociologists have neglected women's financial contribution to family income or, alternatively, have not recognised the way that inequalities in income and wealth are not simply a matter of class, but also affect individuals differentially according to their gender. Many of those in poverty are women, and women earn less than men and are more likely to live in poverty than men. This reflects the patriarchal nature of society, whereby women are less likely to be employed, more likely to earn less (for the same work), and form with their children the majority of single-parent families.

Sociological explanations of poverty

Culture of poverty

Anthropologist Oscar Lewis first developed this explanation of poverty. He argued that the poor developed their own culture as a response and

Wealth, poverty and welfare

> **FACTFILE**
> - A report published by the Joseph Rowntree Foundation in 1998, produced evidence indicating that Pakistanis and Bangladeshis are the poorest groups in the UK, experiencing approximately four times the amount of poverty found in the white population.
>
> Source: *Sociology Update* (1999)

adaptation to living in poverty. In particular, the poor develop a different value system, and take a fatalistic approach to life. This fatalism prevents the poor from acting to improve their situation and to escape from poverty. According to Lewis, the poor are best characterised as passive, and lack the determination to succeed. This culture is seen as causing poverty because it is transmitted to each successive generation, making it difficult to escape from poverty.

A variation of this explanation focuses on the cyclical nature of poverty. The term 'cycle of poverty' was popularised by New Right thinker and Conservative politician Sir Keith Joseph in the 1980s.

Situational constraints

The idea of 'situational constraints' is associated with American sociologists such as Liebow and Hannerz, who developed the theory as a way of modifying cultural explanations. This explanation is critical of the culture of poverty theory, and argues instead that the actions and attitudes of the poor are a rational response to the situation in which they find themselves. According to this view, the poor have much the same norms and values as the rest of the population; they are just poorer. The reason why the poor become fatalistic and passive is simply because their situation is, indeed, a hopeless one from which it is very difficult to escape.

Unlike the culture of poverty theory, this explanation assumes that if the 'situational constraints' leading to poverty are removed, it is possible to abolish poverty. Equally, if situational constraints remain, the idea of a cycle of poverty can be raised again.

Dependency culture and the underclass

This explanation of poverty is associated with New Right sociologists such as Charles Murray and David Marsland. Both see the welfare state as creating a dependency culture amongst the poor. It is argued that the generous benefits provided by the welfare state remove the incentive to work, and encourage idleness and antisocial values. The poor become passive and incapable of self-motivation, and increasingly dependent upon the state to provide for them. This is seen by Murray to result in a morally degenerate, frequently criminal and unemployable, underclass.

Feminism

Feminists such as Glendinning and Millar (1992) have argued that there has been a feminisation of poverty, and indeed, research by Oppenheimer and Harker (1996) demonstrates that more women than men were living in poverty in 1992. Feminists argue that these patterns are the result of women's secondary position in the labour market.

Although more women are now working, many women work part-time, and they earn less than men. This finding, combined with the patriarchal assumptions built into the benefit system, support Glendinning and Millar's notion that poverty has been feminised (become something associated mainly with women).

Weberian/social democratic approaches

Weberian explanations of poverty see it as a result of inequalities in the labour market. It is linked, therefore, to the fact that capitalist societies are inevitably stratified, but for Weberians poverty itself is not an inevitable aspect of capitalism as it is in Marxist explanations. Weberian approaches argue that poverty can be reduced or eradicated by state intervention, for instance through progressive taxation policies, employment creation schemes, or through providing state benefits such as free education.

The explanation for poverty given by Professor Peter Townsend takes a Weberian approach. Townsend sees poverty as the result of exclusion from the labour market (work). The various groups of people who constitute a large proportion of the poor (the sick, the disabled, the old, single parents, the unemployed) are often those who are excluded from work.

Marxist explanations

Marxist explanations of poverty see it as an inevitable consequence of the capitalist system. Indeed poverty and inequality are seen as a necessary part of wealth generation, and fulfil an important function in ensuring that the capitalist system is reproduced. As Kincaid points out, the existence of, and threat of falling into poverty has several important benefits for employers:

Wealth, poverty and welfare

- It divides the working class between those with higher wages and standards of living and those with lower wages or no wage at all.
- It, thus, creates a reserve army of labour.
- It helps to keep wage levels low.
- It helps to keep benefit levels low, which can in turn help reduce taxes.

CHECKLIST

A number of key evaluative points can be made of sociological explanations of poverty:

✓ **Those advocating the 'culture of poverty' explanation need first to demonstrate that the poor do have a very different set of norms and values to that of the wider society. Studies, such as those by Coates and Silburn and, more recently, Taylor-Gooby and Dean, seem to indicate that this is not the case. Culture of poverty theories, like cultural deprivation theories, also seem to involve researchers in making value judgements about the values of particular social groups.**

✓ **A problem with situational constraints or cycle of poverty type theories, is that they only give a partial explanation, and fail to explain why poverty comes into existence anyway.**

✓ **Dependency culture and the notion of underclass has been criticised for being highly value laden, for empirical inaccuracy (the poor are not welfare dependent, again according to Taylor-Gooby and Dean), and because the notion of underclass is so broad as to be meaningless.**

✓ **Marxist explanations of poverty can be criticised as being too general, and lack the ability to explain the incidence of poverty amongst particular social groups, e.g. women and ethnic minorities. Marxists themselves though would be critical of Weberian-based explanations of poverty which, viewed from a Marxist perspective, simply fail to acknowledge that poverty is a systemic inevitability in capitalist society.**

✓ **While feminists have rightly stimulated interest in how poverty affects women, Feminism can be criticised for providing an explanation of poverty only amongst certain groups.**

Defining and measuring poverty

Definitions of poverty

Any attempt to measure the extent of poverty must start with a definition of poverty which can be operationalised to enable conduct of empirical research. There are two main ways of defining poverty: absolute poverty and relative poverty.

Absolute poverty

Absolute poverty is based on the idea that there is a minimum of resources which is needed to keep a human being alive and healthy. This is sometimes referred to as subsistence poverty.

Measures of absolute poverty are usually defined in terms of the nutrition, clothing, and shelter required. They are said, therefore, to refer purely to 'material deprivation', a lack of the physical resources necessary for survival.

Relative poverty

The concept of relative poverty considers poverty in a different way. This concept argues that poverty must always be measured relative to the average standard of living expected and encouraged in a particular society.

This means that a person having sufficient food, clothing and shelter to survive may still be considered to be in relative poverty if their standard of living is a long way below the average expected in their society. This concept of poverty does not define it purely in terms of material deprivation.

Thus, a person with sufficient food, clothing and shelter, may still lack the comforts, benefits and services enjoyed by the majority in their society, such as adequate educational provision, adequate time for leisure, and the ability to participate in social and cultural activities by visiting friends and relatives.

FACTFILE

- **Poverty is a contested concept – sociologists disagree on how it should be defined and how it should be measured.**

Measuring poverty

The different approaches to defining poverty invariably lead to different ways of operationalising and measuring poverty. As a consequence, there have been competing estimates of the extent of poverty in Britain over the course of the twentieth century.

Wealth, poverty and welfare

The Rowntree surveys

Seebohm Rowntree (1871–1954) was a Director of Rowntree (the chocolate company) and was also one of the first social researchers to investigate poverty in the nineteenth and twentieth centuries.

Rowntree used an absolute definition of poverty and distinguished between primary and secondary poverty:

- Primary poverty – where resources were insufficient to sustain the individual.
- Secondary poverty – where earnings were sufficient but were spent on non-essentials (e.g. beer).

Rowntree constructed a list of essentials that he deemed necessary for survival, established how much these goods would cost, and then investigated the income and expenditure of a sample of households in York.

Using these criteria, Rowntree conducted three extensive surveys examining poverty in York in 1899, 1936, and finally in 1950. From these studies Rowntree estimated that 33% of the population in York were living in poverty. This percentage declined to 18% in 1936 and 1.5% in 1950. Findings such as this encouraged a belief in the 1950s and 1960s that poverty had been eradicated from British society.

Poverty in the UK – Professor Peter Townsend

Professor Peter Townsend conducted a major survey into poverty in Britain in the late 1960s. The results of the survey were finally published in 1979. The survey used a sample of some 2000 households, comprising 6000 individuals, drawn from 51 parliamentary constituencies across the country.

Townsend used the notion of relative deprivation to measure poverty. This involved measuring respondents' standard of living against that seen as customary and which was encouraged and approved of in British society. Townsend rejected the government definition of poverty, seeing it as too close to a subsistence view of poverty. He also rejected measuring poverty by using respondents' income to estimate their standard of living. Townsend argued that this last method confused inequality of income with poverty.

Townsend operationalised poverty by creating a 'deprivation index', which consisted of a list of essential items, services, and facilities. Townsend based his estimate of poverty on 12 key items, the lack of which he argued meant that an individual was in poverty. Using this method, Townsend calculated that 22.9% of the population of Britain (12 million people) were living in poverty. This contrasted to the Government estimate of 6.1%.

Criticisms of Townsend – Piachaud and Wedderburn

David Piachaud has been highly critical of the methods used by Peter Townsend. Townsend used the relative deprivation index precisely because he wanted to demonstrate that his estimate of poverty was an objective measure, Piachaud argues that it is a subjective measure.

Piachaud questions why Townsend picked 12 key items without which respondents were considered to be in poverty. Piachaud gives the example of a lack of fresh meat or cooked meals, which Townsend considers to be essential. Piachaud argues that people may dislike these foods, and since the 1960s many people have adopted different eating habits, e.g. vegetarianism. Townsend's method may be imposing his own value-judgements of what is an essential item.

Dorothy Wedderburn points out that, rather than finding what the customary standard of living included, Townsend made assumptions about what it was. As a result, Townsend's measurement of poverty is arbitrary (opinion not fact).

Mack and Lansley

Joanna Mack and Stuart Lansley conducted research in the 1980s which aimed to avoid the criticisms made of Townsend's study. The study was based on a sample of 1174 individuals.

Mack and Lansley used a relative definition of poverty. However, in asking respondents about their standard of living, they asked further questions to distinguish between taste and inability to purchase certain items. To avoid the criticisms of subjectivity, Mack and Lansley used a deprivation index which was constructed by asking respondents to comment on what they considered were the essential items needed to live in modern Britain. The most common responses were then measured; all items which over 50% believed to be essential were included in the index. Individuals lacking three or more were classed as poor by the researchers.

Using this index and generalising from their sample, Mack and Lansley estimated that, in 1983, some 7.5 million of the population (13.8%) were living in poverty. A repeat study in 1990 by the researchers found an increase in the numbers living in poverty, estimated then to be around 11 million.

Wealth, poverty and welfare

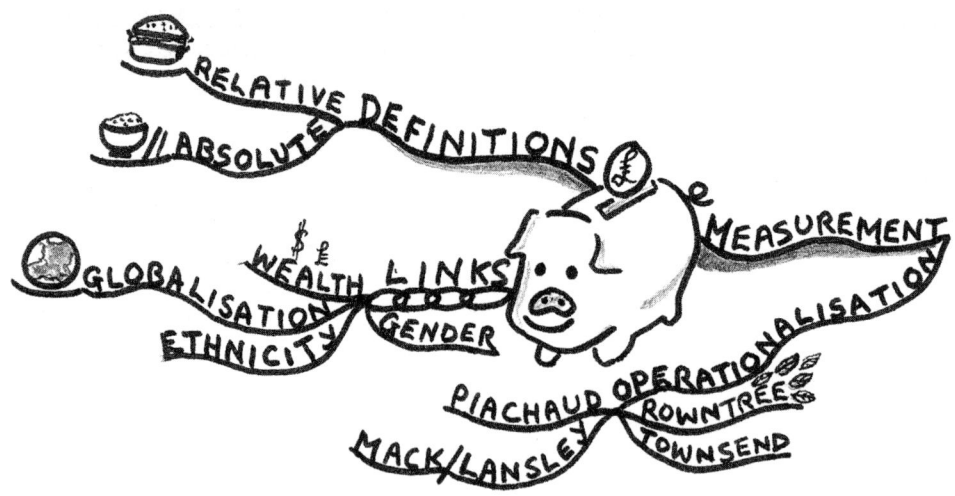

Key concepts in poverty

FACTFILE

- The extent of poverty revealed by empirical studies has varied, partly due to the lack of agreement over how poverty should be defined, operationalised and measured.

Welfare, poverty and social policy

The creation of the welfare state

The term 'welfare state' refers to the institutions that have been created by the state to provide for the healthcare, housing, and education needs of the citizens, as well as providing benefit payments to the sick, disabled, old, or unemployed. In Britain, the welfare state aimed to provide a minimum standard of living for all citizens from 'the cradle to the grave'.

The welfare state can be seen as developing over a long period of time in Britain. Nevertheless, the most important legislation occurred in the late 1940s as a result of the Beveridge Report of 1942. This led to the creation of unemployment benefits, other welfare benefits, and the National Health Service.

The Beveridge Report promoted the idea of universal provision of benefits (universalism), that is benefits to which all citizens were entitled as a matter of right, for example Child Allowance. The welfare state legislation of the 1940s can be seen as a practical application of social democratic principles.

Recent welfare policy issues

Since the late 1970s, the welfare state has been seen by many politicians and commentators to be in a state of crisis as costs have increased, and more demands have been placed on its services. These pressures led to debates about the possible extent of welfare provision and, since the late 1970s, a range of new policies have emerged.

The principle of universalism has come under increasing criticism. Some sociologists (e.g. Walker) have argued that welfare has become increasingly selective – benefits are increasingly being paid on a discretionary basis, some charges have been introduced (e.g. for medical prescriptions) and some benefits or grants have been converted into repayable loans (e.g. social fund). There has been extensive privatisation or marketisation in some welfare services, such as the NHS and the state education service.

In the 1980s and 1990s there was increasing use of 'community care' policies which aimed to reduce the amount of institutionalised facilities for the mentally ill, those in the care of social services, and other sick, disabled, or elderly individuals. This policy has been seen as the result of government attempts to reduce welfare expenditure and to place responsibility for care upon the family and the individual.

Welfare provision is now termed by some sociologists as 'welfare pluralism' since the comprehensive support network provided by the 1940s legislation has been slimmed down. Welfare provision is now available from the state and from a range of private providers, such as private medical care, and private residential and nursing homes for the elderly.

Wealth, poverty and welfare

> **Summary**
>
> **Universal provision**
> - Advantages:
>   - Easier and cheaper to run with less bureaucracy since all are eligible.
>   - Avoids poverty trap since benefits are not withdrawn if individuals start to earn their own income.
>   - When benefits are universal they are much more successfully delivered to the needy since they are easy to claim.
> - Disadvantages:
>   - Critics claim that it encourages welfare dependency.
>   - It may be very expensive since many who do not really need benefits will claim them, therefore depriving the really needy of resources which they could have received.
>
> **Selective provision**
> - Advantages:
>   - Only the most needy receive benefits. This makes the system less expensive and more efficient.
>   - Reductions in costs by being selective could mean the services provided could be improved.
> - Disadvantages:
>   - Selection involves means testing (assessing individuals' financial resources) which is expensive, bureaucratic, and stigmatising.
>   - Selection becomes complex and bogged down in red tape and this discourages claims – often from those most in need.

Sociological explanations of the role of the welfare state

Functionalist explanations

Functionalists such as Parsons use the concept of structural differentiation to explain the way the needs of complex industrial societies change. Complex societies require integration, in order to function effectively and to transmit value-consensus throughout society. Welfare is provided more effectively by the state in a complex society, and in taking on this role, the state is able to promote and reinforce social norms and values, thus strengthening social integration.

Marxist explanations

The Marxist view of the role taken by the welfare state is also a functionalist one, but it sees the welfare state in a much more critical way. Marxists argue that the welfare state increases the efficiency of capitalism, by maintaining the working population to minimal standards of health and welfare. However, this is purely to enable capitalism to function efficiently.

Accordingly to Marxism, the welfare state is simply an ideological device which legitimates capitalism (makes it seem fair), and is, therefore, a form of social control. The welfare state diffuses political and social unrest by providing minimum standards of free healthcare, unemployment benefits, state pensions for the elderly, and other benefits. It is the capitalist class who benefit most from the existence of the welfare state, since it maintains their privileged position.

Marxists such as Offe and O'Connor provide a more complex analysis. They agree that the welfare state plays a legitimating role, but argue that this creates a contradiction in modern capitalist societies. The welfare state increases the desire or need for services, but at the same time there is likely to be increasing unwillingness to payer higher taxes to fund them. This creates a strain in capitalist societies which is difficult to resolve and likely to cause conflict.

New Right explanations

New Right thinkers have been critical of the role of the welfare state. Sociologists such as Charles Murray and David Marsland argue that the welfare state has a number of negative consequences for society:

- It reduces freedom for individual citizens and leads to expensive, bureaucratic government which is needed to provide and organise state welfare.

- State-run services tend to be inefficient and badly organised, and are unable to cope effectively with individual needs and changing or developing situations.

- It encourages and creates dependency, and stifles individual initiative and self-reliance. Reducing state welfare services would save money and, since capitalism is a self-regulating system (if something goes wrong it will automatically be

Wealth, poverty and welfare

corrected), lead to the creation of alternative sources of welfare, e.g. family, voluntary organisations, the Church, etc.

Social democratic explanations

Social democratic views of the role of the welfare state are critical of the capitalist system, but argue that carefully organised welfare provision can create a greater degree of equality and fairness. In particular, social democratic theorists would argue that:

- Capitalism and the markets it creates are not self-regulating (as claimed by the New Right). They create huge inequalities and hardship, but these can be minimised by welfare provision.
- The state has to act as a referee, enforcing rules which make capitalism fair, and protecting the weak (the poor and the powerless) against the strong.
- If the market forces created by capitalism are not restrained, the whole system will be highly unstable and divided by conflict. The creation of a welfare state will allow capitalism to gradually evolve into a fairer society.

Feminist explanations

Feminist views of the role of the welfare state vary (liberal, Marxist, and radical feminist), but most see the welfare state in terms of patriarchy which maintains women's place in the home and the family. Feminists make several key points:

1. Welfare policies have incorporated dominant patriarchal assumptions about the role of women. These assume that women's primary role and responsibilities are as housewives and mothers.
2. The welfare state maintains and reinforces patriarchal and familial ideology, making it difficult for married women to gain the same rights as married men or single women.
3. Sociologists, such as Glendinning and Millar (1987), and Townsend (1987), have identified a 'feminisation of poverty', whereby the poor are disproportionately likely to be female. This reflects women's inferior employment opportunities, and their dependency within the family on a male breadwinner.

Esping-Andersen

A more complicated view of the role of the welfare state has been provided by Danish sociologist Esping-Andersen. Esping-Andersen conducted a comparative analysis of welfare provision in 18 countries, and argued that the role of the welfare state varies according to factors such as the class structure and culture. Esping-Andersen makes several important points:

- The form of welfare state influences the class structure of a society. Esping-Andersen identified three types of welfare systems; liberal, conservative, and social democratic.
- Liberal systems are not very generous and are typical of countries with a strong work ethic and belief in the free market, such as the USA.
- Conservative systems are very traditional and tend to be paternalistic, as in France and Germany for example; however this means that welfare benefits are distributed unequally according to class and status.
- Social democratic systems aim to promote equality amongst all classes and frequently provide 'universal' benefits available to all. Benefits are, however, distributed on the basis of earnings.
- In liberal welfare systems there is a sharp distinction between those receiving welfare and those who do not.
- Conservative welfare systems tend to reinforce the class and status differences already existing.
- Social democratic welfare systems are more likely to promote equality between different class and status groups.

This analysis suggests that the role of the welfare state will vary from country to country. Esping-Andersen's theory is a social democratic one. Contrary to a Marxist view, Esping-Andersen takes the view that welfare policies can successfully moderate the effects of the free market; it is simply the case that some systems are more effective than others.

Who benefits from the welfare state?

As seen above, theoretical answers to the question of who benefits from the welfare state vary. However, empirical research seems to give little scope for optimism.

Professor Julian Le Grand (1982, 1987), an economist based at the London School of Economics, argues that it is the middle classes who benefit most from the welfare state. The state for instance, funds further and higher education, a service which disproportionately benefits the middle classes (who have a higher participation rate). Similar patterns are found in the health service.

Wealth, poverty and welfare

Le Grand argues that the provision of council housing is one of the few areas where the working classes seem to benefit most. However, even this finding is negated by the considerable tax advantages which the state gives to homeowners.

In a study for the Institute of Fiscal Studies, Giles and Johnson (1994) calculated that the tax burden for the poor increased between 1985 and 1995, while for the rich it declined. Over this period Giles and Johnson calculate that the poorest paid some £3 per week more, while the richest found their tax bill reduced by £31.30 per week.

FACTFILE

- Fulcher and Scott (1999) show that the distribution of assets has not changed significantly since the 1970s, while inequalities in income distribution have increased. In 1995 the richest 20% earned approximately 40% of all income after tax, whereas the poorest 20% earned approximately 8% of all income, whereas in 1979 these figures had been respectively approximately 36% and 9%.

Sample questions and answer advice

'Some have argued that the major reasons for the continuation of poverty are the behaviour and attitudes of the poor.' Critically discuss the sociological arguments and evidence in support of this view.

(AEB, 1996)

Answers should highlight the differences between perspectives which support the quotation, such as the New Right, culture of poverty theories and functionalist views, and those opposed to it, including the situational constraints approach, structural theories such as Marxism and the Weberian/social democratic approach, and Feminist views. Discussion could usefully draw on Murray, Marsland, Townsend, and Mack and Lansley. The latter, particularly, could be useful to focus attention on the nature, extent and persistence of poverty, highlighting the way in which social policies may be based upon moralistic views of the poor, rather than sociological explanations of poverty.

'Despite many sociological studies on poverty, it is still not possible to define a "poverty-line" which will be supported by all.' Critically examine the argument for and against this view.

(AEB, 1994)

Answers should explain the differences between relative and absolute, and primary and secondary poverty. A full explanation of the concepts of operationalisation, validity, and indicators should be given, and should be clearly related to empirical studies of poverty. Discussion can focus on relevant studies of poverty, such as Booth, Rowntree, Townsend, Mack and Lansley, Wedderburn and Piachaud, for example. The notion that poverty is a contested concept could be used as part of a conclusion to the question.

TEST YOURSELF

P	O	I	U	Y	V	C	D	F	E	W	Q	R	T	Y	K	L	P	O
V	S	X	Z	T	O	W	N	S	E	N	D	M	Y	G	E	A	V	S
Q	S	W	R	A	Z	Y	N	P	I	A	C	H	A	U	D	G	Q	S
Z	A	X	E	B	C	C	C	C	V	B	N	M	L	K	J	H	Z	A
P	L	A	L	E	S	D	F	D	G	M	U	R	R	A	Y	D	P	L
E	C	O	A	V	I	U	Y	T	N	R	E	W	A	Q	S	N	E	C
N	R	V	T	E	B	N	M	L	K	E	J	H	G	F	D	U	N	R
I	E	C	I	R	X	Z	A	S	D	D	P	F	G	H	J	F	I	E
L	D	P	V	I	L	M	E	A	N	S	T	E	S	T	K	L	L	D
Y	N	O	E	D	I	I	N	D	E	X	U	I	D	Y	T	A	Y	N
T	U	K	J	G	H	G	F	D	S	A	Q	N	W	E	R	I	T	U
R	L	Z	X	E	C	V	B	N	M	K	L	C	H	G	F	C	R	L
E	P	O	U	N	I	V	E	R	S	A	L	O	A	S	D	O	E	P
V	T	A	R	G	E	T	T	I	N	G	I	M	U	Y	T	S	V	T
O	O	P	K	L	M	N	B	V	C	X	Z	E	Q	W	E	R	O	O
P	Y	T	R	E	V	O	P	E	T	U	L	O	S	B	A	W	P	Y

Solution on page 126

Study and Revise AS and A2 Level Sociology

Wealth, poverty and welfare

Summary

1. Poverty is a contested concept and sociologists and other social scientists do not agree on how it should be defined. The definition of poverty used by a researcher or commentator will have a crucial bearing on for instance, how much poverty is identified, what policies are advocated to reduce it, and which factors are identified as causes of poverty.

2. There are considerable differences in the way that sociologists operationalise and measure poverty. This has lead to debate as to the validity of the key studies in this area. Students should ensure that, where relevant, the issues of methodology, validity, and operationalisation are fully discussed and evaluated.

3. Poverty disproportionately affects certain groups in society; the old, children, women, ethnic minorities, and those from the working class.

4. Despite the existence of the welfare state for over half a century, poverty has not been eradicated, and there is evidence that inequalities widened in the last decade of the twentieth century. These failures may lead some to lean towards a Marxist influenced view of the welfare state as merely a set of institutions which legitimate capitalism. The more optimistic may turn to the comparative analysis of Esping-Andersen.

The mass media — CHAPTER 5

PREVIEW

You need to know:
- theories of the mass media
- sociological debates about who owns and controls the mass media
- explanations of the selection and presentation of the content of the mass media
- explanations of the influence of the mass media on audiences
- the role of the mass media in representing class, gender, ethnicity, and age groups in society.

Theories of the mass media

Functionalism

A functionalist analysis of the role of the media would see it as a key part of the cultural system, providing an effective means of socialisation and integrating society around a set of shared norms and values.

Lazarsfeld and Merton argued that the media has become dysfunctional and is responsible for the 'narcotisation' or stupefying of society due to the provision of too much information and media output, most of it shallow and of little worth. The audience is seen as passive.

Pluralism

The pluralist approach to the media is centred around the view that all groups in society have sufficient power to gain access to and contribute to the mass media. Modern society is seen as essentially democratic and, in terms of the media, this means that the views of all social groups are represented, if not equally, at least proportionately.

Pluralists see the audience for mass media products as discriminating, active, and differentiated. People are selectively exposed to the media (they decide what to watch, read and listen to), thereafter they are subject to selective perception (they perceive media products in different ways), and they selectively recall what they have encountered. Thus, the media may not have much effect at all, apart from reinforcing views which the audience had already acquired.

Marxism

It is important to distinguish between different Marxist views. The main differences are between Marxist instrumentalists and Marxist structuralists.

Marxist instrumentalism

This view, also called the 'manipulative view', is seen as simplistic by some and claims that the mass media directly reflect the interests of the ruling classes. The media are owned by capitalists such as Rupert Murdoch, who ensure that their companies reflect the interests of the capitalist classes. The role of the media is to reproduce capitalist ideology, and to maintain capitalism and the dominant ideology. The audience are seen as passive.

TEST YOURSELF

Daily newspapers and the swing to the Conservatives in the 1992 General Election

Newspaper	Vote intention prior to election (%)		Actual vote (%)		Swing to Conservative (%)
	Con	Lab	Con	Lab	
Daily Telegraph	76	9	72	11	−3
Independent	18	44	25	37	7
Guardian	10	57	15	55	3.5
Sun	36	42	45	36	7.5
Daily Mirror	14	68	20	63	5.5

Source: Crewe in Taylor et al. Sociology in Focus (1995)

1 According to the data in the table, which newspaper's readers had the biggest swing to the Conservative Party in the 1992 General Election? Amongst which social class is this newspaper most popular?

2 Which newspaper had the highest percentage of Conservative voters?

3 Does this data suggest that the media are able to influence people's behaviour?

Study and Revise AS and A2 Level Sociology

The mass media

Answers

1. The *Sun*. Working class.
2. The *Daily Telegraph*.
3. It depends on how you interpret the data, and this in turn will depend on your theoretical perspective. Marxist-influenced sociologists, or those who see the media in terms of hypodermic or 'magic bullet' theories, will tend to argue that the media do have tremendous power to influence people's beliefs and behaviour. Sociologists more persuaded by pluralist views, will argue that people are able to think critically, and that they are selectively exposed to media influence, which is then selectively perceived and recalled. According to this view, *Sun* and *Daily Telegraph* readers would be predisposed to vote Conservative anyway, perhaps due to socialisation, or class-cultural factors, so their choice of newspaper would only reinforce their previously held views. To fully answer this question one would also have to apply knowledge of sociological theories of voting behaviour. However, the question does highlight sociological approaches to media effects in general.

Marxist structuralism

This view, also called the 'hegemonic view' is associated with Gramsci and aims to avoid the 'economic reductionism' which the previous view is seen to involve. The media is not seen to be under the direct control of the capitalist ruling class. Instead, it is claimed that the ruling class dominate through ideological means, or hegemony (leadership, dominance).

The media is dominated by media professionals, who because of their social background, inevitably reproduce the dominant ideology. Hegemony is maintained and alternative views, while they are represented, are marginalised, patronised, or ridiculed (e.g. the 1980s example of 'the loony left', or the popular caricature of lesbian and gay rights issues). The audience is seen to be active.

Feminism

There are different varieties of feminist theory (liberal, radical, and socialist). The key insights of feminist theory as applied to the media, would be that the media reproduce a patriarchal image or stereotype of women and their role in society.

The media is central in the process of reproducing patriarchy, which 'genders' female identity and enforces a separation of the public and private spheres. When women do appear in the public sphere of the media, many feminists would agree, it is in the guise of various stereotypes, usually centring around sexuality, and focusing on their body and their appearance. Whether the audience is seen as active or passive varies according to which version of feminism is examined.

Postmodernism

Postmodernism is an approach to sociology which sees the mass media playing a key role in society. Baudrillard argues that we live in a 'media-saturated' environment, meaning that our whole existence is permeated and framed by the signs and symbols produced by the media. We live in a 'hyperreal' world where what we know about the world is drawn from the media.

At the same time, postmodernism argues that individuals are able to use the media to create their own identity, unhampered by social structures such as class, gender, or ethnicity. The effect of media is global, moreover, since media products (including news) are transmitted rapidly from country to country; we live in a 'world information age'. The audience is seen to be active.

FACTFILE

- In 1995–96 government statistics indicated that 97% of households had a colour television and 2% a black and white set.
- Figures for 1996 indicated that watching television was the most common home-based leisure activity, with an average of 25.1 hours spent watching television each week.
- Older age groups tended to watch more television, with the 35–64 age range watching an average of just over 26 hours, and the over 65s watching around 36 hours per week.

Source: *Social Trends* 26 (1996)

Ownership and control

Whilst it is not too difficult to obtain details of who owns mass media companies, there is some debate amongst sociologists as to the significance of the patterns of ownership. The different views on this issue allow some more evaluation of the two Marxist views, and can be usefully applied to questions concerning media bias.

Marxist instrumentalist views

Ownership of the mass media is restricted to a small elite. This elite controls the production of media products, sometimes in a very direct manner, e.g.

The mass media

> ### CHECKLIST
> - ✓ Both Marxist and Functionalist views tend to portray the media audience as passive.
> - ✓ Critics of the pluralist view argue that the notion of choice is exaggerated by this perspective; in reality the public has a limited choice, and minority views are marginalised in various ways.
> - ✓ It can be argued that Marxist hegemonic views do little to rectify the economic reductionism in other versions of Marxism. According to Marxist hegemonic views, culture is closely related to the dominant ideology and, if this is the case, then it is hard to see how people and institutions can act autonomously.
> - ✓ Critics of Marxist instrumentalism argue that ownership does not always lead to control of media output. This theory again assumes that the audience is passive.

editorial decision-making. There are numerous examples, including Rupert Murdoch, owner of the *Sun* and *The Times*.

A restricted group also controls the distribution (sales) of media in the UK. Trowler notes that WH Smiths control approximately 53% of newspaper wholesaling. TNT are responsible for the distribution of 40% of the newspapers in the UK, while one other company, Newsflow, delivers the remaining 60% (Trowler, 1995).

Instrumentalists argue that this tight restriction on ownership means that the media is inevitably biased, and directly represents the interests of the capitalist class. The state (which is controlled by the dominant classes) reinforces the control of the press, by restrictions on what can be published or broadcast, e.g. through the Official Secrets Act and the D Notice system. (A 'D Notice' refers to a form of government warning to the press and media not to publish material that may be considered a threat to national security. Editors who neglect the warning of a D Notice may find that they become liable to prosecution under the Official Secrets Act.)

Other marxist views

Golding and Murdock argue that it is helpful to distinguish between allocative and operational control:

- Allocative control refers to cases where the owners have strategic and financial control, but do not interfere in editorial decisions.
- Operational control refers to cases where the owner plays a big part in all decisions, including daily editorial decisions.

This approach would suggest that, even if individual owners do not take a direct part in editorial decision-making, the media will still reproduce dominant ideologies. Neo-Marxists influenced by Gramsci's concept of hegemony would also find much in this to agree with. They would argue that, while ownership is no longer (in many cases) restricted to a few individuals, nevertheless the structure of capitalism remains and with it other classes who act to reproduce the hegemony of the dominant class.

Pluralist views

Pluralists would argue that ownership and control, while not entirely unrestricted, is remarkably wide. It no longer makes sense to speak of individual proprietors; most media companies are now owned by groups of individual shareholders, so ownership is diversified and rarely controlled by any one individual. There is little restriction on what is published or broadcast and new technology (the Internet and desk top publishing) opens up the prospect of increased communication, not a reduction, and not the monopoly by those with power and money.

> ### Summary
> 1. When evaluating Marxist and Pluralist approaches to the ownership and control debate remember to note contemporary changes such as digital and satellite television, as well as concepts such as globalisation.
> 2. Globalisation can be seen as increasing the power of the trans-national media corporations who produce media products.
> 3. It is also important to apply and evaluate the theoretical perspectives to this issue (see above).

> ### FACTFILE
> - In 1995 News International had 37% of the UK newspaper market and the Mirror Group had 26%.
> - In 1998 the BBC had 41.7% of the television audience, ITV had 32.4%, and Channel 4 had 10.4%.
>
> Source: *Sociology Update* (1996) and *Guardian Media Guide* (1999)

The mass media

The selection and presentation of media content

A focus of sociological interest on the media has been on whether or not it provides a biased source of information on the world. This question has led many sociologists to study the processes of newsgathering and the production of news programmes and journals.

The manufacture of news

A variety of studies indicate that, far from being a spontaneous production of the day's news, news programmes are a manufactured product just like any other. They are carefully planned in advance and routinely produced using a variety of easily available news items, press packs, press releases, and articles, which are themselves produced by specialist suppliers.

Major national and provincial newspapers and television news producers, acquire many news items from press agencies, companies who provide (sell) brief reports of world or national news 24 hours a day. Well-known agencies are The Press Association, Reuters, Associated Press, UPI, and Agence France Press. In addition to these sources, the media receive many press releases from companies, government organisations, pressure groups, and private individuals, all wanting to gain media coverage for their own purposes.

Schlesinger's (1978) study of news production, demonstrated the importance of the news diary in helping to create the routine of newswork. The 'news diary' consists of important national events, social, political, and economic, around which journalists and editors can start to plan coverage, months in advance. For instance, the date for the Chancellor of the Exchequer's autumn-time presentation of the budget is publicly known, and journalists can research and line-up well in advance economic experts to be interviewed on budget day.

Several studies argue that the production of news is not a neutral process, but is guided by the norms and values of dominant groups and the professional values of journalists, or 'news values'.

News values

The term 'news values' refers to journalists' professional definition of what counts as news, or what it is that makes a good news 'story' (or what is newsworthy).

Galtung and Ruge (1965)

These sociologists studied foreign news reporting and argued that there were two sets of factors which influenced news values: bureaucratic and cultural.

Bureaucratic factors

Bureaucratic values referred to the routines of journalism and the form which these imposed on news items.

Key examples here are time, space, novelty, and clarity:

- News needs to have a sense of immediacy, and to refer to recent events. Historical events are of less interest, and hard to make interesting and relevant to the viewer or reader.
- News events have to be, or be made, clear and simple if they are to have maximum impact and grab attention.
- News items also have to be brief in order to fit into a programme or paper and to allow for a variety of items.

Cultural factors

Cultural values include the following:

- Novelty – the unexpected is highly valued. As so much news is routine, the unexpected gives opportunities to get a 'scoop'; a story which other providers do not have. Unexpected events or disasters are highly newsworthy. Similarly, once an issue or story is ingrained in the public consciousness (e.g. the 'Sleaze' issue in British politics, BSE or Genetically-modified food), it does not go away easily and is automatically newsworthy.
- A focus on elite decision-makers in national and international politics – it is important that the focus is on personalities, the media assumption being that these are always more interesting than organisations or governments.
- An ethnocentric bias – the richest and most powerful nations (the Western nations, Europe, USA) are deemed to be more newsworthy than others. In media folk wisdom 'McLurg's Law' holds that a human disaster, such as an air crash, is only of importance if westerners are killed and, the more westerners killed, the more important the story becomes.

As Stuart Hall and others have argued, one other important aspect of news values is the belief that the media themselves are not biased, but this is a view of which sociologists are sceptical.

The mass media

Agenda setting and the presentation of news

Various studies have argued that the selection of news items presented by the media is not objective, but biased in favour of the issues and concerns which are of interest and relevance to the social groups represented by the media. The processes of agenda setting and gatekeeping are two of the key ways in which bias is claimed to occur.

Tuchman (1972) emphasised the central role of a belief in objectivity in journalists' occupational culture.

Hall (1978) argued that the routine structures, sources and practices of the media, allied to the pressure of regular deadlines, meant that, ironically, it is members of elite social groups who become what he calls 'primary definers'. By this, Hall implies that the elite are able to define the terms on which public debates are carried out; what the key issues and relevant questions are. Hall argues that it is the views of social and cultural elites which are represented in the media, not a true consensus.

McQuail (1994), and McCombs and Shaw (1993) develop and articulate the idea that the media act as agenda setters. Through the selection of what is newsworthy, it is the media which shape the way public debate is conducted. If an issue or point of view is not newsworthy, it will get little or no media coverage.

Gans (1980) suggests that key personnel in the media, specifically editors, act as 'gatekeepers'. They are seen as occupying the key role in terms of the selection of items as newsworthy, and thus the characteristics of this group of people, their social background and values, have been seen by some sociologists as an important area of study.

The Glasgow University Media Group (GUMG) in several studies have focused attention on the process of gatekeeping, and have argued that media professionals are generally white, middle class, and predominantly male, despite increasing recruitment of women in recent years. GUMG argue that the media, especially in the selection and presentation of news, frequently reflect the common assumptions of certain social groups.

Presentation of news

Despite the claims to objectivity of journalists, Tuchman and the GUMG studies identified a number of methods which are used frequently by the media, and which can have the effect of creating bias in the presentation of news items. Tuchman notes the way in which print journalists can edit quotations to create a misleading impression. Quotes may even be printed without attributing them to a source.

In studies of the presentation of industrial disputes, the GUMG note the different contexts of interviewing and filming:

- Company directors were interviewed in plush offices, but trade union shop stewards were often interviewed while standing on picket lines, or against a background of a crowd of men, giving an impression of an unruly and potentially violent mob.
- News items on the economy were frequently presented either before or after items on strikes. GUMG argue that the implication was that strikes and workers' wage claims were solely responsible for Britain's poor economic performance.
- GUMG's evidence suggested a disproportionate focus on industrial disputes in mass production industries; more industrial disputes actually occured in smaller firms. This is an example of the media selecting one set of events as more newsworthy than another.
- Television interviewers' questions were biased; they put the emphasis on strikers to justify their actions, rather than on employers.

The influence of mass media

Another key focus of sociological interest has been on the effects which the mass media might have on the audience. Research in this area has been influenced by a variety of theories; a key difference though is between theories or models which focus on the media and the effects it has on the audience, and those which focus on how the audience actively interpret, criticise and make use of media output.

The hypodermic model

One of the earliest models of media effects was the hypodermic or 'magic bullet' model. This made the assumption that the mass media was a powerful force able to have significant effects – usually for the worse – on behaviour. The work of a number of sociologists could be considered to reflect elements of this model, including the Frankfurt School Marxists and the psychologist Albert Bandura. The model makes the assumption that audiences are manipulable, passive, and dependent.

The mass media

The two-step flow model

The two-step flow model was developed by American sociologists Katz and Lazarsfeld, and Lazarsfeld introduced the theory in a study of the 1940 Presidential elections in the USA. Rather than seeing the media as having a 'magic bullet' effect on all individuals, Lazarsfeld argued that the media influenced key opinion leaders, who in turn influenced other individuals. Opinion leaders could be found at different levels in society and would include teachers, parents, bosses, or friends and colleagues.

The uses and gratifications model

This theory was developed by Trenaman and McQuail (1960) and Rosengren and Windahl (1972). The model departs from the above models by acknowledging that people are not passive in their use of the media, and that they may select or choose to use certain media for certain purposes. They may, for instance, choose to watch a soap opera every day in order to relax and 'switch off' after work. They may even be happy to acknowledge that the programme has little artistic merit; nevertheless they find it 'useful' for their own leisure purposes.

Cultural effects theory

The term 'cultural effects theory' can be used to represent a range of sociological studies which emphasise the long-term effects of media output, while also acknowledging that responses to media output may vary according to social factors which differentiate the audience. So, the influence of the media will be dependent upon the social situation (e.g. class, ethnicity, gender, age, region) of the audience.

Media effects are more likely to influence the audience over a long period of time. Media products contribute to the cumulative build up of beliefs and values. Hence, proponents of this theory refer to the 'drip effect' or 'sleeper effect' – indicating a gradual seeping of certain ideas into the mind of the audience.

Cultural effects theory is reflected in the work of Stan Cohen and Stuart Hall.

'Active audience' theories

The above is a term that can be used to describe theories which emphasise the ability of audience to actively interpret and act on media output. Morley provides a good example, though he refers to his own work as offering a 'structured interpretation model'.

Morley's study, *The Nationwide Audience* (1980), is a well-known example. Morley shows how the audience response to a programme varies according to social position. Morley argued that, according to social position, viewers of *Nationwide* took either a dominant, oppositional, or negotiated response.

Morley's study has the advantage over the theories considered above, that it attempted to recognise the active way in which audiences interpreted media content. However, Morley used panel viewing and group discussion and it can be argued that such methods may have lacked validity, as respondents' answers could have been influenced by the artificial environment.

Morley's analysis appears to have difficulty in explaining why bank managers and apprentices would have the same dominant responses to the programme, while shop stewards and black students were oppositional. These results do not demonstrate a clear class or ethnicity effect; if that were the case, one would expect all working-class respondents' (apprentices and shop stewards) to share a similar response.

Semiotics or textual analysis

Semiology is the study of signs, developed by the Swiss linguist Saussure. Semiology suggests that signs or symbols have meanings which may not be initially obvious. Signs denote (stand for) certain objects, but they may also have other connotations, (suggested or implied meanings), which leads us to form associations with other signs. This has an influence on how we interpret the signs, and semiotics is the study of this process. This theory is highly applicable to the media and to the ways in which audiences interpret the media. However, several key criticisms have been made of semiotic analysis:

- It can lead to a neglect of the economic structures in which any symbolic system must be based (i.e. broader structural factors).

- It can be easy for researchers to assume that their interpretation of the meaning of a media item (or any sign or symbol) is correct, and this will influence the analysis of the audience response. There are, thus, many debates about how many readings there can be of signs, and whether any reading can be seen as the correct one and, if so, how it can be detected.

- Semiology is, therefore, seen by some sociologists as lacking in validity and reliability.

The mass media

CHECKLIST

✓ Hypodermic models of media effects can be criticised for neglecting the many other influences on behaviour, for failing to put human action into a social context, and for portraying human actors as passive recipients of media output.

✓ The two-step flow model, while it examines media effects in a social context, does not satisfactorily explain why or how the opinion leaders are influenced by the media and why the mass of the population might attend to the views of opinion formers. It also fails to consider the view that there could be more than two steps in the process of media influence.

✓ The uses and gratifications model, while it is able to examine audience responses in a social context and able to differentiate between different social groups in the mass audience, fails to explain why different social groups have different ways of 'using' the media. It can also be seen as exaggerating the power audiences have to choose which media they will use and how they will use them. This model assumes that the media fulfils certain needs which people have. However, this assumes that there is agreement over what constitutes a 'need', and indeed how needs can be operationalised and measured.

✓ The cultural effects model has many advantages over the other models discussed here, since it examines behaviour in a social context, differentiates between social groups, and takes account of other social influences. However, it still faces the difficulties of explaining why there are variations in the effects which the media has on groups, and of finding accurate ways to measure media effects.

FACTFILE

In 1997, the programme which attracted the highest number of viewers was the coverage of the funeral of Diana Princess of Wales, with 19.2 million viewers. Various episodes of *Eastenders* and *Coronation Street* dominated the top ten rankings of 1997, taking places 4 to 10 and with viewing figures ranging from 16 to 18 million.
Source: *Guardian Media Guide* (1999)

Media effects and violence

One of the most frequently debated topics in this field is whether the portrayal of violence in the mass media causes violent behaviour. Clearly there is much scope here for students to apply their knowledge of the general theories of media effects, as well as the theories of the role of the media. However, knowledge of some specific studies and some of the key theoretical and methodological issues is also needed. Two studies which may be particularly useful here are those by Belson, and Hagell and Newburn, though other texts will provide further examples.

Belson (1978)

Belson conducted 1565 detailed interviews in London (at home and at a research centre) with a sample of boys aged 12–17. At one stage in the research, Belson gave respondents a list of violent television programmes and asked them to indicate how many times they remembered seeing any of the programmes. Comparing boys who had high exposure with those who had low exposure to violence on television, Belson found a high correlation between committing violent acts and watching television.

Hagell and Newburn (1994)

This study involved interviewing 78 young offenders and comparing their responses with the results of questionnaires completed by some 500 school children. The aim was to discover whether there were significant differences in the sorts of programme watched by each group, in an effort to establish whether violence in the media could be a cause of violent behaviour.

The study found that there were no significant differences in the programmes favoured by each group; young offenders and their peers in school, watched the same programmes. This seems to suggest that television viewing has no effect on violent behaviour. Indeed, Hagell and Newburn

FACTFILE

- One of the key problems which questions on this issue frequently require students to address, is that of operationalising 'violent behaviour' and proving a causal link between media violence and violent behaviour.

The mass media

comment that if anything, television seemed to play a much greater role in the lives of the non-offenders.

Deviance amplification and moral panics

The terms 'moral panic' and 'deviance amplification' are usually associated with the work of Jock Young and Stan Cohen. Cohen's research on youth culture in the 1960s, argued that the 'riots' between mods and rockers were reported in an exaggerated and symbolised manner. This, Cohen argues, lead to the development of an inevitable spiralling of events and a self-fulfilling prophecy whereby more violence occured, thus, having the effect of amplifying the deviance identified and creating a 'moral panic'. The concept was also used by Stuart Hall in *Policing the Crisis*. Hall claiming that the media created a moral panic over 'black crime'.

The links which Cohen identifies in the process of deviance amplification appear to constitute an inevitable chain of events. However, this may not always happen:

- It may be the case that the role of the media in any such process is vastly exaggerated by Cohen.

- Cohen neglects the variety of opinion in the press; not all journalists would give the same account of events. The black press (e.g. *The Voice* newspaper) took a very different line on the reporting of black crime and, indeed, many other issues.

- Pluralists could argue that the media only pick up on news events which they think will genuinely concern their audience. The focus on the 'black crime wave' or the mod and rocker disturbances were not panics, but legitimate reporting of real events with important influences on the wider society.

The representation of class, gender, ethnicity and age in the media

Various studies indicate the extent of stereotyping on the basis of class, gender, ethnicity or age in the media. The effects of such stereotyping can be evaluated using the general theories discussed above.

In terms of gender, media representations have tended to portray women as sexual objects rather than as people. Women frequently appear as passive and subservient to men. Ferguson (1983)

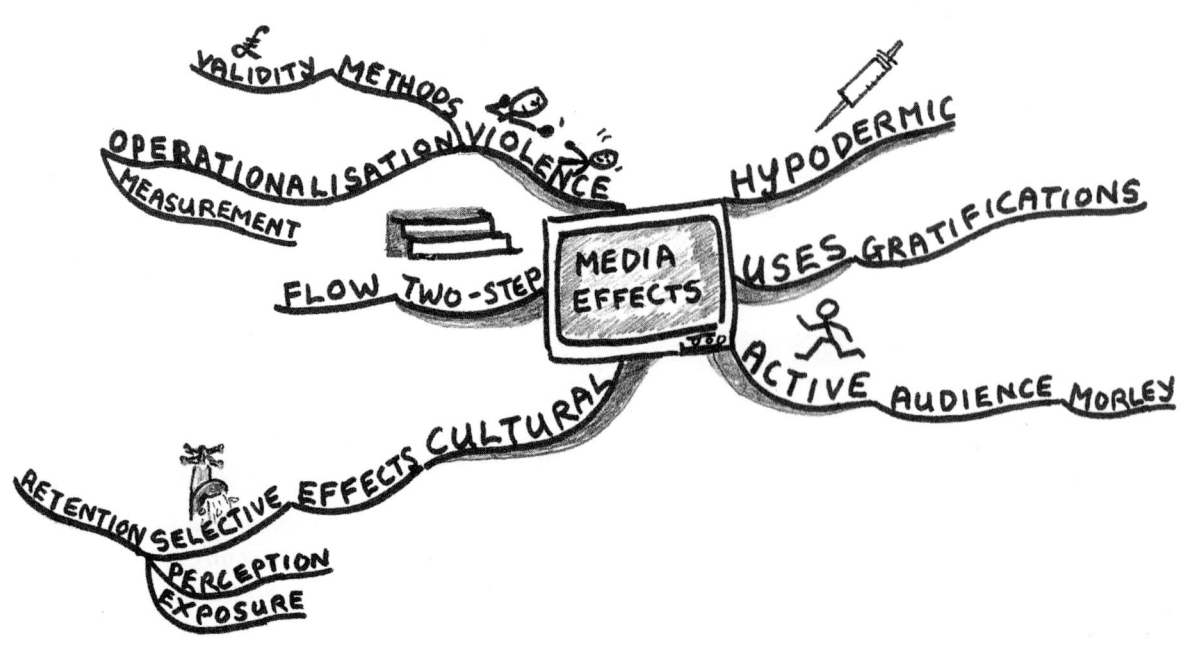

Media effects

demonstrates the way in which the media image of women contributed to gender socialisation.

The media has often portrayed ethnic minorities in terms of stereotypes, as Hartmann and Husband found in their study in 1974. Hall's study *Policing the Crisis*, demonstrates how the media created the myth of the 'black mugger'. However, media portrayals change and ethnic minorities do not passively accept stereotyping. Perhaps the Asian-produced television programme *Goodness Gracious Me* manages to reject such stereotypes?

An American study by Jhally and Lewis (1992) found over-representation of middle-class characters. Further studies would be needed to confirm the extent of this bias. It may be more interesting to consider the extent to which media representations either stereotype or neglect the reality of class differences. In terms of age, Featherstone and Hepworth (1991) argued that negative stereotyping was becoming less common, but at the cost of presenting an unrealistically idealised picture of the elderly.

TEST YOURSELF

Across
1 Key criteria which news professionals look for (10)
3 Glaswegians who watch lots of telly (4)
6 Second half of a double partnership of Marxist-influenced political economists, starts with M (7)
8 French postmodernist who thinks the media is all-important (11)
12 This model assumes the media influence in several stages, or steps (3,4)
15 Editors can fulfil this function (11)
17 Many theories of the media assume that the audience is passive, rather than ... (6)
18 Crude Marxist theory of media (12)
19 Marxist theory of media associated with Gramsci (9)
20 Type of control which most annoys editors (11)
21 The media set it (6)

Down
2 The study of signs (9)
4 He studied the *Nationwide* audience (6)
5 Type of control beginning with A (10)
7 He studied the media's role in deviancy amplification (5)
8 He studied violence and the media (6)
9 This model argues that people have uses for the media which lead to this ... (14)
10 Galtung and Ruge studied values beginning with a B (12)
11 This sociologist did a study on news production (11)
13 Theory of media with lots of needle (10)
14 First half of a double partnership of Marxist-influenced political economists, begins with G (7)
16 Model which looks at the context and effects of media messages (8)

Solution on page 125

Study and Revise AS and A2 Level Sociology

The mass media

Sample question and answer

'The output of the mass media is largely shaped by the demands of their audiences.'

Assess the sociological arguments and evidence for and against this view.

(AEB, 1999)

This quotation reflects a pluralist view of the role of the mass media. Sociological views of the mass media have often tended to reflect either a structural approach or an action approach. Structural approaches have tended to emphasise the role of the media as a means of social control or an ideological device, while action-based theories have tended to emphasise the variety of ways in which the audience may interpret and use media products for their own ends.

Pluralists, such as Whale, argue that the output of the mass media does indeed reflect the demands of audiences. For this reason, the pluralist view is often referred to as the liberal or market view. Pluralists take the view that mass media have to appeal to an audience if they are to be successful, since the public cannot be forced to purchase products they dislike; even in the case of television or radio, pluralists would argue that programming which continually disregards public tastes will lead to a decline in viewing or listening figures, and programmers will have to respond. Pluralists may argue that the relationship between ownership and control of the media is not particularly important, since ultimately the media must be responsive to the audience.

On the issue of concentration of media ownership, pluralists argue that there are regulations to prevent monopolies from gaining a foothold in the British media, as evidenced by the 1990 Broadcasting Bill (amongst others) which imposed limits on media interests. In the context of the widespread availability of cheap desk top publishing and the ability for individuals or minority groups to post information on the Internet, pluralists could undoubtedly argue that just about any view or information can be publicised in some way. In this way, the pluralist view can be presented as a coherent and plausible position.

However, Marxist-influenced views would be highly critical of the quotation, and would argue that it is simplistic to see the media as simply providing the material which audiences desire. The pluralist view appears to neglect to consider both the social background of those who work in the media, and the importance of the concentration of media ownership. There are though important differences within Marxism, in this case between two different Marxist views, the Marxist instrumental view, and the hegemonic or structural Marxist view.

Marxist instrumental (or manipulative) approaches, such as those of Miliband or Althusser, are based on analysis of the relationship between base and superstructure. Such views applied to the mass media, would suggest that the media would inevitably reflect the ideas and interests of those who own the mass media, and these would again inevitably coincide with the interests of the ruling classes. Research by Golding and Murdock on the concentration of media ownership could be interpreted as evidence for this sort of view, although it should be noted that Golding and Murdock would not consider themselves to be Marxist instrumentalists. The Frankfurt School theorists present another articulation of this sort of view. For the Frankfurt School, popular culture and the media represented a commodified and devalued culture, which simply acted as an ideological device. Sociologists such as Adorno believed that mass culture deluded the masses, and duped them into a passive acceptance of capitalism.

The Marxist instrumentalist view is, however, open to several criticisms. The key theoretical criticism is that it is deterministic, and conceives of the audience as passive and incapable of critical thought. It can also be argued that, while there is clear evidence of the concentration of media ownership, it is not so easy to demonstrate the intervention of all owners in what Pahl and Winckler term 'operational control'. The manipulative view also seems to imply that the media works as a form of social control reflecting the interests of the ruling class, but this carries the important implication that all the ruling class share the same interests; it, therefore, may neglect conflicts or competition between different elements of the ruling classes.

Marxist hegemonic (or structural) theory reflects Gramsci's concerns to avoid the problems of economic reductionism. Marxist hegemonic theories, therefore, take the view that dominant groups have to compromise, and that ideological dominance is never completely achieved. While the media and its productive processes may be owned and controlled by individuals from a limited range of social groups, the hegemonic approach would highlight the fact that audiences actively interpret media output, and indeed the media do present some range of alternative views. Examples of studies which use a broadly hegemonic or structural approach are the work of the Glasgow University Media Group and Morley's study of *The Nationwide Audience*. Studies such as these tend to show that, while the media transmit dominant ideologies, these are not passively accepted by an uncritical audience.

The Marxist structural approach is compatible with several studies which show the way in which news gathering and production is socially structured. Galtung and Ruge, for instance, demonstrate the professional values of journalism which structure the way news is defined and selected, through such processes as agenda setting and gatekeeping, and Schlesinger's study of the BBC in the 1970s provides a demonstration of the same processes. These studies, thus, provide evidence against the view that the media simply provide what the public want.

In conclusion, it can be argued that, while there does seem strong evidence to suggest that the output of the media is not strongly shaped by the demands of the audience, this does not mean that the audience are simply passive recipients of media output. This has the implication that, if sociologists are to explain adequately the role of the media, an understanding of both the active role of the audience and of structures of power is required; sociological explanations, therefore, need to examine structure and action.

The mass media

Summary

1. A key factor in all media theories is their view of human agency; are people capable of reflecting freely and evaluating media views, or are they the puppets of structural forces? In some theories the audience is seen as passive, in others it is seen as active. Theories which see the audience as passive have been heavily criticised.

2. Sociological studies have cast doubt on the idea that the media provide a neutral and unbiased view of world events. News media work on the basis of shared professional and cultural assumptions, or news values, and are seen as manufacturing news and 'setting the agenda' for the way many events are seen, and indeed, setting priorities and assumptions about what is newsworthy.

3. Studies of the media and violence involve considerable methodological problems. Where relevant students should discuss in detail the issues of how sociologists operationalise the concept of 'violence' and the indicators which are used. These problems mean that the validity of such studies can be questioned.

4. The media are particularly important in the context of globalisation. Postmodernists such as Baudrillard have argued that the media are now the source of all information and that we now live in a media-saturated environment.

Chapter 6: Work and leisure

PREVIEW

You need to know:
- definitions and theories of work
- theories of the management and organisation of work
- theories of alienation, conflict, and work satisfaction
- the effects of technical change
- explanations of unemployment
- the relationship between work and leisure.

Definitions and theories of work

Defining work

- Work is generally defined by sociologists as paid employment.
- Non-work can include activities such as voluntary work, domestic housework, and leisure.

These definitions can be problematic. Playing football, for instance, is leisure for most people, but for others it is work. Feminists argue that the fact that domestic labour is not paid employment reflects the biases of patriarchal society.

Pahl and Gershuny have argued that sociologists' definition of work as paid employment has obscured large areas of social activity. They suggest that work as paid employment refers only to the formal economy, that is work which is declared to the government and tax authorities. They argue that this neglects the informal economy and the household economy. The informal economy consists of 'work' which is not declared to the authorities. The household economy refers to domestic work, which is unpaid.

FACTFILE

- Sociologists point out that definitions of work are socially constructed.
- When we call an activity 'work', we are not commenting so much on the nature of the task, but rather on the social situation in which it is being conducted.

Theories of work

The main sociological perspectives all have their distinctive views on the nature of work.

TEST YOURSELF

Employees by gender and occupation in the UK, 1991 and 1998

	Males* 1991 (percentages)	Males* 1998 (percentages)	Females* 1991 (percentages)	Females* 1998 (percentages)
Managers and administrators	16	19	8	11
Professional	10	11	8	9
Associate professional and technical	8	9	10	11
Clerical and secretarial	8	8	29	26
Craft and related	21	17	4	2
Personal and protective services	7	8	14	17
Selling	6	5	12	12
Plant and machine operatives	15	15	5	4
Other occupations	8	8	10	8
All employees (millions)	11.8	12.2	10.1	10.6

*Males aged 16–64, females aged 16–59.
Source: Adapted from *Social Trends* 29 (1999)

1. What percentage of men were employed as plant and machine operatives in 1998?
2. What was the most common area of employment for women in 1998?
3. Briefly summarise the employment trends indicated in the table.

> **Answers**
>
> 1. 15%
> 2. Clerical and secretarial.
> 3. The labour force as a whole increased from 1991 to 1998. The data show more women working, and increases in most categories of employment. However, women continue to be most heavily represented in clerical and secretarial work, though jobs in this category may vary in quality. Some categories of work also show an increase in the number of men working, however, men still seem to predominate in managerial and administrative jobs, and slightly less so in the professions. Manual work still appears to be very much a male-dominated area.

Marxism

Marxism is a conflict theory and, thus, sees work as best characterised by the conflicting interests of the different parties involved in the work process. Marx argued that workers in capitalist society are inevitably exploited, since they never gain the full value of their labour. While industrial technology meant a massive increase in productivity, Marx argued that it simply turned the worker 'into an appendage of the machine'. Workers are, thus, said to be alienated, as they gain no personal satisfaction from their work.

Workers become commodities, just like the objects they produce. Marx argues that inhuman working conditions and the different interests of capitalists and workers inevitably lead to conflict. Conflict is built into capitalist relations of production and can only be overcome with the overthrow of the capitalist system.

Functionalism

Durkheim draws a contrast between work in pre-industrial and industrial society. Work in pre-industrial society is less specialised. Since people often have similar sorts of role, society is held together, or integrated, on the basis of these similarities. Durkheim calls this mechanical solidarity.

Work in industrial society is much more specialised. People have very different sorts of role, and may not have much in common. Society, therefore, has to be integrated in a different way. In industrial society the different roles and the different specialised parts of society have to be compatible. They also have to share the same norms and values. Durkheim argues that this is achieved through organic solidarity. The different roles and different parts of society fit together and function like the specialised organs in a living being.

Since industrialisation occurred very rapidly, Durkheim claims that the shared norms and values necessary for organic solidarity may be absent; a situation of normlessness. In such a situation, people think of themselves purely as individuals, and society becomes increasingly based on self-interest and individualism. Durkheim uses the term anomie to refer to such a situation of normlessness. Work in industrial society may be characterised, therefore, by anomie. This can be countered or eradicated by creating a strong consensus and moral order. Durkheim sees this as best achieved by having strong codes of practice governing the behaviour of professionals and workers.

Weber and social action theory

Weber's study of the concept of rationalisation has noted the importance of the hierarchical and bureaucratic organisation of modern work organisations. Weber argues that in modern bureaucratic work organisations, a new form of authority is dominant, whereby action is governed by a set of impersonal rules.

Weber was also an important figure in social action theory, which argues that sociologists must focus on the meaning which actions have to individuals. In this respect Goldthorpe and Lockwood's *Affluent Worker* study provides a good example of a Weberian approach. Goldthorpe and Lockwood reject the concept of alienation, arguing that workers displayed an 'instrumental orientation' to their work.

Feminism

Feminists have pointed out the malestream bias of much sociological writing on work and leisure. Ann Oakley for instance has argued that the sexual division of labour, which has excluded women from work altogether or restricted them to certain types of work, is socially constructed. Feminists now tend to refer to the 'gendered division of labour'.

Walby has argued that the idea of work as paid employment is a patriarchal structure. The study of work, thus, has to examine capitalism and patriarchy. Catherine Hakim has claimed that women's inferior position in the labour market is the result of choice. Hakim claims that some women choose to make a lesser commitment to work, often so as to devote more time to their family. Crompton and Le Feuvre argue that Hakim underestimates the importance of structural constraints which deny women free choice.

Work and leisure

> **CHECKLIST**
>
> ✓ Marxist accounts of work focus on alienation, exploitation, and conflict. Functionalists might point to considerable evidence of co-operation in the workplace and could argue that the concept of alienation is very abstract and hard to measure.
>
> ✓ Functionalists' accounts of work in modern society emphasise the complex and specialised division of labour and the tendency of industrialisation to lead to anomie. Marxists and other critics of functionalism might argue that functionalists put too much emphasis on consensus; indeed, it might be argued that the workplace is more commonly characterised by conflict than by consensus.
>
> ✓ Weber's writing on bureaucracy and rationality offers important insights to sociologists' understanding of work. However, studies, such as those by Selznick, Blau, and Gouldner, suggest that Weber's model of bureaucracy may be inaccurate.
>
> ✓ Feminists point out that much sociology of work and leisure reflects 'malestream' concerns. Work has to be seen as gendered.

Different theories of the management and organisation of work

Scientific management

Scientific management is most closely associated with the work of F.W. Taylor in the early twentieth century. Taylor argued that the scientific study of work would reveal the most efficient work methods and, thus, enable employers to increase both the quality and the quantity of production.

Taylor assumed that workers could be motivated purely by economic gain and that the different interests of employers and employees could be eradicated. He believed that such differences would disappear in successful companies where increased productivity would lead to increased profits for employers and high wages for employees.

Human Relations School

Human relations theory was developed by Elton Mayo, and is exemplified by his well-known studies of the General Electric Company's Hawthorne Plant, which also gave rise to the term 'Hawthorne effect' in sociology. Human relations theory was important for demonstrating that any attempt to understand what motivated workers had to acknowledge that workers were members of social groups.

Mayo found that key factors affecting the effort made by workers were the norms and values of their peer group; this was frequently more important than the prospect of a relatively small economic gain. Mayo's study also helped to demonstrate the view that workers have social needs, including the need for social recognition and self-esteem.

Contemporary management culture

More recent management styles and techniques can always be traced back to their roots in scientific management and the Human Relations School. Many reflect the influence of Japanese and American styles, and manage to combine a focus on making work more satisfying (human relations) with increasing efficiency (scientific management).

There has been a focus on 'quality', as exemplified by techniques such as quality circles, TQM (Total Quality Management) and Kaizen (continuous improvement). However, while involving increasing worker participation in some aspects of work, they also require greater commitment and conformity from workers. They can, thus, be seen as renewed attempts to increase control over labour.

In addition, managers have focused on the flexibility of workers and on techniques such as kanban or JIT (just-in-time). JIT enables companies to save money by reducing the quantity of materials in stock, and flexibility allows the saving of labour costs, since a smaller number of core workers is 'multi-skilled' and can perform a broader range of jobs.

The globalisation of work

The idea that there is now a globalised division of labour carries implications for the management and organisation of work in Britain:

- A globalised division of labour may mean increases in part-time work and in work for women, as trans-national companies (TNCs) relocating in Britain attempt to reduce labour costs.

- There may be an increased risk of redundancy, particularly for those employed by TNCs, which may transfer work or relocate to cheaper sites if necessary or if the opportunity arises. The risk of redundancy may be increased for everyone in an increasingly competitive global economy.

Work and leisure

CHECKLIST

✓ The assumption in scientific management theory that workers are motivated purely by economic factors is widely criticised for being too simplistic.

✓ Marxists have been critical of the Human Relations School (and neo-human relations theory), arguing that it is simply a more subtle method of improving productivity and gaining a very limited form of 'co-operation' from workers; work, therefore, remains exploitative.

✓ A similar critique can be made of contemporary management theories, some of which exhort employees to strive for 'excellence'. These theories can be seen in the light of a Foucauldian analysis – they encourage workers to become self-governing, thus eradicating the need for such stringent management controls as were common in much of the twentieth century.

✓ Critics of the theory of globalisation (e.g. Paul Hirst) might argue that this phenomenon is vastly exaggerated. The risk of unemployment due to global competition is in this sense nothing new, and the nation-state is still able to exert influence and some control on business corporations.

Conflict and co-operation in the workplace

In describing and explaining what goes on in the workplace, some sociologists have emphasised conflict, while others have emphasised co-operation. These differences reflect the various theoretical perspectives taken by sociologists. The key views relevant here are functionalism, pluralism and Marxism.

Functionalist views

- Functionalists see society as characterised by value consensus and shared interests.
- They, therefore, see work organisations as functioning most effectively on the basis of co-operation.
- The concept of anomie can be used to explain any conflict that is observed in work organisations.

Pluralist views

- Pluralists acknowledge that different social groups have different interests. Pluralists, however, argue that the conflicting interests of employers and employees have been institutionalised.
- This does not mean that the conflict has been resolved, but rather that a mechanism has been designed which allows both sides to express their views and work together to create compromises.
- Pluralists are referring here to the development of trade unions, to legal arbitration boards, and to the regular consultation that occurs in many industries between management and trade unions.

Marxist views

- Marxists argue that work in capitalist society always involves the relationship between a capitalist class and the working class.
- This is an exploitative relationship, since workers produce far more wealth than they receive back in the form of wages.
- Capitalists and workers, thus, have different interests: capitalists wish to maximise profit; workers wish to maximise wages.
- The relationship will always involve conflict, although this may not always be easy to identify. Some Marxists argue that conflict can be disguised, and consent manufactured or legitimated in various ways.

Explaining conflict at work

Conflict in the workplace may take various forms, including strikes, industrial sabotage, and various forms of work stoppage. Sociologists also argue that other phenomena, such as high rates of absenteeism, may reflect conflict.

Sociological interest has focused on the most overt forms of conflict, such as strikes and industrial sabotage. The various theoretical perspectives referred to above can be applied to explain strikes, but a number of more detailed factors can be offered to explain why strikes occur in any particular case, including the following:

- community integration and solidarity
- changes in technology
- forms of negotiating practice
- demands for higher wages
- threat of redundancy
- resentment of managerial authority or style.

Work and leisure

Industrial sabotage

Strikes are not the only form that conflict in the workplace may take and workers can sabotage or undermine the work process in many different ways.

Taylor and Walton identified several different reasons why workers might take such action:

- to release tension and frustration
- to make the job easier
- to try and gain some control over the work situation.

CHECKLIST

✓ Some sociologists have concluded that both conflict and co-operation are clearly visible in the workplace.

✓ Edwards and Scullion suggest that the amount of conflict and consensus will vary according to a range of factors. Nevertheless the potential for conflict cannot be eliminated.

✓ Clegg and Dunkerley offer the view that the methods of control used by management will vary as the nature of capitalism changes. This is relevant to current developments.

The effects of technical change on work satisfaction

In recent years a number of changes in the nature of work have been identified by sociologists. In particular, sociologists have noted the following features:

- an increase in the number of part-time workers
- an increase in the flexibility expected of workers and companies
- an increase in the number of women in the labour force
- an expansion in the service sector of the economy and a contraction in the manufacturing sector.

There is debate about how these changes should be interpreted and, in particular, about whether changes in the nature and organisation of work and the workforce are caused by technology or not.

Deindustrialisation

American sociologist Daniel Bell argues that we now live in a post-industrial age. The success of industrial society is such that material (economic) needs can now be adequately met in modern industrial society. The manufacturing sector in such societies has, therefore, declined and there has been a concentration on non-material needs which has meant an increase in the service sector. Bell concludes that industrial society is now best understood as a knowledge society. This inevitably involves a decline in manufacturing work, an increase in white-collar jobs and changes in the organisation of work.

Deskilling

American Marxist Harry Braverman has suggested that work in modern capitalist society is being consistently deskilled as capitalists take control of the work (labour) process. Capitalism involves the separation of the conception and the execution of work. Management takes control of the planning of work and simplifies it into routine repetitive tasks.

This increases productivity and thus helps to increase profit. It also means that workers need lower levels of skill and, therefore, can be paid less. Work satisfaction and the workers' control over their own labour are considerably reduced.

Braverman argues that this process is also applied to white collar clerical work. The theory of deskilling, therefore, complements a Marxist belief in the polarisation of the classes, as the middle and working classes find themselves in the same position as their work is deskilled and wages fall.

Post-Fordism

Post-Fordist theorists, such as Piore and Sabel, argue that capitalist societies have now developed into a new form of economic organisation. New technology has enabled the growth of flexible production methods, allowing firms to produce a wider range of more specialised and customised goods than was possible in the era of mass production (Fordism). Post-Fordists argue that the decline of mass production has involved the re-invention of craft skills and craft technology, and that workers are given new opportunities for developing skills and creativity.

Neo-Fordism

Neo-Fordism argues that, although there have been changes in economic organisation in capitalist societies, there is a lot more continuity than post-Fordism suggests. In particular, Neo-Fordism is much more pessimistic about the opportunities for workers to develop creativity in the new production methods.

Work and leisure

Technology and the experience of work

Many sociologists have studied the relationship between technology and workers' satisfaction. There is much debate around the issue of whether advanced industrial technology inevitably leads to alienation or not. Some of the main studies are indicated below.

Blauner

In a well-known study, Blauner attempted to measure the relationship between different production technologies and alienation. He argued that alienation was high in factory and assembly work, but that it declined with the advent of automated process technology. Blauner reported that workers in the chemical process industry required higher levels of skill and more opportunities for autonomy.

Mallet

Marxist Serge Mallet also conducted research into the effects of automation but argued that automation would increase class conflict, since in giving workers more control over the work process they would become increasingly aware of the nature of their position, that is as exploited labour.

Gallie

Duncan Gallie conducted a cross-cultural study, examining automated plants in Britain and in France. Gallie found that there were differences in workers' job satisfaction and attitude to management. He argued that these were not determined by the production technology, but reflected cultural differences between the French and British workers. He concluded that technology does not impose any particular set of work attitudes.

Goldthorpe and Lockwood *et al.*

In the *Affluent Worker* study, Goldthorpe and Lockwood claimed that they could find no signs of alienation amongst their sample workers. The workers' attitudes to their jobs were instead described as 'instrumental'. The authors argue that the workers had chosen their jobs because they would offer high rates of pay; they did not expect to find the work interesting as well.

Goldthorpe and Lockwood argue that technology does not determine attitudes to work and job satisfaction; on the contrary, these are formed by factors outside the workplace. Goldthorpe and Lockwood argue that job satisfaction is influenced by cultural norms and values, not technology.

Information Technology

Several recent studies of the impact of information technology on the process of work tend to support the view that it is the social organisation of technology which determines work practices and, thus, job satisfaction, not the technology itself.

Studies by Zuboff, Clarke *et al.*, and Kling, all reach this conclusion, although there are differences between them and detailed debate as to whether they have successfully avoided technologically deterministic explanations.

Summary

1. The studies above reflect different approaches to the issue of technological determinism.
2. Blauner supports this idea, arguing that worker attitudes reflect the type of technology in the workplace.
3. Gallie, and Goldthorpe and Lockwood though, take the view that social factors are more important, and that technologies may be used in many different ways.

FACTFILE

- Some sense of the transformation of work in the UK can be gained from the fact that in 1981 one-third of all male jobs (as employees) were in the manufacturing sector and by 1998 this had fallen to a quarter.

    Source: *Social Trends* 29 (1999)

Explanations of unemployment

Sociologists have offered numerous explanations of unemployment. However, the first difficulty to recognise in studying this area, is that definitions of unemployment vary.

Definitions of unemployment

The government definition

The government's official unemployment statistics define and measure unemployment in terms of those claiming unemployment benefit. Claimants must be actively seeking work. However, government regulations exclude many categories of people from claiming unemployment benefit, such as married women (who may not have made sufficient national

Work and leisure

insurance contributions to be eligible) and young people who are unemployed but eligible for government training schemes.

The International Labour Organization (ILO) definition

The ILO defines unemployment as those without work but who are available to start work within two weeks, and who have been seeking employment for a month. This definition excludes anyone with a part-time job.

These variations in definition can, in theory, make a considerable difference to the unemployment statistics. However, more importantly they reflect the fact that defining and measuring unemployment is a politically sensitive process.

Different types of unemployment

Economists and others have identified several different types of unemployment. These may indicate different causes of unemployment.

Frictional unemployment

This refers to a small degree of unemployment that inevitably occurs as people change jobs and have a short temporary break between employment contracts.

Cyclical unemployment

This refers to unemployment that is related to changes in the business cycle. Firms respond to a recession or fluctuation in the market by laying off surplus staff and reducing output.

Structural unemployment

This refers to unemployment caused by a change in the structure of the economy. This may be the result of new production methods (e.g. computerised manufacturing) which lead to a decline in the need for some jobs and an increase in demand for new skills. Labour market vacancies exist, but the unemployed do not have the required training or skills needed for the new employment opportunities.

Structural unemployment is illustrated by the decline of the British coal industry in the 1980s and early 1990s, and the Sheffield steel industry in the same period. There have been very high levels of unemployment for those involved in these industries. New employment opportunities have often required different skills to those needed in the old industries.

Structural unemployment may occur on a regional basis, as indicated by the examples above. Labour shortages may exist in other regions, although here too, they may be in new industries, requiring new skills.

FACTFILE

- Unemployment can be defined and measured in several different ways.
- Governments have an interest in defining and measuring unemployment in such a way as to minimise the proportion of the workforce who are counted as unemployed.

Sociological explanations of unemployment

Unemployment is sometimes explained in individual terms; those who are unemployed may be seen as idle, and as not wanting to work. Sociological explanations reject such theories, and are critical of the lack of consideration of the role of social factors in explaining unemployment.

New Right explanations

Unemployment is seen as resulting from high wages and wage claims from workers and trade unions. This reduces the profitability of industry and trade, and employers reduce costs by shedding labour. Employers may also be burdened by high rates of taxation, and can recoup such losses by reducing employment. In addition, high taxation of the working population discourages spending, thus adversely affecting industry.

New Right thinkers thus argue that workers put themselves out of a job by excessive wage demands. The way to avoid unemployment is for workers to accept lower wages.

Marxist explanations

Marxists see unemployment as an inevitable result of capitalism and the free market. They would argue that unemployment arises as employers try to maintain and increase the rate of profit by reducing the cost of labour. They may do this by paying workers less, by using more part-time workers (who are cheaper), or by making some of their labour force unemployed.

Marxists argue that having a pool of unemployed workers (called the reserve army of labour) is beneficial to capitalism. It keeps wages low, as the employed will be prepared to accept lower wages rather than risk unemployment.

The relationship between work and leisure

Leisure can be defined as what remains after work and non-work obligations have been fulfilled. Stanley

Work and leisure

FACTFILE

- Government statistics indicate that the highest levels of unemployment occur amongst ethnic minority groups.
- For young people in the 16–24 age range, those in the category 'Black' had the highest unemployment rate (39%) in 1997–98.
- For those aged from 45 to retirement, the highest unemployment rate (26%) was found amongst Pakistanis and Bangladeshis.

Source: *Social Trends* 29 (1999)

Parker argues that, in industrial society, the type of leisure activity an individual indulges in will be related to their occupational class. Parker identifies three patterns of work–leisure relationship:

1. The oppositional or segmented pattern is common amongst unskilled workers or routine clerical workers who have little control over their work and use leisure as an escape.
2. The extension pattern is typical of professionals or skilled workers who gain job satisfaction from their work and, thus, find that their work interests often overlap with leisure activities.
3. The neutral pattern occurs where there is no strong contrast between work and leisure, and is found amongst unskilled workers and clerical workers.

More recent views have been critical of this approach. Feminists have argued that the separation of work and leisure cannot be easily applied to women. Postmodernists such as Lash and Urry have identified a number of key changes in leisure in contemporary society. Firstly, consumption has become a key source of identity and leisure, therefore, revolves much more around consumerism. Secondly, there has been a blurring of the boundaries between work and leisure. Lash and Urry give as an example the extension of trading hours and the increase in businesses that trade throughout the week. This is eroding the idea of 'the weekend', and thus blurring the difference between work days and the weekend. Thirdly, leisure has become more privatised. Satellite television is an example of the globalisation of leisure, since viewers can watch programmes from around the world. Lash and Urry claim that it increases the tendency towards individualised or privatised use of leisure time, rather than partaking in group leisure activities.

The postmodernist view implies that the relationship between class and leisure is of declining importance. A Marxist-inspired criticism of this postmodernist approach would have to pose the question of whether leisure has not simply been turned into yet another set of products to be bought and sold for profit. Leisure has been commodified.

In the 1970s some sociologists predicted that technology would reduce the need for long working hours, and that a leisure society would be created. Arguably, this now seems a remote possibility for most, with the UK having the longest average working hours in Europe.

Sample questions and answer advice

Assess the extent to which more flexible ways of organising work are likely to decrease workers' sense of alienation.

(AEB, 1998)

This question could be suitably tackled by starting with a discussion of sociological work on alienation, using Marx and Blauner, and Braverman. However, the question also requires consideration of more recent theories on flexibility and post-Fordism. Writers such as Piore and Sabel have argued that post-Fordism leads to increased flexibility and job satisfaction for workers. Others, such as Pollert, are critical of the extent to which post-Fordism succeeds in this and, indeed, argue that it can lead to increased stress and exploitation. Theories of alienation can be applied to this debate, as can the older studies by Blauner and Braverman; it could be that flexible production will merely intensify the work process.

Evaluate the view that recent social, economic, and technical change are creating more diverse patterns of work, non-work, and leisure.

(AEB, 1999)

To start with, this answer requires careful definition of the terms work, non-work, and leisure. It can then continue to discuss debates about the nature of change in these areas. Key theories which should be discussed here are, on the one side, those who argue in favour of a shift from Fordism to post-Fordism or neo-Fordism. Against this, cite those sociologists or theories which argue in favour of continuity, such as Pollert, Kumar, or the Marxist view. An emphasis on change can refer to concepts such as globalisation, changing work patterns, and the erosion of boundaries between work and leisure. An emphasis on continuity can refer to and apply Marxist theory to reinforce the view that exploitation and conflict continues, as does a sharp contrast between home and (for many) meaningless work. A suitable conclusion might be that although work and leisure have changed considerably over recent years, a postmodernist-influenced conclusion that the patterns are ever more diverse is at present a distorted view for all but a minority.

Work and leisure

TEST YOURSELF

A	Y	J	N	L	B	T	M	I	K	A	H	A	C	Q	E	W	E	Z
G	N	F	E	K	P	O	S	T	F	O	R	A	I	S	M	P	O	X
V	O	R	P	U	V	W	J	E	N	A	D	S	B	P	Y	J	L	W
F	I	C	N	W	T	X	R	V	B	Q	C	P	R	I	U	K	H	Q
E	T	N	B	X	U	C	F	N	T	Z	V	T	N	C	S	L	T	P
U	A	U	N	R	E	T	T	A	P	N	O	I	S	N	E	T	X	E
I	N	P	O	Z	H	A	N	O	M	I	E	U	Y	K	P	M	V	Y
K	E	L	Y	S	G	M	R	E	N	U	A	L	P	N	H	E	F	M
S	I	K	W	D	W	O	B	R	Y	X	R	Y	L	F	O	L	C	O
N	L	G	N	W	S	U	K	K	A	I	Z	E	N	B	L	F	X	N
O	A	M	A	E	P	F	G	S	H	B	U	G	G	I	W	M	P	O
I	I	B	M	F	L	O	E	R	U	S	I	E	R	A	Q	S	D	C
T	G	A	R	L	E	R	L	H	Q	H	P	N	K	D	D	I	E	E
A	A	X	E	J	A	D	C	L	I	J	J	D	F	V	A	R	F	L
L	F	Z	V	U	X	I	S	G	K	F	R	S	M	X	J	O	H	A
E	E	C	A	K	C	S	J	Y	M	V	G	F	O	R	P	L	G	M
R	H	V	R	I	J	M	Y	Q	F	M	M	J	J	O	H	Y	K	R
N	I	Q	B	B	M	R	T	W	R	U	Z	T	D	T	K	A	J	O
A	P	A	A	H	F	L	E	X	I	B	I	L	I	T	Y	T	L	F
M	M	U	Q	V	B	M	R	Z	I	L	B	W	K	Y	N	B	D	N
U	F	G	T	U	D	E	S	K	I	L	L	I	N	G	V	K	C	I
H	V	D	T	N	O	I	T	A	S	I	L	A	N	O	I	T	A	R

Solution on page 126

Summary

1. Sociologists distinguish between work, non-work, and leisure. It is a good idea for students to show that they understand the differences between these definitions where it is relevant, or even just to give some acknowledgement of the difficulties, e.g. simply referring to 'paid work' in a question about flexibility.

2. The re-structuring of the economy has led to the use of new technology and new work practices. These have changed the structure of the workforce and the nature of work.

3. Many sociologists have seen the workplace as characterised by both conflict and co-operation. This is a useful point to consider if answering questions which require an evaluation of competing theoretical perspectives on work and leisure.

4. Leisure can be seen as an increasingly important source of identity, or as becoming increasingly commodified.

Power and politics — CHAPTER 7

PREVIEW

You need to know:

- sociological definitions and theories of power and politics
- the role of the state
- decision-making and the political process
- sociological explanations of voting behaviour
- the influence of the mass media in politics.

1 Definitions of power

Sociologists do not agree on how power should be defined, and there are several definitions which are commonly referred to.

Weber's definition

Max Weber defined power as the ability of an individual or group to achieve their own goals or aims, even when others are trying to prevent them from realising them. Weber makes a distinction between power and authority: people accept the right of others to make decisions and give orders if they have the authority to do so.

In modern society, Weber argues that authority is usually based on what he calls 'legal–rational' grounds, that is on impersonal rules which may be applied by an appropriate official. He sees this as very different to societies in which people act on the basis of tradition and decisions are accepted because 'things have always been done like this'. It is also very different to a society in which a charismatic ruler is able to rule on the basis of personal appeal.

TEST YOURSELF

How Britain voted in the 1997 General Election

	Social class*				Gender*		
	AB	C1	C2	DE	Men	Women	Total
Conservative	42	26	25	21	31	32	31
Labour	31	47	54	61	44	44	44
Liberal Democrat	21	19	14	13	17	17	17

*Percentage of the total vote

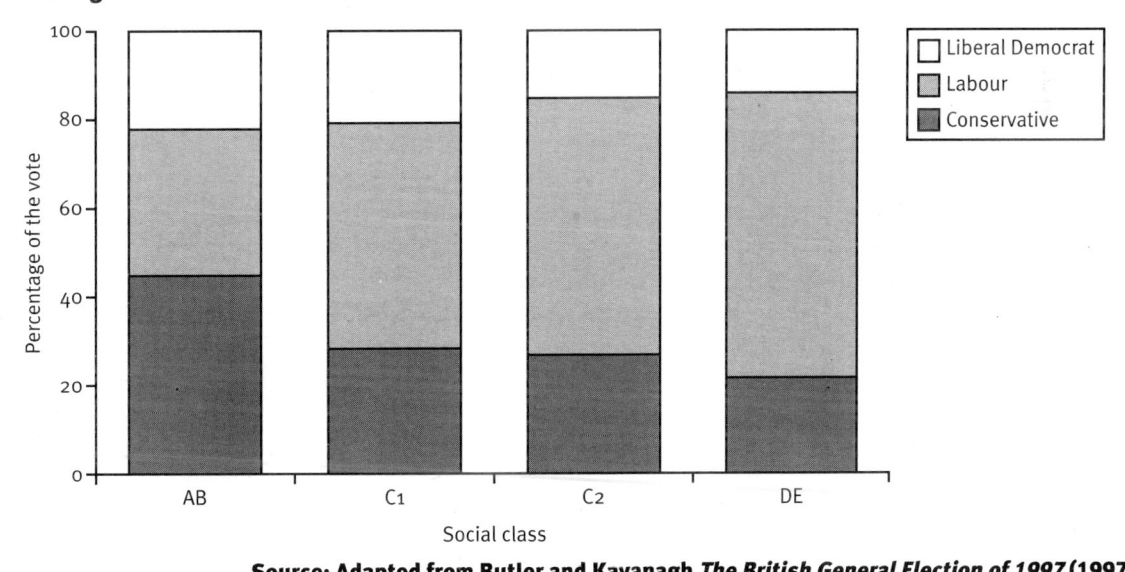

Class voting in the 1997 General Election

Source: Adapted from Butler and Kavanagh *The British General Election of 1997* (1997)

1. From which socio-economic group did the Conservatives gain the highest percentage of votes in the 1997 General Election?
2. From which socio-economic group did Labour gain the highest percentage of votes in the 1997 General Election?
3. Does the data in the table provide support for the dealignment theory of voting?

Study and Revise AS and A2 Level Sociology

Power and politics

> **Answers**
>
> 1 The AB group (42%).
> 2 The DE group (61%).
> 3 This is open to much interpretation. It could be argued that the figures give very little evidence of dealignment, since the data seem to indicate strong relationships between voting and the social 'class' categories used here (note that these are marketing categories, and do not strictly correlate to sociological definitions of class). However, there are large proportions in each socio-economic category who vote 'against' what some theories would see as their 'natural' class choice. Also, it has to be remembered that these figures only show the results for one election — voters may well have chosen different parties at different elections, and those arguing for dealignment could make this point as evidence for their case. It could be concluded that, while there has been evidence of a weakening in the link between class and voting, and while it is not an automatic link, class and voting behaviour do correlate in a significant way (see Heath, Jowell and Curtice, page 66).

Lukes' definition

Lukes conceptualises three main forms of power: decision-making, non-decision-making, and shaping desires.

Decision-making

This is the most obvious form of power. Sociologists can consider how decisions are reached and find out which groups are able to influence decisions and policies.

Non-decision-making

This refers to the idea that power may involve being able to set or fix the boundaries of discussion so that some options or decisions are never considered. Some options are simply not on the agenda for discussion. A government, for example, may suggest that the population has the choice of paying more income tax or paying tax on luxury goods instead. However, the population are not given the option of paying less tax.

Shaping desires

This term refers to the idea that people's preferences and desires can be the result of conditioning over a long period of time. It suggests that power frequently works in much the same way as an ideology, so people accept conditions which are, in fact, not in their best interests.

Lukes gives the example of the population of a town polluted by its dominant employer. People accept their polluted environment which creates high levels of disease because they want jobs. Lukes argues that they do not have the power to make a rational decision.

There are also two ideas about the nature of power which sociologists debate.

The constant sum view of power

This view assumes that power is a limited (or finite) resource; there is a fixed amount of power, so if one party or group has most of the available power, there will only be a small amount left for others. It is also possible that one group may have all the power, leaving the rest with nothing.

The variable sum view of power

This view assumes that there is an infinite amount of power available. Just because one group is more powerful than another, it does not follow that other groups will always have a smaller amount of power. Even in the most extreme conditions, the weakest social groups will always have some power. From a base such as this, groups with less power always have the opportunity to gain further support and, therefore, more power.

> **FACTFILE**
>
> - Power is a contested concept and sociologists cannot provide one definition which all will agree with.

Sociological theories of power

Functionalist

Functionalist sociologists such as Parsons, take the view that power is a general resource which can be used to the benefit of the whole society. Power is not seen in terms of a constant sum view of power, as something that a social group either has or lacks. Parsons' functionalist view of power is termed a 'variable sum' view of power. This means that power is possessed by a whole society, not simply particular groups within it.

Pluralist

Pluralists see power as distributed equally throughout a variety of interest groups or power centres, such as political parties and organisations, pressure groups, occupational and professional organisations, state institutions (e.g. the civil service), and other organisations.

Power and politics

In sharp contrast to functionalists, however, pluralists do not assume that there is value consensus and, moreover, see individuals as having a variety of interests. It is quite possible for an individual to belong to different interest groups and, indeed, some interests may conflict. Pluralists take a constant sum view of power. They see a variety of interest groups competing (on an equal basis) for dominance.

Elite pluralism developed from pluralism. This version of pluralism takes the view that power is not distributed equally between or within different interest groups. Elite groups are seen to dominate the decision-making process.

Elite theory

Elite theory sees society as dominated by a small minority. Elite theories can be divided between those that are supportive of elite rule (such as Mosca and Pareto), and those who are critical of it, such as C. Wright Mills.

Marxist

Marxism sees power as deriving from economic ownership. Economic power becomes political power. Therefore, power is monopolised by the ruling classes, the owners of capital. Marx argues that the ruling ideas in any society are always those of the ruling classes. The ruling ideas of capitalist society act as a dominant ideology which legitimates capitalism.

Politics and political systems

Politics

Politics can be defined in many ways, but is essentially concerned with the way a society is governed through political institutions such as the state, how decisions are made, and the struggle for power between various social groups and political parties.

Sociologists are also keen to point out that much activity at a lower level in society is political activity, thus, they may refer to 'the politics of the workplace', or to 'sexual politics'. These phrases indicate that there are frequently struggles for power at all levels in society.

Political systems

Sociologists have identified several key types of political system: totalitarianism, oligarchy, and democracy.

Totalitarianism

Totalitarian political systems are usually dominated by a single party or a dictator. No opposition is tolerated. There is usually a party or state ideology, and again no alternative ideologies are permitted. In totalitarian societies the state controls all economic and state institutions.

Oligarchy

An oligarchic political system means literally one that is 'ruled by a few'. An example would be a self-regulating elite group.

Democracy

A democratic political system means literally one in which there is 'rule by the people'. Unfortunately, the terms 'rule' and 'people' can be interpreted in different ways. Sociologists and political scientists usually distinguish between direct democracy and representative democracy.

- Direct democracy – this refers to a system in which a whole population have voting rights and participate directly in the decision-making process.
- Representative democracy – this refers to a system whereby a whole population has voting rights, but exercise these on a periodic basis, electing others to represent them in a political institution such as a parliament. The elected representatives then act on behalf of the population and are said to represent the views of the public in the decision-making process.

Power and the role of the state

The functionalist view

Functionalists believe that society requires value-consensus in order to exist. The role of the state, therefore, is to reflect value-consensus. The state functions as an institution which enables societies to define their moral values and rules, which in turn helps to promote social solidarity.

The state promotes the interests of all groups and sections of society and helps to maintain order. Durkheim argued that participatory democracy was impossible in modern industrial society, due to the scale of such societies. However, representative democracy was possible.

Pluralist views

Pluralists see power as distributed throughout a number of different centres or 'sites' of power, e.g.

shared amongst different social groups or institutions. Politics is a matter of the way these different participants have plans and interests which conflict, how they compete to win their own way, and how compromises are reached, since it is unlikely that any group will get its own way. Pluralists, thus, reject the idea of value-consensus.

Pluralists apply this view to understand how the state itself works. Dahl's classic study *Who Governs?* examined local politics in an American city and argued that several interest groups influenced the decision-making process, and no one elite was predominant. In short, Dahl argues that those with power had to listen and respond to other groups if their decisions were to be accepted.

Elite theory

Elite theorists take a constant sum view of power, and argue that domination by elites is inevitable. In some versions of elite theory, this is explained in terms of a natural superiority between individuals and, indeed, social groups, which means that there are natural leaders in society. Thus, the state is dominated, rightly and necessarily, by elites, since these are the only groups capable of ruling effectively.

However, radical elite theorists such as C. Wright Mills offer an alternative view. Mills sees power as a limited resource which elite groups monopolise and use for their own ends. In contrast to a Marxist view, however, Mills argues that the dominant classes in American society are formed by a white, Anglo-Saxon, Protestant cultural elite, who are employed in the higher ranks of the military, the government, and industry.

Mills terms this the 'military–industrial complex', and sees the state as subordinated to the interests of these groups. This is a structural view; the particular individuals may change, but the state will continue to serve the interests of this elite.

Marxist views

Marxists take a zero sum view of power. Power is a limited resource which is monopolised by the ruling classes. Likewise, the state is seen as an institution which always acts in the interests of the ruling classes, legitimating capitalism. However, it is important to note that there are different views of the role of the state within Marxism.

Miliband represents an orthodox Marxist view, broadly as outlined above.

One alternative view is that proposed by Poulantzas, who argues that the state is not under the direct control of the ruling classes but, rather, has relative autonomy. Poulantzas argues that it is the structure of the state and its place in capitalist society which ensure that the interests of capital are always served. This means that the state may not be run by ruling class elites but, nevertheless, the structure ensures that it continues to work in their interest.

Neo-Marxists, such as Gramsci, take the view that the state operates in a more subtle manner. The state reflects the interests of the ruling class, but does so subtly, by creating ideological hegemony. The state is seen as legitimate by the working classes.

The New Right

New Right thinkers take the view that the state in modern society has become too large and powerful. They see the state as hampering individual freedom and sociologists influenced by these ideas, such as Marsland and Murray, argue that the welfare state has created a dependency culture.

The New Right argues that the correct role for the state is simply to protect the freedom of the market, and to enable it to function effectively. In this way, the state would not act in a biased way protecting the interests of one class, but would enable all to have the opportunity to maximise their potential. Reducing the state to the minimum institutional framework necessary for this task would empower all citizens equally.

Decision-making and the political process

Detailed studies into decision-making have tended to be carried out by pluralist sociologists. This is a reflection of the fact that pluralists argue that there is competition for power, that all interest groups have access to power, and that compromises will invariably have to be made. It follows from this that empirical research can identify who has power and how it is used in different situations.

Sociologists from a variety of perspectives, though, have also been concerned to investigate the role which pressure groups may have on decision-making and the political process.

More recently some sociologists have argued that class-based political organisations have been in decline, and it has been argued that there are now political interest groups which form on the grounds of other social characteristics. These groups are known as new social movements.

Power and politics

Pressure groups

Sociologists describe pressure groups as organisations which aim to influence governments and government policy on a limited number of issues. The AA (Automobile Association), for instance, aims to represent the interests of road-users to the government, while Friends of the Earth lobby the government on environmental issues.

Pressure groups are distinct from political parties because they do not aim to form a government and do not enter candidates in elections; their only aim is to pressure the government on particular issues.

Sociologists identify two main types of pressure group: promotional and protective groups.

Promotional pressure groups

These aim to promote and publicise the interests and views of a particular group.

Protective pressure groups

These have the aim of protecting the rights and privileges of a particular social group.

Grant has argued that pressure groups are vital to a democratic political system, providing access to government for a range of views, including minority views. However, others might argue that pressure groups simply help legitimate an undemocratic system, or apply radical elitist views to argue that pressure groups and their leaders simply form another elite, far removed from the grassroots.

New social movements

The term 'new social movements' (NSMs) refers to less formally organised networks or non-institutional groups which aim to promote a socio-political cause. They frequently involve large numbers of people, sometimes in different countries, although they do not have members in the way that institutions or pressure groups usually do. Political action undertaken by NSMs is usually done on an informal basis; there is no policy or formal plan (e.g. the green movement – a wide variety of actions are undertaken).

Some sociologists, influenced by a variety of theories including postmodernism, have seen new social movements as reflecting a move away from class-based politics, which mainly focused around economic issues. New social movements encompassing gay rights, animal rights, or environmental issues, are seen as drawing support from individuals across class divisions.

Paul Bagguley argues that a key difference between traditional pressure groups, which he terms old social movements, and the new social movements is that the latter are less interested in economic issues. In a postmodernist sense, new social movements can be seen as focusing on lifestyle or identity politics.

Ulrich Beck in his book *Risk Society* argues that we now live in a society where class is of less importance, but where individuals face huge uncertainties and risks (such as ecological disaster). It has, thus, become important for individuals to avoid risk. Beck argues that joining new social movements can be a way for individuals to try and manage risk in their lives, for instance, by joining the green movement. It can also lead to the adoption of 'alternative lifestyles', e.g. vegetarianism, as a way of minimising the risks involved in modern life.

For those attracted to postmodernist ideas, NSMs are important as they indicate the existence of a new type of society and a new type of politics. In this view, class divisions are no longer a central political issue around which debates may focus. Others, such as Marxist sociologist Alex Callinicos, would argue that class conflict remains central to understanding contemporary politics.

Decision-making, the nation-state and globalisation

The concept of globalisation has become extremely popular in recent years. Globalisation refers to the idea that we now live in an increasingly interconnected world, where events in one part of the globe can have important effects elsewhere. The role of trans-national corporations (TNCs) gives a good illustration of the effects of globalisation.

Lash and Urry argue that there is now a new stage of capitalism, which they call 'disorganised capitalism'. This involves TNCs which are so wealthy that they are able to have branches in many different countries. This means that they can often rival or surpass the economic and political power of governments.

The implication of this is that a TNC based in Japan or the USA may close down operations in the UK, with devastating effects on the national and local economy. Whereas in the mid-twentieth century, British governments would have considered providing economic help or exerting political pressure to avoid such problems, in a globalised economy the government of any nation-state has less power to influence. So, the political implications of globalisation are that individuals may be affected by events which their government is unable to control.

Power and politics

Sociological explanations of voting behaviour

Voting behaviour is the subject of considerable sociological interest and sociologists have generally been keen to demonstrate the relationship between voting and structural factors, particularly class. In more recent years, the relationship between voting and class has become more hotly debated and remains controversial.

Class and voting behaviour

Classic twentieth-century studies into voting behaviour, such as those of Butler and Stokes, maintained that there was a strong relationship between occupational class and voting behaviour.

In the heyday of the two-party system, Butler and Stokes argued that about four-fifths of the middle-class electorate voted Conservative, and two-thirds of the working classes voted for Labour. Butler and Stokes argued that this partisanship was learnt early in life, through a process of political socialisation.

Those voting against the 'natural' party of their class were termed 'deviant voters'. McKenzie and Silver argued that the deviant working-class voters could be explained in terms of deference (voting for their betters), while others voted on a more pragmatic basis.

Class dealignment

In the 1980s political scientist Ivor Crewe presented a number of studies of voting behaviour in Britain and argued that the partisan relationship between class and voting behaviour was breaking down.

Crewe claimed that knowing a voter's occupational class was no longer sufficient information on which to predict which party he or she would support. He, therefore, claimed that class could no longer be the key factor determining voting behaviour.

Crewe argued that class dealignment was the result of changes in the labour market which led to the decline of traditional heavy industries. In turn, this led to a decline in class solidarity and to the creation of what Crewe termed the 'new working class', usually employed in the private sector and owning their own houses.

Crewe concluded that, although still significant, class had declined considerably in importance, and that voters had to be seen as acting rationally when voting, rather than simply automatically voting on the basis of their class and class-based political socialisation.

Consumer or issue voting theories

This theory argues that rational choice is the key determinant in voting behaviour, and that class-based political socialisation is of far less importance. The view is exemplified in the work of Himmelweit, who argues that voters decide which party to vote for much in the same way that consumer choices are made. Himmelweit suggests that consumers choose products by matching their preferences with the products on offer. The voter or consumer may not have accurate information, but they will decide rationally on the basis of the information which is available.

The changing class structure

Other sociologists argue that the apparent decline in class-based voting simply reflects changes in the class structure, and a more complex political system.

Heath, Jowell and Curtice argue that how class is defined and operationalised is a key factor in electoral studies. Their study used the Goldthorpe classification and a statistical technique called the 'odds ratio' to calculate the relationship between class and voting. Using this technique, Heath *et al.* argue that class-based support for the major parties

CHECKLIST

✓ The traditional class-based explanation of voting behaviour has always had the problem of trying to explain so-called 'deviant voters'. As voting patterns have changed, it can be argued that the class-based explanations of voting has become over-simplified, and that a number of other key social factors need to be taken into account, e.g. age, ethnicity, gender, region.

✓ Critics of dealignment theory (e.g. Heath *et al.*) argue that class remains an important, if not *the* most important determinant of voting behaviour, but that the class structure in late twentieth-century Britain has undergone considerable change.

✓ Critics of Heath *et al.* (e.g. Crewe) argue in reply that the methodology and operationalisation of class used by Heath's team lacked validity, and resulted in an inaccurate conceptualisation of the working class. It is argued that this distorted the results produced by Heath *et al.*

✓ The consumer-type model preferred by Himmelweit, can be criticised for neglecting structural factors such as class.

Power and politics

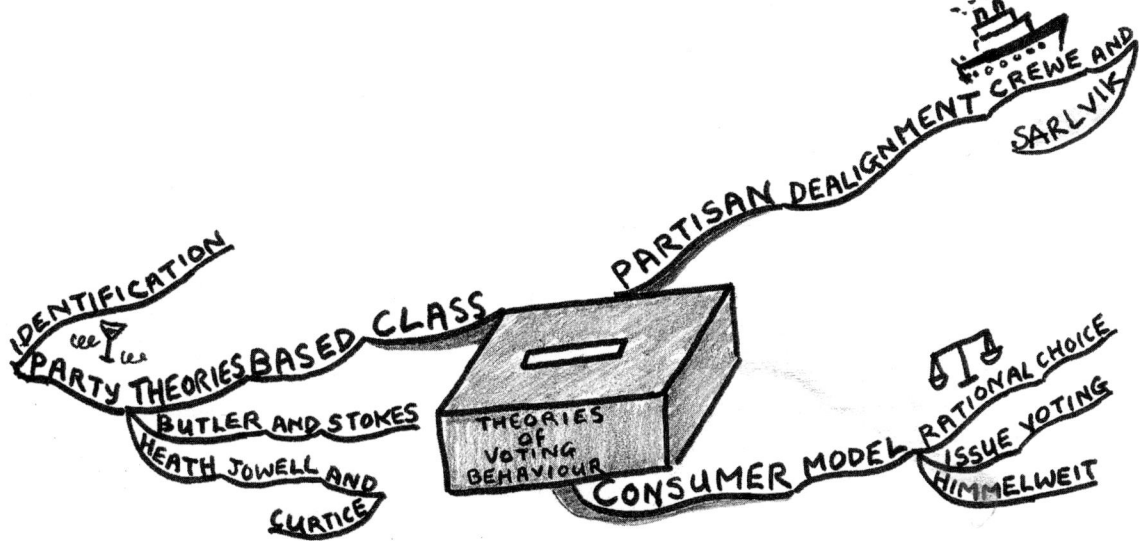

Theories of voting behaviour

has remained at a significant level since the 1960s, although there has been some slight decline in the relationship between class and voting.

Heath and his colleagues argue that the results of their analysis lead to the conclusion that a lot of the changes in class-based support for the main political parties has, in fact, been as a result of shifts in the class structure. The working class has contracted, while the service class and routine non-manual classes have expanded.

Summary

1. A key factor in the debates on voting behaviour is how class is operationalised and measured.
2. Arguably, class remains an important factor but, increasingly, sociologists are aware that other factors are also important, and they acknowledge that sociological explanations of voting behaviour have to examine the way in which class interacts with other determinants.

FACTFILE

- **According to Saggar in *Parliamentary Affairs* (Oct 1997), in 1996–97 25% of 'Asians' and 8% of 'Blacks' intended to vote Conservative at the next general election, and 70% and 86% repetively, intended to vote Labour.**
  Source: Butler and Kavanagh *The British General Election of 1997* (1997)

The influence of the mass media on politics and voting behaviour

The mass media has been seen as an important influence on voting behaviour, but precisely how important it is remains open to debate. Research by Curtice and Semetko (1994) found that the influence of the press in elections appeared to be minor. Research by Ivor Crewe on the 1992 General Election, suggested that tactical voting by Liberal-Democrat voters (voting Conservative) may have helped to give the Conservatives a victory. Liberal-Democrat tactical voters may have been influenced in their behaviour by the reporting of opinion polls in the media.

Power and politics

Sociological theories on media effects can be usefully applied to this issue. Marxist theories (instrumental or hegemonic) would suggest that the media do have an important role, but this would be hard to measure. Equally, issues of ownership and control are also relevant, and many political scientists and commentators have noted the importance for British political parties of gaining the support of the key media institutions. Students may also take the opportunity to apply the work of the GUMG to this topic (see Chapter 5).

The importance of the media is also apparent in the use of the media by Conservative governments in the 1980s and 1990s and by 'New' Labour following the 1997 election victory. Parties are increasing the amount of money spent in campaigning and advertising. According to Taylor *et al.* (1995), expenditure on advertising in the 1980s more than doubled. Increasingly, the parties are employing press officers ('spin doctors') and other 'consultants' to help with 'media management' and policy presentation.

Postmodernist theories also present more opportunities for application. Postmodernist theory, as expressed by Baudrillard, implies that the media is the source of all knowledge, and political knowledge would be no exception. Political choice would seem to become rather like shopping, and based more on the appeal of parties in terms of their 'image' rather than on the basis of a choice between rational alternatives.

> ### FACTFILE
>
> A Gallup survey for the BBC in 1983 estimated that 6% of all voters claimed that their vote had been influenced by a Conservative broadcast, 5% by a Labour broadcast, and 9% by an Alliance broadcast. This could be interpreted as evidence that the mass media have the greatest influence on undecided voters. However, if the link between class and voting behaviour has weakened and the electorate is increasingly volatile, this could be a small, but relatively important difference.
>
> **Source: Jones and Jones *Mass Media* (1999)**

Sample questions and answer advice

Critically examine the usefulness of pluralist theories to an understanding of the relationship between power and the state in modern societies.

(AEB, 1994)

The key strengths and weaknesses of pluralist theory can be usefully examined and discussed in contrast with other theories. It should be pointed out that pluralist theories vary, e.g. the differences between classical and elite pluralism can be emphasised. The answer should include discussion of different concepts of power, including the Weberian view, Lukes' view, as well as Functionalist and Marxist approaches to power and its relationship to the state. Examples of studies which apply pluralist theories, such as Dahl's study *Who Governs* should be discussed. Discussion could also include Wright Mills, Miliband, Poulantzas and Gramsci. More recent examples of relevant case studies could include discussions of the role of NRMs, or globalisation.

Critically examine the view that voting behaviour in the United Kingdom during the last 30 years has been increasingly influenced by factors other than social class.

(AEB, 1996)

Answers should discuss the various class-based models of voting and evaluate by comparing with alternative models. Discussion should include Butler and Stokes, McKenzie and Silver, as well as the alternative models, e.g. class dealignment (Crewe), and the consumer model (Himmelweit). More recent versions of a class-based explanation from Heath, Jowell, and Curtice also need discussion. Some coverage of methodological issues, such as operationalisation of class, and the validity of research based on different class categorisation schemes should be given. Answers can also bring in consideration of other forms of stratification, such as ethnicity and gender, and relate these to the issue of whether the class structure is changing or even fragmenting.

Power and politics

TEST YOURSELF

Q	E	T	N	A	I	R	A	T	I	L	A	T	O	T	U	P
T	D	E	F	E	R	E	N	T	I	A	L	Y	P	O	I	R
A	E	E	S	D	S	A	Z	T	N	A	L	U	O	P	F	E
A	M	L	A	P	F	Y	T	I	L	I	T	A	L	O	V	S
Z	O	P	X	L	C	V	B	N	M	L	K	J	U	H	G	S
P	C	I	O	U	I	U	I	Y	T	Q	W	D	K	J	K	U
Y	R	H	X	R	B	G	Y	N	O	M	E	G	E	H	M	R
G	A	S	Z	A	C	V	N	S	M	B	T	H	S	Y	W	E
O	C	N	N	L	C	L	I	M	J	M	B	V	W	Q	P	G
L	Y	A	Z	I	V	B	U	E	E	K	F	P	O	W	E	R
O	P	S	O	S	Q	W	E	L	R	N	T	Y	H	J	K	O
H	Z	I	M	M	X	C	W	I	V	R	T	Y	S	D	K	U
P	X	T	S	E	N	V	N	T	H	C	J	K	E	F	X	P
E	E	R	M	U	S	O	R	E	Z	Z	F	J	T	N	V	S
S	R	A	J	T	D	I	V	S	T	A	T	E	V	Y	I	A
P	Z	P	M	N	O	I	T	A	S	I	L	A	B	O	L	G

Solution on page 126

Summary

1. Power is a contested concept and sociologists do not agree on how it is best defined. However, this provides students with many opportunities to demonstrate a detailed knowledge and understanding, and to evaluate in a sophisticated manner, by demonstrating – for example – how the answer to a question might differ if an alternative definition of power is used.

2. Politics can be defined narrowly in terms of political parties and decision-making, but increasingly sociologists are interested in the role played by pressure groups and new social movements (NSMs).

3. The study of voting behaviour is a key area of interest for sociologists, but it is an issue which has to be seen in the context of changes in the class structure. Particularly important is the issue of whether the class structure is fragmenting, and whether aspects of stratification, such as ethnicity and gender, are becoming as or more important than class. In evaluating this debate, an important issue which must be considered in detail is how class is operationalised in studies of voting behaviour.

4. The role of the media in politics is difficult to evaluate. However, if postmodernist theory is only partially right, it may be that the media is becoming an increasingly important influence on politics and directly or indirectly on voting behaviour.

Study and Revise AS and A2 Level Sociology

Chapter 8: Religion

PREVIEW

You need to know:

- how sociologists define religion
- sociological explanations of how religion functions in society
- classifying different types of religious organisation
- the relationship between religion and social change
- explanations for the growth of cults, sects and new religious movements
- the secularisation debate – have religion and religious values become irrelevant in modern industrial society?

Definitions and theories of religion

Defining religion

Anthony Giddens has defined religion as having two key characteristics:

1. It must involve a set of symbols which invoke a sense of reverence or awe in believers.
2. The symbols are linked to ritual or ceremonial activity which is carried out by a community.

However, it is important to note that sociologists do not have an agreed definition of religion, and definitions tend to fall into two groups, broad and narrow.

Broad definitions

Broad views would be typified by Durkheim's view of religion, which defines religion as the division of the world into the two categories of sacred and profane. Broad views of religion do not have to involve belief in the supernatural, or in a deity, and religion is defined chiefly in terms of its functions. Durkheim's definition of religion is so broad that it can be interpreted as allowing phenomena such as nationalism, or supporting a football club to become defined as religious.

Narrow definitions

A narrow definition of religion is closer to the commonsense meaning of the term 'religion'. It would, in practice, confine the study of religion to the main world religions and to other groups which could be seen as religious in terms of mainstream definitions, that is a focus on spiritual issues, beliefs in the supernatural, and beliefs in a god. Sociologists using this definition may tend to focus their interests on the significance of religion at a particular period of time.

FACTFILE

- These various definitions of religion are important, since they lead sociologists to focus on different aspects of religion, and they can mean that sociologists give very different answers to the question of whether the significance of religion has declined (see page 75).

Theories of religion

Functionalist perspectives

Functionalists make several key points about the role of religion:

- religion works to maintain social order and social integration
- it reinforces solidarity and value-consensus

TEST YOURSELF

People in the UK belonging to a religion

Religion*	1990 (millions)	1995 (millions)
Trinitarian Churches	38.6	38.1
Non-Trinitarian Churches	1.1	1.3
Other religions	2.5	2.8

*Those stating that they belong to a particular religion or denomination
Source: Adapted from *Social Trends* 28 (1998) (original source: Christian Research)

1. By how many million did membership of Trinitarian churches decline between 1990 and 1995?
2. Give at least one example of each of the following: a Trinitarian church; a Non-Trinitarian church; 'Other religions'.
3. Explain the word 'Trinitarian'.
4. Does the data provide evidence for the secularisation thesis?

> **Answers**
>
> 1. 500,000
>
> 2. Trinitarian churches: Anglican, Roman Catholic, Methodists, Baptists, Presbyterians.
>
>   Non-Trinitarian churches: Church of Scientology.
>
>   Other Religions: Muslim/Islam, Sikhism, Hinduism, Jewish.
>
> 3. Trinitarian churches are those Christian churches which believe that God consists of Father, Son, and Holy Spirit.
>
> 4. The data is hard to interpret. On the one hand, Trinitarian churches in the UK have seen a decline in membership over these years, which should be seen in the general context of a decline in their membership over a longer period. The data are extracted from *Social Trends* 28 (1998), and the table is titled 'People Belonging to a Religion'. A footnote explains that this has been defined in terms of people stating that they belong to a religion. Interpretivist sociologists might well argue that such data lacks validity, because it does not probe into the meaning which religion has for the respondents. It could be argued further that religion has lost its importance for many respondents, who say that they 'belong' to a religion merely because they have been asked if this is the case. It could be argued, then, that the data does provide evidence of secularisation.
>
>   Having said this, it could be argued that church membership, whatever the difficulties in measurement, is not a sufficient indicator on which to base the secularisation thesis. Sociologists, such as Bryan Wilson argue that secularisation would involve a decline in religious thinking, practice, and institutions. On this basis, the figures only relate to institutional membership; it is possible to be religious without being a member of a church. In conclusion, it can be suggested that the secularisation thesis is not something which can be evaluated purely on the basis of quantitative data.

- religion acts as a support mechanism, helping individuals and society deal with change, uncertainty, and the various disasters which can beset human existence.

Functionalist views on religion have been developed by Durkheim, Parsons, and Malinowski, although there is considerable overlap between their contributions to the topic. Durkheim's work is amongst the most important of functionalist contributions to religion, for his definition can imply that religion will not fall into decline, rather that the nature of religion will change.

For Durkheim, religion divides the world into two categories, the sacred and the profane. By worshipping what it defines as sacred, a society reinforces social solidarity and integration. It is, in a sense, worshipping itself, since it is society which defines what is sacred and what is profane. This division will continue even in industrial society so, although superficially such societies may seem irreligious, religion may continue under the guise, for instance, of nationalism. Nationalists may see their own symbols and beliefs as sacred, and those of other nations as profane.

Marxist perspectives

Marxism is a conflict theory, and so it tends to see the role of religion in society as more beneficial for the dominant social groups, since:

- religion obscures social problems and conflicts
- religion obscures the process of exploitation
- religion maintains social order by obscuring and legitimating exploitation and inequality.

A key concept in the Marxist analysis of religion is that of ideology. Marx argued that 'the ruling ideas in any epoch are the ideas of the ruling classes'. It is, thus, suggested that the interests of the ruling classes are directly related to those of organised religion, and that religion is, in Marx's famous phrase, 'the opium of the masses'.

Social action and phenomenological perspectives

In contrast to the structural theories discussed, social action and phenomenological approaches see religious beliefs as things that are actively created by people in the course of their everyday lives. These approaches see people as 'skilled actors', who do not simply react automatically to structural forces, but who have various motives and reasons for acting in the way they do.

Max Weber was chiefly interested in the role of religion in creating social change, which will be discussed in greater detail below. However, in contrast to Marx, Weber believed that religion was not to be seen as a consequence of the economic structure of society. Weber is, thus, an important figure in the social action tradition, since he insisted upon the need to examine how religious ideas influenced people's behaviour and how this, in turn, could have important effects on economic behaviour.

Other views which represent a similar approach are well typified by phenomenologists Berger and Luckmann. Berger and Luckmann see religion in the following terms:

- Religion is not part of a functional system, nor a functional prerequisite, nor a system of social control. It is a socially constructed 'universe of meaning' (way of thinking), which enables people to categorise and make sense of their lives.

- Berger and Luckmann call the universe of meaning a 'sacred canopy' – a protective covering under which every aspect of human life can be sheltered and fitted into a 'universe of meaning'.
- This is a reflexive theory. Religion is socially constructed – it is made by people's own activity, but it then has its own influence upon society.
- Social action and phenomenological views ignore the relationship between religion and economic or cultural power.

Postmodernism and religion

Postmodernist concepts can be applied to provide several insights into religion in contemporary society. The concept of globalisation – the idea that there is a global culture – has several consequences for religion. Firstly, in a global culture it is possible for individuals to have access to information about a wide range of religious organisations. Those who wish to be involved in a religious organsation, thus, have greater choice. Secondly however, one response to globalisation is fundamentalism. This can be defined in several ways but, in this context, it may be seen as a desire to return to traditional values. Sociologists have explained the rise of Islamic and Christian fundamentalism as a response to the pressures and uncertainties of modern society.

The work of the post-structuralist philosopher Michel Foucault can also be applied to the analysis of religion. In terms of Foucault's theory, religion can be seen as a discourse – a type of ideology which governs social behaviour. In terms of this theory, however, religion would be seen as a discourse or ideology which is no longer a major form of social control in contemporary society, as other belief systems have become more important.

Religious organisations

Sociologists have been particularly interested to explain the role which religion plays in society, and this has involved them in examining the institutional structures which religious groups have constructed and in examining the relationship between religious groups and wider society.

Church and ecclesia

The term 'church' is now used very loosely to refer to many religious groups. For this reason, many sociologists now use the term 'ecclesia' in preference. In its original sense, a church or an ecclesia refers to a religious organisation which is closely allied to the political power of a state. The key characteristics of a church or ecclesia would consist of the following:

> **CHECKLIST**
>
> ✓ Functionalist accounts of religion may be criticised for exaggerating the integrative function of religion; religious faith could be seen as equally likely to cause conflict as to integrate. Durkheim's view and definition of religion may be more applicable to small-scale societies and have less relevance to large-scale industrial society.
>
> ✓ The Marxist view of religion can be criticised for its economic determinism. Religion may not always act in the interests of the ruling classes or the state, and there are many historical examples of cases where organised religions have been critical of political authority, e.g. the Catholic Church in Poland in the 1970s and 1980s.
>
> ✓ Phenomenological or social action approaches to religion can provide many insights, but they do reflect the weaknesses associated with all theories which focus on action at the expense of structure. Discussions of theoretical perspectives on religion can usefully apply insights from the structure/action debate.

- the church would claim universal authority – it would be the one, true, religious faith
- a church would have a clear set of beliefs to which all members would adhere
- a church would have a hierarchical priesthood
- membership would be compulsory for all who lived within the state in which it was based.

Examples of ecclesia would be the Roman Catholic Church in the Middle Ages, or the Church of England in the sixteenth century. In contemporary society, these churches clearly do not have all the characteristics identified above. This reflects the declining influence of the church and perhaps religion in general in contemporary society, an issue which will be examined in greater detail below.

Denominations

Denominations are similar in some ways to churches, and they may develop from an offshoot of an established church, as Methodism and the Baptist Church did in the eighteenth and nineteenth centuries in Britain. However, they differ importantly from churches in the following ways:

- they are not tied to the state in any way, and have a distant relationship to political authority

> **FACTFILE**
> - In 1990 the Church of England had some 1.5 million members in the UK, 3.9% of the adult population.
> - In 1900 there were around 20,000 Church of England clerics, but by 1984 the number was around 10,000, while in the same period the population had increased from 32.5 to 55 million.
>
> Source: Bruce *Religion in Modern Britain* (1995).

- they insist on fewer controls on members, and membership is voluntary
- they tend to be more tolerant of other religions, and avoid claiming to be the sole possessors of religious truth.

Cults and sects

The terms 'cult' and 'sect' are applied to a range of more loosely organised religious organisations. As these forms of religion have become increasingly common in the latter part of the twentieth century, more sociological attention has been devoted to them and to the problems of categorising them.

The following features have been seen as typical of sects:

- a claim to possess religious truth, and hence an antagonistic relationship with other faiths, and indeed the wider society (note the pejorative use of the term 'sectarian')
- charismatic and non-hierarchical leadership (no organised hierarchy of officials)
- a high degree of commitment from members is demanded and it is hard to gain entry
- worship tends to be emotionally charged
- frequently regarded as deviant by wider society.

Cults have been characterised as involving the following key features:

- a wide range of beliefs, very open to accepting beliefs from other faiths and no claim on a monopoly of truth
- relatively few demands are placed on members and it is easy to gain entry
- often short-lived
- frequently regarded as deviant by wider society.

Not all sociologists would agree, however, that this is a useful way of distinguishing between different religious organisations, and Roy Wallis has devised an alternative set of categories (termed a typology) of what he terms new religious movements (NRMs).

Wallis' typology

World-affirming NRMs

These accept most of the values of society, but provide a new way to achieve them, e.g. Scientology.

World-rejecting NRMs

They reject the wider society, seeing it as corrupt. They frequently predict a spiritual revival, or the return of Christ and separate themselves off from the rest of society, e.g. Moonies.

World-accommodating NRMs

These neither accept nor fully reject the values of the wider society. They co-exist and tolerate the wider society. They believe that religion has lost its key role in society, but that this can be regained.

> **FACTFILE**
> - While established churches have generally seen a decline in membership, there has been a growth in the number of NRMs, particularly during the 1960s and 1970s, although caution has to be exercised in interpreting the significance and validity of this trend.
> - It is hard to compare the increase in membership with other periods in history.
> - Those joining may not remain members for long, and indeed membership figures have the same problems as those for any other religious group.

Religion and social change

The influence of religion upon social change has been an area of interest and debate for many sociologists.

Functionalism

Functionalist views tend to emphasise the role of religion in maintaining social stability. Parsons' concept of structural differentiation implies that the functions carried out by religion would be taken over gradually by other institutions, leaving formal organised religion in industrial society responsible for maintaining and legitmating general social values.

Religion

Marxism

Marxist views of religion generally see religion as maintaining the status quo, and functioning so as to prevent social change.

Both Marxism and Functionalism are structural theories and both see religion as something derived from and determined by social structures. This can mean that they underestimate the role which religion can play in causing social change.

Max Weber and *The Protestant Ethic*

Weber's work on religion is particularly important because he offers an alternative to structural theories, and demonstrates that religion can be a powerful force for change in society. Weber's views are developed in his book, *The Protestant Ethic and the Spirit of Capitalism*, which argues that it was the rise of the Protestant religion which led to the development of capitalism in Europe. This contrasts to a Marxist view, which would see the development of capitalism as leading to forms of religion which reflected the interests of the ruling classes.

Weber's theory makes several key points:

- Calvinist Protestantism preceded the rise of capitalism. Capitalism developed first where this religion was present (i.e. Europe, not India or China).
- A key belief in this religion was the idea that some individuals (the elect) were predestined to go to heaven.
- A sign that an individual was one of the elect was worldly success in business. This led Protestants to lead a frugal life, avoiding ostentatious spending on luxuries, and wasting time on leisure pursuits. This was the 'Protestant ethic'.
- The Protestant ethic – the work ethic – lead Calvinists to work exceptionally hard, saving their money and reinvesting it in their business, in order to achieve success. This would give them reassurance that they were the elect, since in a Protestant catchphrase, 'God helps those who help themselves'.
- The rise of Protestantism is thus the key reason why capitalism first developed in western Europe.

Explanations for the growth of new religious movements

A growing alternative to the main world religions in the late twentieth century has been a range of sects and cults. As mentioned above, this has caused sociologists some problems in trying to categorise the whole range of organisations accurately and meaningfully. It has also raised the interesting sociological problem of trying to account for this growth of interest.

> ### Summary
> 1. The relationship between religion and social change is not a fixed one, but may vary according to a variety of factors, including the nature of the religion itself, the culture in which it is located, and the nature of the social structure and the place of religion in that structure.
> 2. Equally, a reflexive view of religion may be applied to this problem. Giddens, for instance, might argue that religion, while a social construct, becomes a structure which can influence society in many, often unforeseen, ways.
> 3. Therefore, religion may lead or prevent change, depending upon other social factors; it is not intrinsically conservative or radical.

Deprivation

Some sociologists have explained the growth in NRMs as a consequence of economic or spiritual deprivation. Such views may be based on a Marxist view of religion, and see religion as an ideological form of social control. Weber, though, also refers to the 'theodicy of suffering', whereby religion becomes a way of explaining and justifying suffering. Scott and Fulcher (1999) see deprivation as a good way of explaining what they refer to as religions of ethnic protest – Black Pentecostalism, the Baptist Church, Rastafarianism, and the Nation of Islam.

Roy Wallis argues that recruits to NRMs are frequently idealistic, young, and middle class. He argued that the excessively materialistic values of twentieth-century society are frequently experienced as alienating and meaningless. NRMs offer a heightened sense of meaning and community for many recruits, who Wallis argued were 'relatively deprived' spiritually.

Eileen Barker's study, *The Making of a Moonie*, offers further support for this view. Barker found that, far from 'brainwashing' young people into joining the cult, those joining did so under their own free will.

Secularisation

Bryan Wilson sees NRMs as the result of secularisation (page 75) which has weakened the power of the established churches. Herberg sees religion in the USA as having 'sold out', thus losing its character and true meaning. The desacralisation of contemporary society and contemporary religion creates a situation in which some NRMs become popular because they offer something which is recognisably religious in more traditional terms. As Bruce notes, many 'converts' to fundamentalist Christian groups are young people already predisposed towards conservative forms of religion.

Disengagement

The concept of 'disengagment' offers a similar interpretation. As churches have disengaged (separated) from the wider society, they have come to be seen by some as irrelevant and out of touch, thus opening the way for more spectacular forms of worship, such as evangelism, and what Bruce has termed 'televangelism'.

Summary

1. **The growth in NRMs can be explained by a variety of factors, and sociologists will be influenced by their general theoretical stance in coming down on one side or another.**
2. **Conflict-influenced theories will tend to see the growth of NRMs as the result of economic inequalities or the alienation which these cause.**
3. **Consensus-based theory might see them more as the inevitable result of a dislocation of cultural and spiritual values.**
4. **A postmodernist approach might suggest that globalisation and the end of metanarratives makes it feasible for all to seek their own answers to questions of faith and, hence, an end to the dominance of the major world religions.**

The secularisation debate

Secularisation can be defined as the decline in the significance of religion. Those who argue that industrial society has undergone a process of secularisation, are claiming that religion no longer has the power and influence which it had before industrialisation. The key issue posed then, is whether we live in a society where religion is of little significance.

There is a lot of evidence both for and against the secularisation thesis, so questions on the subject provide students with a good opportunity to demonstrate their evaluation skills.

Evidence used in the debate

For secularisation

- Survey evidence (e.g. *Social Trends*, *British Social Attitudes Survey*, 1997) shows a decline in the number of those attending church services.
- The laws against Sunday trading have been substantially modified. Many businesses now trade on a Sunday.
- Fewer people are getting married in church, and the divorce rate is high.
- There has been a decline in the number of clergy (see page 73).

Against secularisation

- The validity of statistics on church membership and attendance has been criticised by sociologists such as David Martin.
- There has been an increase in the membership of non-Trinitarian religions in the UK.
- Religious broadcasting continues to be popular, with large audiences watching programmes such as *Songs of Praise* and *Highway*. Radio 4 has a daily religious item, *Thought for the Day*, and broadsheet newspapers have columns devoted to religious matters.
- The Head of State of the UK, the Queen, is the head of the Church of England. Any subsequent monarch must also be a member of the Church of England.

Key issues

There are several key issues to remember to focus on when answering questions on the secularisation debate.

Definitions

Sociologists have different ways of defining secularisation, and indeed, religion, and these have a large bearing on how they position themselves in regard to the debate. Bryan Wilson defines secularisation as a decline in religious thinking, practice, and institutions. This definition can help you to evaluate evidence in point 4 below.

Validity and interpretation of statistics

If you wish to gain a high mark it is essential to tackle this issue in most questions on this topic. Martin has

Religion

cast doubt on the validity of eighteenth- and nineteenth-century church attendance statistics. Similarly, the validity of contemporary statistics can be questioned.

The issue should be developed fully through a consideration of how or whether religiosity can be measured statistically. The following questions should be addressed:

1. What does church attendance mean to those who go to church? Might they attend for other (maybe non-religious) reasons, e.g. respectability, status?
2. Is it possible to be 'religious' without regularly attending church?
3. How should religiosity be operationalised?
4. What are the best indicators of religiosity?

FACTFILE

- In the 1991 *British Social Attitudes Survey* 75% of respondents believed in some sort of supernatural power.
- *Social Trends* in 1997 reported the results of a survey in 1995 which found only 11% of respondents disbelieved in God completely, while 21% had no doubts at all that there was a God.

Source: Bruce (1995), Fulcher and Scott (1999)

CHECKLIST

✓ In concluding, it can be helpful to refer back to Wilson's definition. Perhaps it can be argued that there has been a decline in the institutional power of religion and in practice (at least as defined by attendance) religion has declined.

✓ However, in terms of religious thinking, there is strong evidence (e.g. BSA surveys) that religion still exerts some influence on beliefs. Equally, since the UK is a multi-cultural society, the development of non-Trinitarian religions should not be overlooked.

✓ When answering questions on the secularisation issue, discussion of the interpretation of statistical data is required in some detail. Concepts such as validity and operationalisation should be used accurately, and as a result evaluation is more likely to be sophisticated.

✓ Do not overlook the significance of religious broadcasting in the UK and the role of religion in politics in the USA (and indeed elsewhere), which serves as a powerful reminder of the need for sociological theory to avoid exaggeration. In many ways, contemporary western societies are secularised; but it would a sweeping generalisation to assert that religion has little or no influence. It seems more helpful to argue that it has changed in many complex ways.

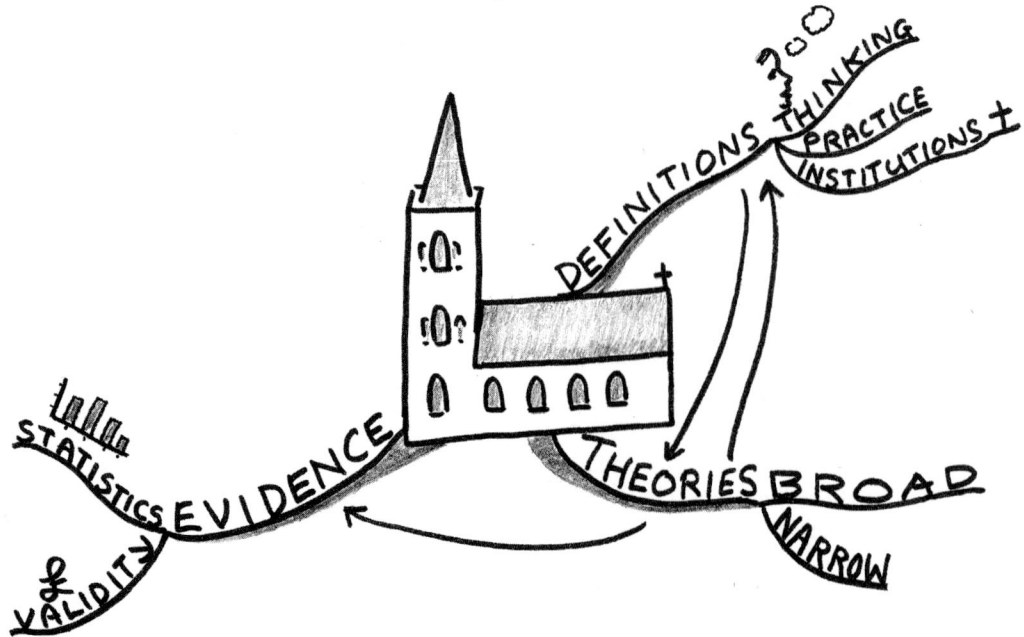

The secularisation debate

Sample question and answer

'In modern society, religious beliefs and religious behaviour are changing rather than declining.' Assess the arguments and evidence for and against this view.

(AEB, 1999)

The sociologist Bryan Wilson has forcibly presented the case for the secularisation thesis, arguing that we now live in a society where religious thinking, practice, and institutions are in decline. However, there are alternative views and indeed empirical evidence, which suggest that this assessment should not be accepted too readily.

The secularisation thesis has drawn upon statistical evidence which demonstrates a sharp fall in church attendance over the course of the twentieth century. However, as David Martin has argued, the validity of attendance statistics from earlier times has to be treated with caution, and may reflect social conventions rather than religious fervour. Recent survey data from Britain suggests a more complex picture. While church membership and attendance is indeed low, in the 1992 *British Social Attitudes Survey* 69% of those surveyed *believed* in God; in Northern Ireland and the Republic of Ireland the figure was 95%. In the USA by contrast, church attendance stands at around 69%, while survey data indicates that 95% of the population profess a belief in God, according to Taylor *et al*. Moreover, *Social Trends* presents data for the UK which indicates that, while Trinitarian churches have declined in membership, non-Trinitarian religions have shown increasing membership. Sociologists might usefully point to the popularity of religious broadcasting on television and radio. Certainly, these programmes appear to be popular enough to ensure that television companies feel a need to retain them. Lastly, research by Melton indicates that, in the USA over the last half of the twentieth century, there has been an increase in what Wallis terms New Religious Movements.

All these findings seem to offer strong support for the view that religious beliefs and behaviour have changed rather than simply declined. This interpretation suggests that examining the complex issues of religious belief and secularisation cannot simply be determined through the use of quantitative data. Trying to understand the findings examined above, requires interpretation of the data by applying sociological theory.

Arguably, it is functionalist theory, particularly Durkheimian functionalism, which offers most insight into the data presented above. Durkheim defined religion in a broad sense as the division of the world into the sacred and the profane, and argued that this symbolic process created a sense of shared meanings and beliefs. These helped to integrate society and create social solidarity around a set of shared norms and values. For Durkheim, the division of sacred and profane is necessary and universal. Thus, while Durkheim foresaw that industrialisation could lead to a decline in traditional religious institutions, he argued that religion would continue to be a feature of industrial society.

However, Durkheim argued that religion would change its character, and the sacred and profane could be identified in other phenomena, for example in celebration of the nation or membership of smaller social units or communities. In this sense, nationalism could be seen as a new form of religion in modern societies. It could even be possible to see football as a religion, since supporting a team means seeing one's own team as sacred and symbolises one's own community. Outsiders can be characterised as profane, and the 'religious' beliefs can, thus, integrate the community and create social solidarity.

Other functionalists, such as Parsons, would draw upon the concept of differentiation to explain changes in religious behaviour. This concept argues that modern societies become increasingly specialised and, thus, organised religion is not necessarily any less important. The church in America, according to Parsons, still provides meaning and a support system for the wider society. Others, however, would dispute this position. Herberg, for instance, argues that what he terms 'disengagement' – the withdrawal of organised religion from playing a role in all social activity – amounts to an acknowledgement that religion is of less significance in modern society.

Another American sociologist, Robert Bellah, argues that in modern society religion has not disappeared, it has simply become privatised. In a highly individualistic society, religion has become something which is restricted to private life; more people are able to practise their religious beliefs privately and without necessarily attending church. In terms of the rise of religious pluralism, ecumenicalism (different denominations unifying), and the rise of NRMs, Bryan Wilson has argued against the idea that these trends somehow represent a refutation of his thesis of secularisation. On the contrary, Wilson argues that such fragmentation reflects a decline in the power of traditional religious groups and beliefs. It is precisely because of this decline that small fringe groups are able to proliferate, and in the case of NRMs, Wilson argues that these are often commercial in nature, or focus on the development of the self. This last point hints that Wilson may use a narrower definition of religion than Durkheim, and this might help to explain the divergence in their views.

In conclusion, it can be argued that in western societies there does seem to have been a decline in the power and significance of religious beliefs, practice and institutions. However, the continued existence of a range of religious groups suggests that the secularisation thesis cannot be accepted without some careful qualifications and modifications. Despite current theories of globalisation, it may be useful to reflect upon the idea that western sociologists have been too hasty and have theorised too generally, especially given the importance of religion in non-western societies. In the light of these considerations, it is arguably more useful for sociologists to consider that, rather than evaporating, religious belief and behaviour has changed as society has changed.

Religion

TEST YOURSELF

Across

3. A reassertion of fundamental religious values; Giddens terms it a refusal of dialogue (14)
4. Wrote study on *The Making of a Moonie* (6)
6. Wilson defines this as a decline in religious thinking, practice and institutions (14)
11. Wallis defines these as world-affirming NRMs (4)
12. A movement towards greater church unity (10)
14. He claims that golden age of religiosity and church attendance was a myth (6)
15. Believed that all societies distinguished the sacred and the profane (8)
16. Sociologist who claims that religion reinforces value-consensus and maintains order and stability (7)
17. The idea that the sacred is no longer a force in society (15)
18. A tendency for churches to withdraw from the wider society (13)
19. Important concept to remember when examining church membership and attendance figures (8)

Down

1. Sociologist Steve Bruce describes this American form of televisual religion (13)
2. Commented that religion was the opium of the people (4)
5. Beliefs which prophesy a radical or supernatural change (14)
6. A religious organisation which withdraws from the wider society, often has a charismatic leader (4)
7. He studied NRMs and Scientology (6)
8. American sociologist who argues that religion has become increasingly privatised (6)
9. Sociologist who wrote about the protestant ethic (5)
10. Film star Tom Cruise is one of these (13)
13. Large-scale religious organisation (6)

Solution on page 125

Summary

1. Sociologists do not agree on how religion should be defined. The range of definitions available can be categorised in terms of broad and narrow definitions. This may seem unhelpful at first but, in fact, students can use the differing conceptions of religion to help evaluate theoretical views of religion and its role in contemporary society. In terms of the secularisation thesis, for example, Durkheim's broad notion of religion suggests that religion continues in different forms; those with a different notion of religion may be unpersuaded that it is helpful to equate football or nationalism with religion.

2. Wilson's definition of secularisation is a good example of how definitions can be carefully used to create nuanced and incisive arguments. By arguing that secularisation implies a decline in three aspects of religion, it is possible to argue that, while institutions and practices may have declined, religious thinking is still an important aspect of society.

3. In evaluating the secularisation thesis, students must focus in some detail on the methodological problems involved, and discuss key methodological concepts including validity and operationalisation.

4. While religious institutions in the UK may have declined, and despite the power of science, religious and spiritual thought seems to remain a significant factor in the lives of many, although not perhaps in the same ways that were prevalent prior to industrialisation. More globally, religion still seems to be an important social force in many parts of the world, as the development of various forms of religious fundamentalism demonstrates.

World sociology — Chapter 9

> **PREVIEW**
>
> You need to know:
>
> - sociological definitions and explanations of development and underdevelopment
> - approaches to aid, strategies for development, and inter-relationships between societies
> - explanations of urbanisation and industrialisation in developing countries
> - approaches to various aspects of development, including employment, education, health, gender and demographic change.

Definitions and theories of development and underdevelopment

Definitions of development and underdevelopment

The sociological study of development originated in the study of societies which were in the process of trying to industrialise. More recently, sociological study has turned to examine the way in which different societies are increasingly globally interrelated, hence the term 'World Sociology'.

The term 'development' refers to the process of a society becoming a modern capitalist and industrial society. The term 'developed societies', refers to those societies, generally western countries, which are already industrial–capitalist societies. 'Underdevelopment' and 'underdeveloped societies', are terms that can be applied to those, generally non-western, societies which are attempting to modernise.

A measure of economic development and wealth that is often used is gross national product (GNP) per capita. This is a measure of the output of consumer goods and services produced by a country and converted to an average based on the total population.

However, this is only one measure and economic growth and prosperity does not always lead to a broader social or political development. Moreover, the term 'developed societies' and the comparison it invites with underdeveloped societies can be criticised for its ethnocentric, pro-western bias.

Sociologists have used a variety of terms to categorise the different groups of societies into clusters of more or less developed societies. The

---

> **TEST YOURSELF**
>
> **World population indicators 1995–2000**
>
> | | Infant mortality[1] | Total period fertility rate[2] | Life expectancy Males | Females |
> |---|---|---|---|---|
> | Europe | 12 | 1.6 | 69 | 77 |
> | North America | 7 | 2.1 | 74 | 80 |
> | Africa | 85 | 5.3 | 53 | 56 |
> | Asia | 57 | 2.9 | 65 | 68 |
> | Latin America and Caribbean | 41 | 2.8 | 67 | 72 |
> | World | | | | |
> | More developed | 9 | 1.7 | 71 | 79 |
> | Less developed[4] | 63 | 3.3 | 62 | 65 |
>
> [1] Per 1000 live births.
> [2] The average number of children who would be born per woman if women experienced the age-specific fertility rates of the reference years throughout their child-bearing span.
> [3] More developed: Europe, North America, Australia, New Zealand and Japan.
> [4] Less developed: Africa, Latin America, Asia (excluding Japan) and Melanesia, Micronesia and Polynesia.
> Source: Adapted from *Social Trends* 27 (1997)
>
> 1. In which area of the world is the infant mortality rate (IMR) lowest?
> 2. In which area of the world is the highest fertility rate found? Identify and explain the figure given for the fertility rate in this area.
> 3. What is the average difference in life expectancy for men from the more developed societies compared with men from less developed societies?

World sociology

> **Answers**
>
> 1 North America (IMR 7).
> 2 Africa. The fertility rate is 5.3. This means that every woman will have about five children on average.
> 3 The average difference is 9 years: the average expectancy for men in more developed societies = 71, for men in less developed societies = 62, therefore 71 − 62 = 9.

terms 'first', 'second' and 'third world' have been commonly used. First world societies are modern industrial capitalist nations, the second world refers to the eastern European socialist states that existed prior to 1989, and the third world refers to those other societies that remain.

These terms are clearly dated and lacking in precision, but so too are other distinctions, such as that produced in 1980 by the Brandt Commission, which spoke of the wealth divide between the North and the South. This fails to account for wealthy industrial societies in the Southern Hemisphere such as Japan, New Zealand, and Australia.

Equally, recent years have seen the phenomenal economic development of the Tiger Economies of South East Asia (Singapore, Indonesia, Korea, Taiwan, and Hong Kong). Lastly, it can be noted that sociologists may wish to make distinctions between the poorer societies of the world, where there may be considerable differences between the poor and the poorest.

Theories of development and underdevelopment

Modernisation theory

Modernisation theory was one of the first systematic attempts to explain the process of development. The theory is associated with functionalist thought, and assumes that societies develop in an evolutionary way. Modernisation theory assumed that underdeveloped societies would develop in the same way as developed societies had and therefore, would become increasingly like modern industrial capital nations. Where growth and development have slowed down, modernisation theorists argue that internal factors are to blame; a failure to change traditional attitudes or institutions will hinder development.

One of the best-known modernisation theorists is W.W. Rostow. Rostow argues that there is only one route to development and it entails progressing through five stages. The five stages start in traditional society and end in the 'age of high mass consumption'.

In order to progress through these stages, a society must have certain functional prerequisites, including an education system and sufficient capital investment, financial institutions, and government. Also important are key cultural attitudes, such as work discipline and a desire for economic competition and success.

Classical Marxist approaches

Marxism can also be seen as implying an evolutionary theory of social change; societies are seen as inevitably changing as economic change promotes class conflict.

Some commentators influenced by a classical view of Marxism, such as Warren and Harris, have taken the view that the third world will inevitably undergo change in the direction of the industrial–capitalist route.

Dependency theory and neo-Marxism

Dependency theory was developed by Andre Frank as a critique of evolutionary theories of development. This was a neo-Marxist approach which rejected classical Marxist assumptions that development had to follow the same pattern as development in the West. It also rejected the view that the process of development was mainly determined by internal factors in a society and argued that the development process in any society could only be understood by examining that society in the context of its interrelations with other societies.

Frank argued that underdevelopment was, in fact, *caused* by developed societies. Underdeveloped societies have been systematically exploited and impoverished by colonialism and imperialism. Frank extends this argument, arguing that colonising nations 'developed underdevelopment', meaning that, through their activities, they pushed the colonised societies further 'back', beyond the stage they had been in when the colonisers arrived.

Underdevelopment is claimed to have occurred in three phases; mercantile capitalism, colonialism, and neo-colonialism. In the first two stages, Frank argues that colonising nations introduced the harmful policies of promoting production for export and production of a very limited range of crops. This did not enable colonised countries to develop their own internal markets nor to diversify, both important if a society wishes to expand its economy and develop its infrastructure.

The stage of neo-colonialism is seen by Frank as leading to a system of satellite economies, which each function only to serve a dominating metropolis. This system creates a hierarchical chain of dependency and exploitation, ensuring that those at the lower end of the hierarchy meet the needs of others rather than their own needs.

World systems theory

World systems theory is the name given to the theory developed by Immanuel Wallerstein. Wallerstein has been critical of dependency theory, and in particular of Frank, arguing that the theory of metropolises and satellites oversimplified issues.

Wallerstein argues that there is a world capitalist economy, linked by an international division of labour. This consists of three levels or positions: core, semi-periphery, and periphery.

- The core consists of the western societies and Japan, and these societies specialise in the production of manufactured goods.
- The periphery supplies raw materials to the core and imports manufactured goods from it.
- The semi-periphery exploits the periphery as well, but its intermediate position reflects the fact that it is either a core society which is in decline, or a peripheral society which is on the rise.

The global system

Leslie Sklair has suggested that the process of globalisation has added further complexities to the processes of development and underdevelopment. Globalisation suggests that the world is increasingly economically integrated into one highly interrelated system. Postmodernist influenced geographer and social theorist David Harvey has shown how differences in time and distance are now less important due to improvements in travel and electronic communication. For trade relationships between different societies this is important, since it provides more opportunities for trade and opens up new markets. According to Leslie Sklair, it has also meant that nationally-based corporations have become less important, and that corporations are increasingly becoming trans-national corporations (TNCs). Sklair argues that there is now a trans-national capitalist class which helps to promote a global system of capitalism and which promotes an increasingly consumerist culture.

The new international division of labour

The sociologist Froebel argues that the old division of labour, whereby the richer countries exported raw materials to be used in developing countries, has now been replaced. Companies in the richer nations can now export expensive and labour intensive tasks to third world countries where labour costs are cheaper.

CHECKLIST

✓ **Modernisation theory has been criticised for taking an ethnocentric approach to development. It sees progress or evolution as inevitable, but envisages only one route and one destination – modern industrialised society.**

✓ **Dependency theory or underdevelopment theories usefully focus on the interrelation of national economies, but tend to oversimplify and neglect the importance of internal factors' role in development.**

✓ **World systems theory still maintains some of the ethnocentric bias of modernisation theory. Wallerstein, for instance, argues that economic 'take-off' can only be achieved when the necessary cultural pre-conditions have been achieved. It also tends to imply that there are certain 'correct' paths of development.**

✓ **Global systems theory can be criticised for exaggerating the scope and novelty of the global economy. As Hirst and Thompson have argued, theories of globalisation frequently exaggerate the decline in the power and importance of the nation-state in contrast to that of trans-national corporations.**

Aid and strategies for development

There are three main types of aid:

1. Bilateral aid – this refers to aid whereby two countries arrange for one to give the other aid.
2. Multilateral aid – this refers to aid that finds its way from many national governments to a country through a third party, generally an international organisation such as the United Nations.
3. Tied aid – this refers to aid that is given on the understanding that the country receiving the aid will meet certain conditions demanded by the donor. These may stipulate, for instance, where money can be spent, or what it can be spent on.

In addition, aid may be given by NGOs (non-governmental organisations), including well-known charities, such as Christian Aid and, Oxfam, and the various Live Aid and Comic Relief appeals. However,

World sociology

as *Guardian* journalist John Vidal noted, in 1991 the UK government gave some £1500 million to aid, whereas the top 400 charities managed to raise £300 million between themselves.

International agencies and strategies for development

The increasing globalisation of the world economy was acknowledged by the governments of the major economic powers in the 1944 Bretton Woods Conference. This established the International Monetary Fund (IMF), the World Bank, and the General Agreements on Tariffs and Trade (GATT). These institutions aim to prevent economic protectionism and to promote free trade. This also involves providing aid to developing economies.

The United Nations (UN) provides various forms of aid and co-ordinates aid programme's in developing countries. The UN has recommended that developed countries give 0.7% of GNP as aid to underdeveloped countries. This target has not been met by most contributing countries.

The UN organised a summit meeting in 1992 (called the 'Earth Summit', held in Brazil) to co-ordinate plans to tackle concerns about environmental problems. Underdeveloped countries claimed that the richer nations were making the poor pay for pollution that is largely caused by the richer nations, through policies which were obstructing development. The meeting led to an agreement that all countries had the right to develop, although the USA refused to agree to this clause.

The World Bank and the IMF provide aid to developing countries. However, both institutions take a free market approach to the world economy and apply this to development issues. This means that aid is provided by these institutions under strict conditions. Both the World Bank and the IMF expect developing countries to compete in a world market.

Structural Adjustment Plans (SAPs) which are imposed upon developing countries applying for aid from these organisations also make similar demands. Countries receiving aid are required to restrict public expenditure, increase exports, and carry out privatisation schemes – all free market policies. Critics would argue that this provides aid on the terms of the developed nations, and is not appropriate for extremely poor countries.

The Brandt Commission of 1980 conducted an inquiry into inequality and aid and argued that alternatives to structural adjustment plans were needed. The Commission found that assessments of the aid requirements of particular countries did not take account of the structural nature of the economic inequalities in the world economic system. Such inequalities can be considered as the causes of underdevelopment, not the symptoms.

Arguments for and against international aid

There are several main arguments regarding the usefulness of aid:

1. In terms of modernisation theory, aid could be seen as advantageous – provided it is sufficient and is used wisely, it could enable developing societies to invest in their own infrastructure, enabling them to modernise.

2. The views of New Right theorists would suggest that aid is not a good investment, since it merely encourages the governments of undeveloped societies to depend on aid from wealthier societies, and to neglect finding solutions to their own plight. The New Right, of course, argues that the solution to these problems lies with policies that will promote free trade and the free market.

3. The idea that giving aid may actually be a continuation of imperialism is one that reflects a Marxist approach. Marxist writer Teresa Hayter expresses this viewpoint, arguing that the conditions which western developed societies attach to many aid programmes frequently mean that the West benefits economically in the long term from such arrangements, e.g. through interest payments, establishing home companies in new markets, or gaining geopolitical advantages.

4. In addition, it could be argued that some forms of aid are inappropriate to the needs of developing countries, or that funds may be misspent.

Sociologist Susan George's concept of the 'debt boomerang' indicates that the developed societies will have to tolerate higher levels of pollution, unemployment, tax, and immigration, as long as exploitation of poorer countries continues.

FACTFILE

- The richest 20% of the global population receive 70% of all income, and the poorest 20% receive 2% of all income.
    Source: Plummer and Macionis
    Sociology: A Global Introduction (1997)

Industrialisation and urbanisation in developing countries

Industrialisation

Sociologists have been concerned to examine industrialisation and urbanisation in developing countries, and there are disagreements as to how successful some of the newly industrialised countries (NICs) have been, and whether their success can be repeated.

Industrialisation in developing societies can be seen to have occurred in one of two ways: import-substitution industrialisation (ISI), or export-orientated industrialisation (EOI).

Import-substitution industrialisation

ISI involved countries trying to industrialise by producing for a home market. The aim was to reduce the need for expensive foreign imports and, thus, to build up capital which could then be reinvested in developing infrastructure. However, this strategy ran into various problems.

Much of the productive capacity of developing countries concentrates on agriculture, and it is hard to gain ever-increasing levels of profit solely from food production. Where developing countries did try to industrialise, it was found that up-to-date technology had to be imported. This was very expensive and, rather than reducing imports, the strategy led to an increase. Lastly, trying to make profits mainly by producing for a home market was found to be very difficult in countries with a generally poor population lacking the means to buy expensive consumer goods.

Export-orientated industrialisation

EOI was a strategy that involved developing countries aiming to manufacture goods for export. The idea was to begin with light production, selling to home and export markets, and then to branch out gradually into heavy industry as capital was accumulated and could be reinvested in infrastructure and plant. In some cases, notably some South American countries and the Tiger economies of south-east Asia, this strategy has met with apparent success, with growth rates in some of these countries outstripping by far those of western developed economies.

The success of newly industrialised countries

However, the success of these newly industrialised countries (NICs) has attracted various explanations. Those influenced by the free market philosophies of the New Right have argued that NICs have simply reaped the benefits of applying free market principles. The implication has been that other third world countries should apply the same strategies and, thus, all countries can industrialise and be economic successes.

Others, such as Jenkins, argue that NICs have, in fact, been successful due to huge investments from western countries and/or considerable state planning. This, of course, contradicts New Right views about the unfettered mechanism of the market. It is also argued that many NICs have been associated with dictatorial or authoritarian political regimes and, thus, economic success may have been achieved at the cost of political freedom and human rights.

Further uncertainty remains as to whether the NICs' success is a fragile one; it can be argued that they are uniquely vulnerable to slumps in the world economy, overly dependent on exports, and less protected against marauding attacks from the currency speculators of the global market. However, for the present NICs may be considered by their existence to refute Frank's claim that no underdeveloped society could successfully develop under capitalism. It remains to be seen whether other underdeveloped countries will be able to join them.

Underdeveloped countries may face a variety of obstacles to industrialisation, both internal and external. However, populists have argued that such countries should not aim to industrialise, pointing out the costs and disadvantages of development.

The focus on investment in third world countries can prevent much needed public spending in what are often highly unequal societies. Industrialisation does not occur without social and cultural costs, as older ways of life are replaced. Development also involves environmental costs, such as increases in pollutants and the intensification of the depletion of the Earth's natural resources. However, as mentioned, third world countries are quick to point to western hypocrisy on such issues. Nevertheless, these concerns have lead to the concept of sustainable development: the idea that third world countries should develop in ways which will not harm the environment and should attempt to conserve natural resources.

Urbanisation

Urbanisation in developing societies has had particular characteristics and has not simply repeated the patterns of urbanisation found in developed societies. Third world cities have expanded rapidly in recent years. Much of the population growth in these cities has been a natural increase; that is it has occurred due to high fertility rates and low death

World sociology

rates, but there have also been high rates of internal migration. The population in many third world cities is disproportionately comprised of young people.

Push and pull factors

Urbanisation in underdeveloped societies can be explained in terms of a variety of push and pull factors. Push factors have included the loss of farming land, rural poverty, the mechanisation of agriculture, and unemployment. Pull factors include the various perceived attractions of the city: better job prospects, higher wages, and a higher standard of living.

Dual sector economies

However, the growth of third world cities has not been accompanied by a proportional expansion in the manufacturing sector of the economy. Developing industry has often been capital rather than labour intensive, leading to the development of dual sector economies.

The dual sector economy is characterised by two distinct economies. On the one hand, jobs in the formal sector of the economy are organised in much the same way as jobs in the major industrialised economies of the world, with good rates of pay, career prospects, and other benefits. However, such jobs, whether at professional, white collar, or manual level, are in short supply and extremely sought after. The informal sector of the economy consists of a variety of jobs in small businesses, often run by family members, or in various forms of self-employment. Such work is labour intensive and poorly paid.

The labour force of the informal economy can be seen as a peripheral workforce, or even as a reserve army of labour, helping to keep wages low and always available if extra labour power is needed. The formal economy makes use of this labour supply through a system whereby subcontractors provide casual workers as required, as well as through various forms of 'out work' where work is completed by workers in their own home. Such arrangements reduce costs and provide flexibility for the employer.

FACTFILE

- In 1996 over 45% of the world population lived in cities and this has been projected to rise to 52% by 2010.
- The most rapid rates of urbanisation are projected to occur in developing countries.

Source: *Social Trends 27* (1997)

Aspects of development

Sociological study has concentrated on investigating several key aspects of developing societies.

Health

There are considerable inequalities in health between developed and developing countries, despite some improvements in developing countries in recent years. The nature of ill-health in developed and developing countries also differs. In industrialised countries the key diseases tend to be the so-called 'diseases of affluence', such as various forms of cancer and heart disease. In developing countries life expectancy is lower and the key illnesses tend to be linked to hygiene and diet; dysentery, malnutrition, and other communicable diseases are the main causes of death.

Dependency theorists have seen some of the causes of health problems in developing countries as the result of colonialism. Colonialism brought western diseases to many developing countries, but perhaps more importantly, it brought agricultural policies (monoculture) which helped to create the conditions for the chronic inability to produce sufficiently varied foods. In addition, western domination led developing countries to model their own health service provision on western industrialised models, thus encouraging the building of large hospitals equipped with the latest hi-tech equipment. Some would argue that such facilities were inappropriate to the needs of developing countries (and often still are), absorbing huge amounts of money and taking funds away from modest and effective, but less glamorous, projects.

Development theorists would also point to the involvement of TNCs in developing countries, arguing that the policies TNCs adopt do little to promote the health and welfare of citizens of developing countries. Cases such as Nestlé's selling of powdered baby milk in Africa, the sale of drugs banned by western governments, and the neglect of health and safety precautions in manufacturing plants, all provide evidence that some TNCs tend to show little concern for health issues, whatever their public pronouncements.

The implication of such criticisms is that, in order to make improvements in health, developing countries need a different set of priorities and strategies. These could include improvements in hygiene and the quality of water supply, improved sanitation, and an improved diet. These basic remedies could help bring about significant change. Development theory suggests powerful interest groups in developed societies (e.g. TNCs), as well as those within developing societies themselves (elites), may have more to gain from attempts to promote western-style solutions to health problems than from more modest strategies.

> **FACTFILE**
>
> - The 1998 UN Human Development Report calculated that of the 4.4. billion people living in developing countries, one-fifth were undernourished, one-quarter lived in inadequate housing, three-fifths lacked basic sanitation, one-third had no safe drinking water, and one-fifth lacked access to a modern health service.
>
>   Source: *Sociology Update* (1999)

Education

Modernisation theorists and dependency theorists reach very different views as to the value of education in developing countries.

Modernisation theorists see education as vital to developing countries' attempts to industrialise. Echoing functionalist arguments regarding the role of education in industrial society, modernisation theorists argue that a complex education system is necessary to provide the skills required in such a society.

Dependency theorists take the view that education systems in many developing societies reflect colonial models of education and even colonial curriculum designs, which are often lacking in relevance to the needs of such countries. Paulo Freire, in his book *Pedagogy of the Oppressed*, and Ivan Illich, in *Deschooling Society*, both provide good examples of this type of critique. Both argue that developing societies have particular needs, partly due to their lack of industrialisation, and partly due to the structure of such societies. This means that the hierarchical and bureaucratic structure of western education systems, with the frequent separation of academic and vocational knowledge is not inevitably a good thing.

Stuart Hall, a British sociologist originally from Jamaica, provides a personal insight into the anomalies of colonial education. His education in Jamaica included a thorough immersion in the poetry of Wordsworth and the history of the British Isles, but nothing about the history or literature of his own people. Moreover, none of this prepared him for the realities of life in Britain, especially, he notes, the weather.

Gender

Gender relations and the extent of gender inequalities in developing countries vary considerably, but a UN Report in 1995 found that many inequalities are being reduced. This said, for many women in the third world, considerable inequalities and patriarchal traditions persist. Life expectancy for women in developing countries is lower than for men. The value put on women in some cultures is reflected in the high rates of female infanticide and the increase of 'dowry deaths' in recent years in India. (Dowry deaths occur when brides are murdered due to the failure of their family to pay the dowry expected by the husband's family. The receipt or payment of a dowry is illegal in India, but nevertheless the practice persists.)

For many women in developing countries, career prospects may be non-existent, or where women are encouraged to gain paid employment, work is unskilled and offers few prospects. Even the better industrial work in western TNCs is production line based, often in the electronics industry, where women are stereotyped as suitable workers due to their supposed docility and superiority in light assembly work. Other opportunities may maintain the link with women's domestic roles and, more recently, there has been the development of marriage bureaux, enabling women from developing countries to survive and better themselves through marriage to a westerner, although the scale of this may be relatively small.

Gender inequalities also persist in other aspects of life in developing societies. In education, women seem to lose out again, with women in many African countries having higher rates of illiteracy than men. This has many important consequences, but one is that higher rates of illiteracy are associated with a high infant mortality rate. Attempts to improve health, thus, require more equality between men and women, as well as improvements in educational provision.

> **FACTFILE**
>
> - The UN reports that the literacy rate for women throughout the world stands at 71.2%, while the rate for men is 83.6%.
> - Two-thirds of the world's illiterate adults are women, and most of them live in Africa, Asia, and Latin America.
>
>   Source: Jorgensen *et al. Sociology: An Interactive Approach* (1997)

World sociology

Sample questions and answer advice

Critically examine the contribution of theories of globalisation to our understanding of development and underdevelopment.

(AEB, 1996)

Theories of globalisation can be critically examined by contrasting them with other theories. Modernisation theory and dependency theory consider development in terms of individual and autonomous nations. Globalisation theory argues that development and underdevelopment are interrelated processes, and that the power of nation-states is in sharp decline. Globalisation theory argues that the capitalism and the role played by Trans-National Corporations, has created a new international division of labour (NIDL), and that it is this which explains the systemic inequality in the global system. Globalisation theory can be criticised for exaggerating the decline in the power and importance of the nation-state, and it can be argued that the evidence for a NIDL is weak. In conclusion, however, it can be argued that globalisation theory makes a useful contribution to understanding development and underdevelopment, stressing the new forms of interrelationships between societies in a changing global economy.

'Contacts between rich and poor nations encourage development.' To what extent do sociologists agree with this statement?

(AEB, 1999)

Answers to this question can focus on debates between modernist and dependency theories. This debate can be illustrated and supported with discussion of the different types of aid and the arguments as to the effectiveness of aid, and through focus on one or more aspects of development, such as urbanisation, gender, education, or health. These examples may enable criticism of the two main theories, and drawing in more recent theories, such as Wallerstein's world systems theory, or theories of globalisation. In conclusion, while modernisation theorists would agree with this optimistic statement, many other theories would be far more critical.

TEST YOURSELF

A	M	I	H	J	I	W	U	S	Y	T	N	R	Q	Z	X	Y	U
Y	O	Y	R	O	E	H	T	Y	C	N	E	D	N	E	P	E	D
U	P	U	R	B	O	D	L	J	U	G	M	B	N	Z	B	H	F
Y	U	V	B	I	L	A	T	E	R	A	L	A	I	D	U	G	K
R	F	L	K	W	U	L	H	L	O	J	X	N	X	R	U	L	L
O	B	N	B	D	P	H	E	R	U	T	L	U	C	O	N	O	M
E	S	O	F	G	Q	T	N	C	I	Z	V	X	F	X	C	B	X
H	E	I	E	N	M	S	A	P	P	K	Q	W	U	T	T	A	V
T	I	S	Z	U	V	G	T	F	W	V	A	Z	A	B	S	L	G
N	M	S	A	E	T	I	L	L	E	T	A	S	G	C	I	I	N
O	O	I	S	K	C	I	L	L	I	C	H	G	E	F	L	S	A
I	N	M	R	A	F	U	J	G	M	I	D	H	R	Y	O	A	R
T	O	M	L	O	D	K	B	V	G	O	G	P	I	R	P	T	E
A	C	O	U	C	S	M	K	H	L	S	P	N	E	E	O	I	M
S	E	C	J	N	K	T	D	X	F	Q	N	Y	R	H	R	O	O
I	R	T	C	L	G	B	O	J	W	A	G	P	F	P	T	N	O
N	E	D	O	Y	R	E	E	W	E	R	H	I	G	I	E	V	B
R	G	N	R	E	S	T	G	K	Q	E	J	S	I	R	M	R	T
E	I	A	E	H	Q	W	X	N	A	G	E	B	N	E	T	N	B
D	T	R	H	O	A	Z	V	H	X	J	L	K	N	P	C	V	E
O	Z	B	R	N	I	E	T	S	R	E	L	L	A	W	T	B	D
M	Q	X	D	T	B	X	U	O	B	H	T	F	C	O	T	E	K

Solution on page 126

Summary

1. World sociology is concerned with the study of the ways in which different societies are interrelated in an increasingly integrated world economic and social system.

2. Modernisation theorists have argued that poorer, less industrialised societies can compete with the more economically advanced nations by industrialising. The key barrier to modernisation, according to this theory, is cultural traditions in the poorer countries of the world. Critics of this theory have argued that modernisation theory is ethnocentric and that structural inequalities make it extremely difficult for poorer nations to compete effectively with richer nations.

3. Dependency theory argues that global wealth and poverty can only be understood in terms of the development of a world capitalist economy. This involved colonialism, which disadvantaged less developed societies to the benefit of the richer industrialised nation-states. Dependency theorists argue that, although colonialism has been eradicated, the domination of multi-national companies has created a new form of exploitation, a neo-colonialism. The exploitation of the poor by the rich nations just continues, but under a new guise.

4. Sociologists such as Sklair argue that globalisation has created a world economic system which is more integrated than in previous times. Transnational corporations (TNCs) can be more powerful than the governments of nation-states, and can pressure nation-states into providing beneficial trading environments. In such a system, inequalities between nations may be harder to eradicate, as the power of TNCs grows. It may also lead to the development of a global consumer culture which suppresses local traditional cultures.

Chapter 10: Crime and deviance

PREVIEW

You need to know:
- definitions of crime and deviance
- debates about the accuracy of official statistics
- sociological explanations of crime and deviance
- sociological explanations of the relationship between gender and crime, and ethnicity and crime
- social reactions to crime and deviance, and the role of the mass media.

Defining crime and deviance

Crime and deviance may seem relatively straight forward to define, crime referring to acts which the laws of a society have deemed to be illegal, and deviance referring to behaviour which deviates from the socially agreed norms and values of a society. Deviance is a much broader notion, applying to all behaviour, whereas crime applies solely to those acts which are against the law and which will be formally sanctioned if reported.

Ken Plummer has suggested that sociologists should recognise the difference between societal and situational deviance:

- Societal deviance refers to acts which would generally be seen as breaking social rules, and Plummer argues that there is considerable consensus on what these rules are.

TEST YOURSELF

Offenders found guilty of, or cautioned for, indictable offences in England and Wales: by gender, type of offence and age, 1997

	Rates per 10,000 population				All aged 10 and over
	10–15	16–24	25–34	35 and over	(thousands)
Males					
Theft and handling stolen goods	124	216	85	18	149
Drug offences	12	158	63	8	86
Violence against the person	30	71	32	7	50
Burglary	43	71	18	2	39
Criminal Damage	11	18	7	1	12
Robbery	6	11	2	–	6
Sexual Offences	3	4	3	2	6
Other indictable offences	11	101	59	11	72
All indictable offences	240	651	269	50	420
Females					
Theft and handling stolen goods	58	70	30	7	52
Drug offences	1	17	9	1	10
Violence against the person	11	11	5	1	9
Burglary	3	3	1	–	2
Criminal Damage	1	2	1	–	1
Robbery	1	1	–	–	1
Sexual Offences	–	–	–	–	–
Other indictable offences	3	18	12	2	13
All indictable offences	80	122	57	11	88

Source: Adapted from *Social Trends* 29 (1999)

1. According to the data in the table, which social group is responsible for most theft and handling of stolen goods?

2. Does the data support the view that women are less involved in crime than men?

3. Explain what is meant by a 'rate per 10,000 population'.

Crime and deviance

Answers

1. Males aged 16–24.

2. To some extent it does. However, two interpretative points could be made. Firstly, some of the rates given are perhaps surprisingly high, (e.g. a rate of 70 per 10,000 of population of females aged 16–24 involved in theft), given that some sociologists (e.g. Heidensohn) argue that official statistics give a fairly accurate picture of gender and crime. Heidensohn implies that females tend not to be involved in crime. The rate, however, may seem to give some support to the feminist point that 'malestream' bias simply blocks out the role of women in crime or, at the very least, may indicate social change in this area. Secondly, this data raises the general issue of the validity of official statistics. These figures show those criminals apprehended and charged by the police. Thus, the validity of the data and the ability of sociologists to generalise from them may be limited.

3. This means that, for example, for every 10,000 males aged 16–24 in the population, 216 will be charged with committing theft or handling stolen goods.

FACTFILE

- What counts as a crime varies from place to place, and changes over time.
- Crime is relative across time and place.

Explanations of crime and deviance

Biological and psychological perspectives

There are two views associated with this perspective.

1. Criminal behaviour is caused by inherited physical characteristics (Lombroso, first published in 1876).
2. Criminality is correlated with personality (Eysenck, 1970).

Both explanations assume that criminal characteristics are innate, implying that a tendency to act in a criminal way is something which we are born with and cannot change.

The functionalist perspective

According to Durkheim, any society must have common norms and values. It is inevitable that some of its rules will be broken, and there will be a variance in the strength of individuals' commitment to shared values. He suggests that deviance can be functional for society, since it can strengthen social solidarity, by punishing those who break the law. It can also be beneficial since a change in the law may come about after some individuals have broken a rule or law. If the law is challenged, it may subsequently be changed. This is functional as it allows social rules to develop and change over time.

Robert Merton argues that in American society norms and values vary between different social groups. In such an unequal society individuals do not have an equal chance to follow the approved norms and values. This leads to a strain or tension between the goals of society and the opportunities to achieve the goals. Merton sees this as a key way of explaining crime; much crime is committed by individuals who are simply trying to find a way to achieve the goals of the wider society, e.g. the pursuit of wealth. Merton develops a classification system to describe the various adaptations to cultural goals which individuals may adopt: conformity, innovation, ritualism, retreatism and rebellion.

The Marxist perspective

Ideas of crime and deviance invariably reflect the interests of the ruling class, e.g. much of the law is

---

- Situational deviance suggests that, in certain situations, the dominant norms and values may not apply, or apply with less force. For instance, the general consensus is that men do not kiss and hug each other, yet in the specific situation of a football match it is not deviant for men to act in this way.

This distinction underlines the point that crime and deviance should be understood in the context of both general social rules and in terms of the 'rules' which apply in particular situations.

One of the most influential definitions of crime and deviance comes from the interactionist sociologist Howard Becker. Becker defines deviance as follows:

> Social groups create deviance by making the rules whose infraction constitutes deviance, and by applying those rules to particular people and labelling them as outsiders. From this point of view, deviance is not a quality of the act the person commits, but rather a consequence of the application by others of the rules and sanctions to an offender. The deviant is one to whom the label has successfully been applied; deviant behaviour is behaviour that people so label.

The implication of this definition is that what counts as deviance or crime is socially defined, and may vary between different societies and across time. This leads sociologists to be interested in examining how social rules are constructed and negotiated, and whether the process of making social rules may benefit some social groups more than others.

Crime and deviance

concerned with property. The legal system functions so as to impose social control on the working classes and any group which threatens the capitalist system. Crime is not a solely working-class phenomenon, though the operation of the law defines it as such. Much less effort is made to apprehend perpetrators of white-collar and corporate crime.

The interactionist perspective

Interactionist perspectives offer a sharp contrast to structural theories. Crime is defined as the result of processes of labelling and negotiation:

- Deviance is not a quality that any action has, rather certain behaviour is *labelled* as deviant.
- This may depend on who has committed the act, and on the social situation (i.e. where it has occurred).
- How an act is labelled is the outcome of a process of negotiation.
- Once a person has been labelled, the label will have an influence upon their self-concept and the way others react to them.
- The label will become a master status, and the difficulty of rejecting the label may lead to the creation of a deviant career.

Subcultural theories

There is a wide range of subcultural theories. They all share the idea that some social groups develop a distinct set of values, in response to their social and economic environment (this may include, for example, poverty or racism), forming a subculture, and this can lead them to commit crime. A key difference between subcultural theories is that some are functionalist, and others Marxist influenced.

Functionalist subcultural theories

Albert Cohen (1955) argues that young working-class males, because of their position in the class system will become susceptible to 'status frustration'. They have few legitimate means of gaining high status in their society, so they may reject the dominant values of society and attempt to gain attention and status through criminal behaviour.

Cloward and Ohlin (1961) link crime to the availability of opportunities to become involved in criminal activity. In inner city areas with high crime rates, it is easy for young people to become involved in crime, whereas a council estate in an area with full employment may well offer fewer opportunities.

CHECKLIST

✓ Studies such as those by Lombroso and Eysenck have not used representative samples of the population; both studied convicted prisoners. Neither is it clear whether extroversion is a cause, as Eysenck claims, or an effect of imprisonment. Many sociologists would argue that people's characteristics and personality are strongly influenced by the social environment and are not fixed – they can change their behaviour.

✓ Merton's classification (or typology) only explains the way individuals respond to their position in society; not all members of the same social group, e.g. social class, will respond in the same way to the same structural forces. Merton's theory may not be able to explain crimes which seem to have no financial purpose or gain, e.g. vandalism, assault, rape.

✓ Although care should be taken not to oversimplify Marxist approaches to crime, it can be argued that not all crime may be explained in terms of class conflict or economic and political oppression. The debate between the new criminologists and the New Left realists is of relevance here. A feminist critique could also be applied, since it can be argued that a Marxist analysis would have great difficulty in explaining crimes such as rape or child abuse.

✓ The interactionist approach is often criticised as being superficial and descriptive. Although it can appear to describe how some actions come to be defined as criminal, it is argued that it does little to explain why people act criminally, and why certain acts are defined as criminal. It can be suggested that these questions can only be answered by reference to structural concepts, such as class and power.

Marxist subcultural theories

Key examples of this theory are exposed in the work of members of the University of Birmingham Centre for Contemporary Cultural Studies (CCCS). Dick Hebdige and Phil Clarke argue that working-class crime and deviance is a response, or a resistance, to the oppression experienced by that social group. This is a controversial claim, since it assumes that the working class is oppressed. Furthermore, those committing criminal acts may disagree with this explanation, and see their behaviour in a completely different light.

Crime and deviance

> **Summary**
> 1. Functionalist and Marxist versions of subcultural theory assume there is a dominant set of norms and values (or dominant ideology in Marxist terms), which criminals reject.
> 2. Criminal 'subculture' may share many values with the wider society.
> 3. They tend to neglect white-collar crime, corporate crime, and the issue of gender and crime.
> 4. Marxist subcultural theory may misinterpret the significance of working-class crime.

Official statistics and the measurement of crime

The validity of official statistics on crime

Official crime statistics rely on the public reporting offences to the police, on the police deciding to take action on reported crimes, and on crimes witnessed by officers in the course of their duty.

The public may not report crimes to the police for several reasons:
- fear of reprisals
- may not be aware that a crime has been committed
- embarrassment
- the crime may be perceived as too minor
- they prefer to deal with it themselves
- they lack confidence that the police will catch the offender
- the victim has broken the law themselves.

Holdaway, who conducted participant observation and published his research as *Inside the British Police*, notes that police officers have discretion as to how they apply the law. Police officers frequently have to prioritise which offences and offenders they will take action against. Their activities are influenced by police culture and by their definition of what action is to their own advantage.

Sociologists have used other methods to try and gain a more accurate picture of the amount and type of crime being committed, such as victim studies and self-report studies.

Victim studies

The British Crime Survey (BCS) has indicated that the recorded figures for some crimes, such as theft and burglary, may dramatically underestimate the real rate. The 1998 survey estimates that crimes reported to the police represent only 54% of the total amount of crime.

Professor Robert Reiner (1996) has made several criticisms. Victim studies may have been less accurate as respondents may have a vested interest to under-report crime; higher crime areas will have higher insurance premiums. The BCS may be less accurate in estimating violent crime. Much violent crime is domestic violence and, since the BCS is conducted on a household basis, it seems likely that perpetrators and victims of this type of crime would be unwilling to report such offences.

Self-report studies

Self-report studies involve a researcher giving respondents a confidential questionnaire which provides examples of offences and invites the respondent to identify those which they have committed. This research method was used by Anne Campbell in her study *Girl Delinquents* (1981) which examined a group of females in youth custody. Maguire points out that the range of criminal offences investigated by self-report studies tends to be rather narrow, and neglects crimes such as fraud and domestic violence.

Reliability

As is clear from comparing official crime statistics with those generated by researchers using other methods, it seems that statistical information on crime is rarely reliable, i.e. it is hard to get different researchers to agree on how much crime is committed.

It is worth noting that many theories of crime and deviance have been based on a view of crime which is derived from official statistics and the other sources mentioned. If the view of crime which these methods provide lacks validity, it may well imply that the theories which rely too much on them are also open to criticism.

> **FACTFILE**
> - Official statistics may lack *validity* and *representativeness*.
> - They reflect the behaviour of an unrepresentative sample of the population – young, male, working class, and black.
> - Crime may be committed by other groups in the population, but it is simply unreported and undetected by the police.
> - The so-called 'dark figure' of crime refers to the idea that most crime is unreported and therefore the extent of crime is unknown. It is hidden from view and not as it were, 'brought to light'.

Crime and deviance

> **CHECKLIST**
> - ✓ Official statistics may lack validity, reliability, and representativeness.
> - ✓ The public may not report all crime.
> - ✓ The police may not always take action.
> - ✓ Victim and self-report studies may also lack validity, reliability, and representativeness.
> - ✓ Theories of crime based on the view given by official statistics may be misconceived.

> **CHECKLIST**
> - ✓ Remember to use more recent theories of crime to demonstrate how, for instance, Marxist theory has been modified to counter the criticisms of economic reductionism.
> - ✓ Left and Right realism are useful theories to use to contrast against Marxist views.
> - ✓ New Left realism and the New Criminology are good examples of sociologists trying to synthesise subcultural and structural perspectives.

More recent theories of crime

The New Criminology

The New Criminology is associated with the work of Ian Taylor, Paul Walton and Jock Young, and their book of that title (1973). Taylor *et al.* adopted a conflict based approach to crime which aimed to provide a comprehensive sociological theory of crime combining the strengths of labelling and Marxist based theory, while avoiding the weaknesses of both. It is often criticised for supposedly 'romanticising' crime.

New Left realism

Developed by sociologists such as Jock Young, John Lea and Roger Matthews, this view of crime suggested that previous theorising had been in danger of romanticising crime. Crime was indeed a predominantly working-class phenomenon, and this was seen as the result of relative deprivation, marginalisation and subcultural values.

Right realism

This is a loosely linked group of theories which see crime as the result of cultural deprivation and moral decay. A decline in moral values leads criminals to choose to commit crime, e.g. Charles Murray.

Control theory

Largely oriented to a practical and policy-centred approach, this theory suggests that crime is the result of providing criminals with the opportunities to commit crime. Control theorists advocate a range of preventative measures, such as target hardening by increased surveillance, e.g. closed-circuit television, or other anti-theft devices.

Postmodernism

You can use postmodernism to demonstrate up-to-date knowledge and your ability to apply it. One implication of postmodernism might be that the boundary between crime and deviance, and lawful or normal behaviour, is becoming increasingly blurred in a fast-changing society. Another application might be in terms of the way perceptions of crime are distorted by the media.

Gender and crime

The relationship between gender and crime was largely neglected until the 1980s when feminist sociologists started to study the area in more detail. Feminists have suggested that this neglect reflects the bias of malestream sociology.

There is debate as to the extent of women's involvement with crime. Heidensohn argues that the picture revealed by official statistics is probably accurate. This shows that women are much less involved in crime than men, and that their involvement tends to be concentrated in a fairly narrow range of offences, such as shoplifting, dealing with stolen goods, and prostitution. Women also figure highly as the victims of crime, particularly domestic violence.

Women's involvement in crime can be explained by applying general sociological theories of crime and deviance: e.g. biological theories – women are naturally less disposed to criminal behaviour; labelling theory – women are labelled as 'caring', 'non-violent' etc; functionalist theory – women are socialised into the affective role.

Some of the theories mentioned above focus on factors in the social background of the 'non-offenders' to explain their behaviour. Other theories though, such as labelling, have suggested that police and courts treat female defendants and offenders differently to males. Some sociologists have argued that this has been to the benefit of female offenders, enabling them to receive lighter sentences. Others though, such as Carlen and Eaton, have found that women (and particularly certain categories of women, such as single women, or women whose children are in care) have been treated more harshly.

Crime and deviance

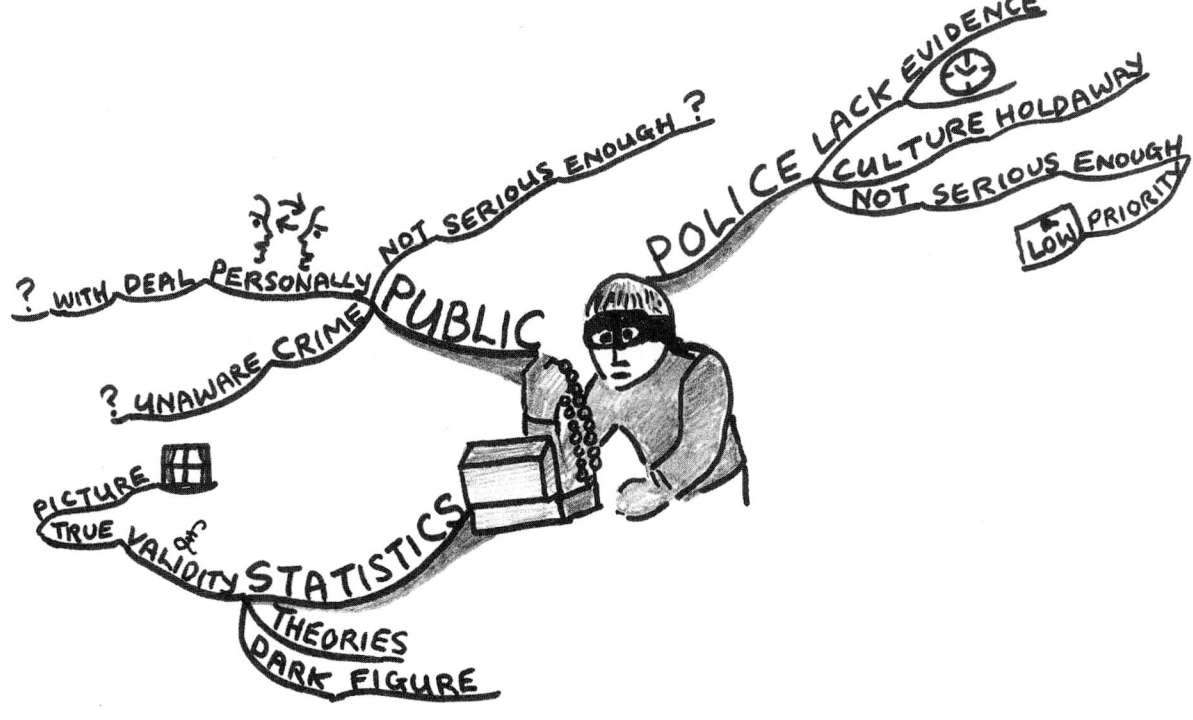

Reasons for and implications of the non-reporting of crime

Some studies, such as Anne Campbell's study, criticise the view of women as in some sense 'non-criminal', and are critical of the validity of official crime statistics. However, it is acknowledged that there may be differences in male and female criminality.

Studying gender and crime necessarily involves examining the roles of men, as well as women, since there are two genders. As Ken Plummer has argued gender is a neglected aspect of crime, and it may be that it can explain as much about crime – men's involvement in it, and women's lack of involvement – as theories which place more emphasis on class.

Ethnicity and crime

Some exam questions may require students to focus on ethnicity and crime. Such questions can be dealt with, in part, by applying general sociological theories of crime and deviance, e.g. crime committed by ethnic minorities can be explained in terms of functionalist or Marxist subcultural theory, or labelling theory could be applied, and the argument that ethnic minorities are labelled as deviant could be examined. However, there are also studies and theories which specifically focus on ethnicity and crime, and these too must be discussed. Recent research highlights three main positions which sociologists have taken on the issue of ethnicity.

Stuart Hall

Stuart Hall, in *Policing the Crisis*, argued that the widespread reporting of 'mugging' in the mid to late 1970s created a 'myth of black criminality'. Hall's argument is that the 'black' population were not more

> **FACTFILE**
> - In 1997 83% of those found guilty of, or cautioned for, an indictable offence were male.
> - Sociologists disagree as to whether this provides an accurate picture of crime, implying a lesser involvement of women in crime.
>
> Source: *Social Trends 29* (1999)

Study and Revise AS and A2 Level Sociology

Crime and deviance

> **FACTFILE**
> - In 1997 about one in eight adult male prisoners were from ethnic minority groups.
>   Source: *Social Trends* 29 (1999)

criminal than other ethnic groups. Hall argues that a myth was created through media stereotyping, and that the moral panic about 'black crime' reflected an economic and social crisis occurring within British capitalism at that time.

Paul Gilroy

Paul Gilroy provides a slightly different perspective. Gilroy argues that there were relatively high rates of street crime in areas with a population containing a high proportion of ethnic minority groups. However, Gilroy argues that much 'black crime' could be seen broadly as 'political' in its motivation and as a form of resistance to living in a white-dominated society. The experience of oppression which this created, combined with sometimes heavy handed policing methods, led to black resistance.

New Left Realism

A third view comes from the sociologists credited with creating New Left realism. This group argues that 'black criminality' was a very real phenomenon in the inner cities, not a myth. However, the New Left realists argue that these high rates of crime were the result of high levels of social deprivation and marginalisation. In other words, this explanation sees crime, to some degree, as situational.

A key issue in these debates is over the validity of official statistics and the picture that is given of high rates of 'black' crime. Some of the views considered here see these as broadly accurate, while Hall argues that a false impression has been created of the 'criminal nature' of ethnic minorities. This view could be supported by reference to labelling theory, and by studies of racism, both within British society generally and within the criminal justice system.

Social reactions to crime and deviance – the role of the mass media

Becker's definition of deviance makes the role of societal reaction of prime importance. This has not been neglected by other sociologists who have focused their research efforts on the role of the mass media in crime and deviance. Stanley Cohen's work on moral panics has argued that the media play a vital role in deviancy amplification (see Chapter 5 for more details of this study).

Other sociologists have argued that the media form an important source of ideas about crime and deviance, and structure public perceptions of crime. The media is selective, for instance, in the way it reports crime, and may simply reinforce popular stereotypes and prejudices about the nature and extent of crime, as well as about who are the perpetrators of crime. Hall, for instance, in *Policing the Crisis*, sees the media as playing a key role in creating the myth of black criminality.

However, it can be argued that these theories give too much importance to the power of the mass media. As examination of sociological perspectives on the media will show, audiences may not respond passively to media messages and Morley, for example, shows how audiences may interpret media output in a variety of complex ways which relate to their social situation. Nevertheless, the media does seem to give high priority to programmes about crime, whether they be news items, documentaries, programmes such as *Crimewatch UK*, plus interminable detective series.

Sample question and answer

Some explanations of crime focus on the background of the offenders, while others focus on the practices of police and courts. Assess the usefulness of these two approaches in explaining the social characteristics of convicted criminals.
(AEB, 1997)

According to official statistics, convicted criminals appear to consist mainly of young urban, working-class males, with a disproportionate number coming from ethnic minority groups. Sociological explanations of these phenomena do appear to focus either on the background of offenders or on the practices of the criminal justice system. It can be argued that, in taking such a course, sociological explanations and perspectives invariably reflect their approach to the structure/action debate.

Functionalist sociologists have offered several explanations of crime, all of which focus on the social background of the criminal. Robert Merton, for instance, argues that not all social groups have the same opportunity to achieve the cultural goals valued in their society. For Merton, this leads to a variety of responses whereby individuals may use alternative means in order to achieve shared social goals. Thus, Merton refers to 'innovators' who share the goals of society, for example, to accumulate wealth but, lacking the conventional means to achieve this, turn to drug dealing or robbery.

Sample question and answer – cont

Other functionalists, such as Albert Cohen, have argued that inequalities lead to cultural deprivation and status frustration. Young adolescents unable to participate fully in their society and gain status in conventional ways, seek to do so through the development of a delinquent subculture; Cohen, thus, develops a functionalist subcultural explanation of crime.

While there are some important differences between the various functionalist explanations of crime, they can all be criticised for offering a deterministic view of crime. These explanations give the impression that crime is an exclusively working-class phenomenon and seem to imply that, if a person is working class, then they will almost inevitably commit crime. Moreover, these explanations can also be criticised for their underlying assumption that society is integrated by value-consensus.

Other subcultural explanations of crime accept that there can be conflicting values, thus rejecting the idea of value-consensus. Walter Miller, for instance, argues that the American working class have a distinctive subculture, emphasising values which may lead young working-class males into frequent contact with the law and encourage them to break it. The work of the Birmingham Centre for Contemporary Cultural Studies (CCCS), influenced by Marxism and other theories, also explains working-class crime as a subcultural response to oppression. Crime is seen as a real working-class phenomenon, but is interpreted by the Birmingham school as a form of resistance to capitalism. Again, however, these views may be seen as deterministic and, in the case of the CCCS work, important questions arise as to whether they interpret the meaning of crime accurately.

Labelling theory, and interactionism generally, offer an alternative set of explanations which seem to focus not so much on the background of the 'offender', but on the way they are perceived by the agents of social control. Becker's famous definition of deviance, for example, stresses that an act itself is not deviant until it is so labelled. Studies for instance by, Cicourel and Stan Cohen, show how the police and courts treat people differently according to their social class background. Indeed, feminist studies have found evidence that women are treated differently from men in the criminal justice system. Labelling theory would seem to offer a potentially useful way of explaining the prevalence of young working-class males, of ethnic minorities, and of the lack of women in the criminal justice system.

However, labelling theory has been strongly criticised, particularly on the grounds that it neglects power and, thus, fails to explain the social and structural basis on which labelling is conducted. In addition, labelling theory is criticised as being deterministic, since it may appear that, once a label has been applied, the person labelled has no alternative but to accept the label.

Ken Plummer has argued in defence of labelling theory, that the criticism over its alleged neglect of power is inaccurate. Plummer argues that the central concern of labelling theory was precisely to focus on the way that certain social groups were criminalised. However, while this may have been the intention, it can be argued that interactionist and labelling theories in themselves do not provide the concepts needed to make them fully social theories of deviance.

Some theories, then, do focus on the background of offenders, while others focus on the actions of police and courts. However, there are theories that attempt to synthesise both of these aspects. Marxist accounts, such as those of Chambliss and Sutherland's work on white-collar crime, make the point that crime is not restricted to the working class, but exists in all social classes. Traditional Marxist views would suggest that crime is an inevitable consequence of capitalist society and, thus, would be able to point out that sociological theories should examine the social background of offenders, as well as the practices of police and courts. Marxist views along these lines would highlight the fact that the predominance of working-class crime simply reflects the workings of the agencies of social control; there is likely to be crime in other social classes, but it is obscured by the process of social control. The police and courts can be seen as acting in the interests of the ruling classes, and the law is applied for the benefit of these classes. Marxist views, though, may be criticised on similar grounds to the other theories discussed thus far. Critics point to the economic determinism involved in Marxist explanations of crime, and the need to examine actors' own explanations of their actions.

It may, therefore, be argued that a synthesis (social background, *and* practices of police and courts) based on traditional Marxism is not wholly successful. For this reason, Taylor, Walton and Young, developed a theory in the 1970s which is termed 'the new criminology'. This aimed to provide a comprehensive explanation of deviance, and stressed the need to examine crime in terms of structure, focusing on inequality and class conflict. Yet, it also utilised some theoretical insights from interactionism, trying to examine the meaning of crime for the perpetrator, and acknowledging that deviant behaviour reflected the conscious decisions of the actor. However, Young, Lea, Matthews, and Kinley, who developed 'New Left realism' in the 1980s, have been critical of this approach. They argued that it tended to romanticise crime and did not focus sufficiently on the fact that most crime was perpetrated by young working-class males, including those from ethnic minorities. For the New Left realists, it does, indeed, seem that explaining crime requires a focus on the background of the offender, since the practices of the courts and police by and large reflect the nature of crime fairly accurately, with the exception perhaps of white-collar crime.

In conclusion, it can be argued that the various attempts to explain crime in terms of either social background or police and court practice are lacking, and that a full sociological explanation has to try and take account of both structure and action.

Crime and deviance

TEST YOURSELF

Across
- **2** Sociologist who wrote on crime and ethnicity (4)
- **4** Wrote about moral panics (5)
- **6** Sociologist who argues that crime is inevitable, and functions as a 'safety valve' (8)
- **8** Theory which suggests that crime is created by society (9)
- **11** Common criticism of interactionist and Marxist approaches (13)
- **13** Crime which does not appear in official statistics (10)
- **16** Sociologist who wrote on white collar crime (10)
- **17** Crime committed by institutions (9)
- **18** Theory which sees crime as related to class conflict (7)
- **19** Official statistics on crime may lack this (8)
- **20** A form of study devised to avoid problems of official statistics (13)

Down
- **1** Key sociologist who developed labelling theory (6)
- **3** Italian who argued that crime was genetically determined (8)
- **5** Theory which suggests that crime reinforces value-consensus (13)
- **7** Psychologist who argues that criminals are extroverts (7)
- **9** This theory argues that crime and justice are negotiated (14)
- **10** Argued that crime reflected adaptations to cultural goals (6)
- **12** Labelling theorists argue that this is created by labelling (10)
- **14** Sociologist who studied police culture (8)
- **15** Theory of crime which aims to reduce crime by minimising opportunities (7)

Solution on page 125

Summary

1. Becker's definition of crime opens up a new way of viewing crime and deviance, and this informs many sociological explanations of crime. However, although it has been an influential definition, it is not beyond criticism, e.g. Plummer qualifies it, and some might argue that certain acts are always seen as deviant, irrespective of time or place. Where it is relevant to the question set, students who show the ability to think critically about sociological ideas will be rewarded.

2. The concepts of white-collar crime and corporate crime should not be confused. White-collar crime refers to crime committed by the professional classes, usually crimes related to their work. Corporate crime refers to crimes committed by corporations and the managers who run them, and may include activities such as fraud, false accounting, neglect of health and safety regulations, e.g. through lack of satisfactory maintenance, or environmental crimes such as allowing the discharge of pollutants into the atmosphere. Notions of white-collar and corporate crime are important because they contribute to changing views about the nature of both crime and criminals.

3. Debates about the validity of official statistics frequently crop up in exam questions. Students need to be aware of the problems involved in using official statistics on crime. As ever, it is important to use accurately terms such as validity, representativeness, reliability, and operationalisation.

4. Questions about gender and ethnicity, and crime can be tackled effectively by applying general sociological theories and concepts about the topic. However, these should not be used as a substitute for more detailed knowledge of studies on gender, ethnicity and crime.

Health — Chapter 11

PREVIEW

You need to know:
- definitions of health and illness
- theoretical approaches to health and illness
- explanations of class, gender, ethnic, and age differences in health
- the availability of healthcare and development of healthcare services
- sociological approaches to mental health.

Definitions of health and illness

Although it may seem a simple matter to define health, and perhaps even easier to define illness, what has struck many sociologists is how hard it is to gain definitions on which all can agree. In 1955, the World Health Organisation (WHO) offered the following definition:

> not the mere absence of disease, but total physical, mental and social well-being.

However it seems possible that no one could ever be considered healthy with such a definition!

Sociologists have noted two broad types of definition of health:

- Positive definitions – these see health in terms of what an individual can do, e.g. play rugby, cycle, run, go to work.
- Negative definitions – these focus on being free of illness, or free of the symptoms of illness or disease, e.g. not having a heart condition, not having chicken pox, not having influenza.

If these definitions are embedded in social policy, they can have an important influence on the type of medical services offered. A negative definition of health can lead to a limited range of health services, while a positive definition may aim for a wider range of services. For instance, the provision of sports injury clinics would generally reflect a positive definition. A negative definition might tend to the view that the most serious sports injuries (e.g. a broken leg or neck) obviously need treatment, but the common range of minor injuries in otherwise 'healthy' people do not warrant expensive treatment.

A study by Blaxter (1990) using a representative sample of 9003 respondents drawn from electoral registers revealed a tremendous range of definitions of health and illness. Professor Bryan Turner (1987) confirms that illness is very much a subjective matter:

> Whereas disease is a concept which describes malfunction of a physiological and biological character, illness refers to the individual's subjective awareness of the disorder, and sickness designates appropriate social roles.

TEST YOURSELF

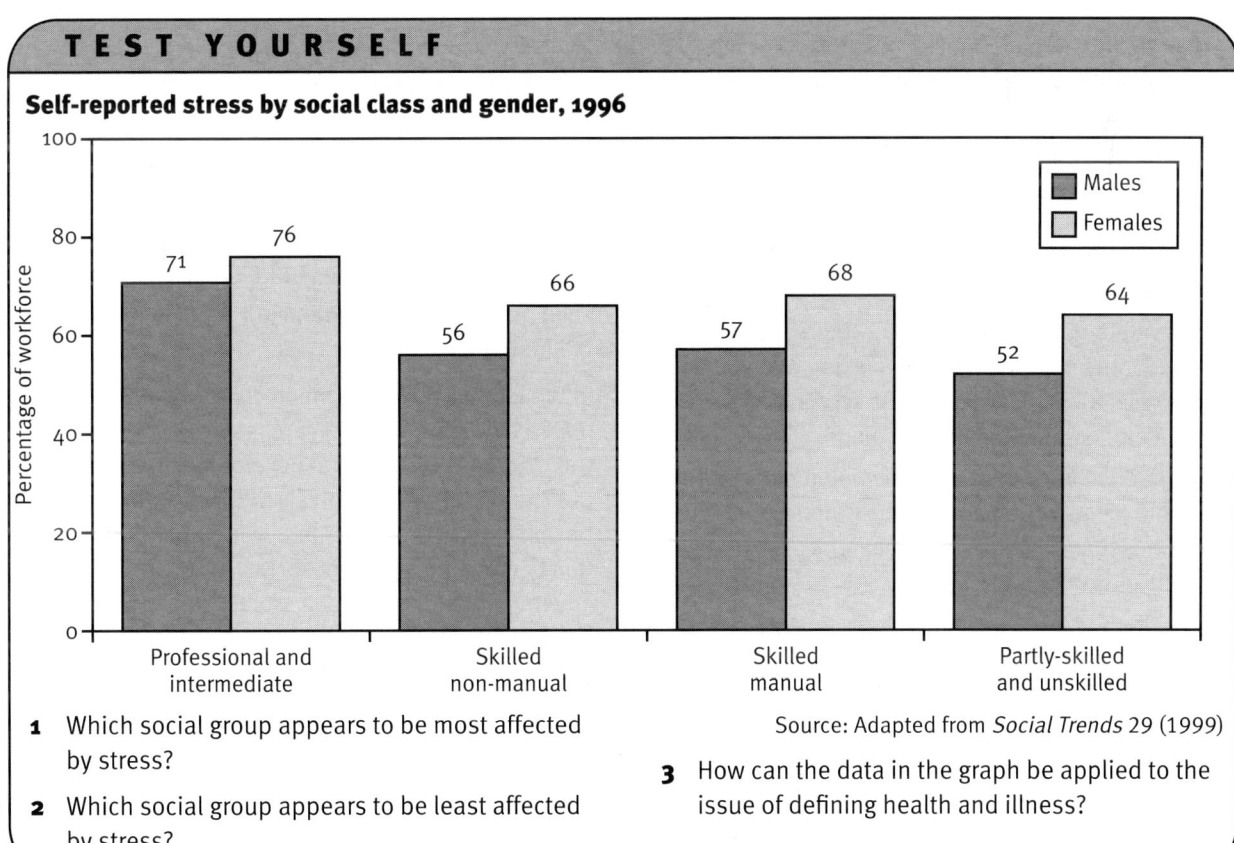

Source: Adapted from *Social Trends* 29 (1999)

1. Which social group appears to be most affected by stress?
2. Which social group appears to be least affected by stress?
3. How can the data in the graph be applied to the issue of defining health and illness?

Health

> **Answers**
>
> 1. Professional and Intermediate class females, 76%.
> 2. Partly-skilled and unskilled males, 52%.
> 3. It is hard to be sure how valid these figures are and, therefore, the accuracy with which they indicate the real levels of stress in the population. It may be the case that those in higher social classes do indeed suffer more stress than others classes, and women more than men. Alternatively, it could be that rates are higher amongst the working classes, but either they do not recognise it as an illness, or material factors (e.g. they cannot afford time off work) mean that it is tolerated. Thus the data in the graph point to the difficulties which sociologists face in defining and measuring health and illness.

It can be concluded that the terms 'health' and 'illness' are an example of essentially contested concepts. This means that agreement about the meaning of the concept cannot be reached. Thus, what counts as health or illness may vary between different societies, at different times in history and, even more problematically, between different members of the same society.

Indicators of health

Despite these disagreements about the definition of health, a number of common indicators are used to measure the health of a population:

- Mortality rates (or standard mortality rates, SMRs) refer to the death rate. A simple measure is the crude mortality rate, which gives a rate of deaths per 1000 of population for a given year. SMRs are more sophisticated and better measures, which can be standardised for sex and age, area and social group, such as class or ethnicity, for specific causes of death, and even for the influence of factors such as unemployment.
- The infant mortality rate (IMR), which provides a rate for the number of children dying within the first year of life, is also seen as an important indicator of health and well-being.
- Morbidity Rates measure the amount of illness within a population and can be produced in various forms, e.g. for particular diseases and by social grouping.

As health and illness are contested concepts, all medical statistics have to be seen as socially-constructed data, in the same way that sociologists treat suicide or crime statistics. Studies by Wadsworth (1971) and Last (1963) indicate that, just as there is a 'dark figure' of crime, so there is an 'illness iceberg'; an unknown number of cases of illnesses which are never reported to a doctor. Statistical data is compiled as a result of clinical diagnoses by doctors and medical staff. Therefore, official statistics on health may lack validity, as they only record 'illnesses' which have been brought to the attention of a doctor and which have been diagnosed by a doctor as an illness.

> **FACTFILE**
>
> - Health and illness are essentially contested concepts.
> - What counts as health or illness is socially constructed, e.g. what is defined as illness can vary in different times and in different places, and between different social groups, e.g. doctors/patients, classes, races.
> - So, health statistics are socially constructed and may lack validity.

Theoretical approaches to health and illness

There are several main theoretical approaches to the sociological study of health and illness. They do not have to be seen as alternatives to each other, or as mutually exclusive. Sociologists frequently borrow ideas from various theoretical sources and create their own synthesis. You should avoid, however, putting together concepts and theoretical insights which are contradictory.

Functionalist approaches

Functionalism provides a number of useful insights into health and illness. The specialist healthcare services and professions of industrial societies are seen as functional requirements in complex societies, maintaining a healthy and effective population.

In industrial society the medical profession is able to offer a better standard of care, as a result of specialist training and technological development. The medical profession receives relatively high rewards and status because its work is functionally important. However, this benefits the whole of society, and the government and regulating professional associations tightly control the profession.

Parsons devised the concept of the sick role. He argues that there are a set of norms and values, which enable us to define the ill or the sick in a particular way:

- Sick people are not seen as responsible for their illness.

- They do not have to undertake their usual activities, such as work,
- They are expected to seek medical help in order to become well.

Marxist approaches

Marxist approaches to health and illness inevitably see them in the context of class conflict and capitalist society. There are though a variety of points of view within this perspective, and not all Marxists would agree with all of them.

A traditional Marxist view would see state-provided health services in contemporary society as a way of maintaining the capitalist system, 'reproducing the labour force', by keeping it healthy. Other Marxists, influenced by Althusser, would see health services more in terms of the concept of social control. Healthcare services legitimate capitalism – it can be seen as 'capitalism with a human face'. Doyal and Pennell (1979) see the health service as focusing on treatment of many ailments which result from the capitalist system, e.g. work-related disease, rather than on preventive medicine. Health comes to be seen mainly as an individual issue. For example 'He died because he smoked too much', is seen as a valid explanation of illness, putting the blame on to the individual, instead of seeing it as the result of government policies which permit advertising and the selling of tobacco.

McKinley (1984) sees medicine as being commodified. This means that medicine has become a product to be bought and sold just like any other, in order to make a profit. This may mean that healthcare provision and professionals may be offering services, treatments, or drugs for reasons other than on strict medical grounds. Equally, the refusal of the NHS in 1999 to provide Viagra (a drug to treat impotence) on prescription is yet another example of cases where a treatment is withheld for economic reasons.

Others influenced by Marxism, such as Ian Gough, would take a more optimistic view and see the British National Health Service (NHS) as a benefit that was won by the working class through political action and protest, in the early to mid-twentieth century. Prior to the provision of the NHS in 1947, the only medical help that was available had to be paid for, although there was also very limited charitable help.

Interactionist approaches

Interactionist theory is readily applied to the study of health. Interactionists reject the structural approach adopted by Marxists and Functionalists, to focus on the interactions between the sick and the healthy, and between health professionals and patients. It is argued that this can provide a deeper insight into the way that ideas of health and illness are socially constructed. Several key points can be made:

- The concept of labelling is important in interactionism. Interactionist studies provide numerous examples of doctors labelling patients. Miller (1989), Dougal (1985), and Gillespie (1993) showed how doctors were able to label patients with HIV/AIDS. Gillespie's study demonstrated that patients with AIDS were seen in a negative light compared to patients with lung cancer.
- Erving Goffman's study of mental patients showed that they were negatively labelled. This negative or stigmatised label became a master status which was difficult to eradicate.
- Becoming ill involves a process of negotiation and individuals become defined or labelled as ill as the result of a negotiation with a medical professional or others.
- Rosenhan's (1973) study provides another demonstration of how doctors label certain behaviour as sick and make diagnoses on the basis of such judgements. Rosenhan's experiment involved a number of his associates posing as mentally ill and attempting to gain admittance to psychiatric departments in American hospitals. They were all successful and, despite being perfectly healthy, the majority were diagnosed schizophrenic. When they claimed to be cured, medical staff were unconvinced and refused to discharge the 'patients'.

Feminist approaches

There are several versions of feminist theory, but they all agree with the view that contemporary society is divided not simply on the basis of class, but also on the grounds of gender differences. Feminists see society as patriarchal, that is, as based around male dominance and power. This view is again, readily applied to the area of health and medicine.

Abbott and Wallace (1996) argue that the medical profession is dominated by men, and mainly works in the interests of men. Abbott and Wallace point to the disadvantages and health risks imposed by men on women through the invention of modern contraceptive methods. They see this as an example of the male bias of the medical profession.

Ann Oakely (1979, 1993) argues that the medical profession has 'medicalised' motherhood. This

Health

means that being pregnant and giving birth have come to be seen almost as 'illnesses', which must be placed under the control of the medical specialists and experts – who are predominantly men.

The New Right

The New Right is a term from the study of politics. It is important to consider the New Right since the ideas associated with it have had such a big influence on social policies throughout the 1980s and 1990s. The New Right has promoted two main ideas:

1. The free market is the best way to regulate society. This means that businesses and service providers should be able to compete and the best providers or businesses will succeed. This will be to the benefit of the consumer, since there will be competition and the goods or services provided, will over time, be of the best quality. Governments should not intervene or, in the view of the New Right, interfere in this process.

2. Individuals should be given the freedom to choose which goods and services they use and buy. They alone are responsible for their choices. Individuals should not have to be dependent upon the state for services, since dependency means that the individual has lost their freedom.

As applied to health and medicine, this philosophy has several implications. An efficient and effective health service will only flourish where competition between healthcare providers (whether private or state services) is encouraged. Individuals are responsible for looking after their own healthcare needs. This can refer to saving their money or buying into a private healthcare plan, but it also involves decisions such as whether or not one chooses to smoke.

Postmodernist approaches

Postmodernism sees contemporary society as having undergone important social, economic, and political changes in recent years. Theoretically, it is also critical of the idea of 'metanarratives', or dominant theories (including science) which attempt to explain everything. Postmodernist theory can, therefore, make several contributions to understanding health and medicine. For example, the decline in the belief in science would explain the rise in alternative medicine, e.g. acupuncture, aromatherapy, reflexology, etc. In addition, different cultures have differing ideas about health and medicine, and it is not possible to say that only one set of ideas are true, and that others are false.

Foucault (a post-structuralist) argued that medicine is best seen as a way of thinking which has become dominant in the West over several centuries. Foucault argues that any specialist form of knowledge, such as medicine, will become a powerful form of control for those professionals who organise it. He, therefore, argues that sociologists need to examine the power of the medical profession to promote a certain way of looking at things. Foucault calls a special form of knowledge a discourse. Science or psychiatry would be examples of specialist discourses.

CHECKLIST

✓ **Functionalist views that the relatively high rewards gained by the medical profession indicate consensus on the importance of medicine can be criticised; it can be argued that this simply reflects the power and strong market situation of the medical profession. The usefulness of Parson's view of the 'sick role' in a multicultural society is also open to question. Functionalists assume that we all share the same culture.**

✓ **Marxist analysis of health and illness can be criticised for exaggerating the importance of economic factors at the expense of cultural factors, e.g. cultural influences on diet, physical exercise, etc.**

✓ **Interactionist studies on health and illness can be criticised for failing to take adequate account of structural factors, such as class, gender, and ethnicity.**

✓ **New Right approaches to health and illness can be criticised for greatly exaggerating the choices which individuals have in relation to their health and lifestyle, and for neglecting or misunderstanding the true nature of markets. It can be argued that markets do not simply create choice, rather that they structure choices in an unequal way.**

✓ **Postmodernist-influenced views, as exemplified by Foucault, can be criticised for distorting the role of medical professionals. It can be argued that modern medicine has, after all, been associated with some great improvements in healthcare, such as increases in life expectancy, reductions in the IMR, and developments in the fight against diseases such as AIDS. Others might argue, however, that these are not necessarily the result of improvements in medical science.**

Social differences in health

A key area of interest for sociologists is to examine whether people's health and the access they have to healthcare resources vary with their membership of social groups, such as class, gender, ethnicity, age and region. There is much complex data available to sociologists and considerable debate about how it can be interpreted.

Class

Infant mortality is higher the lower down the social class scale you go. Conversely, infant mortality is lower, the higher social class.

Gender

Women have a longer life expectancy than men. Women are more likely to report illness to a doctor. It could be argued that some of the health differences between men and women are small, but the differences for 'anxiety and depression', and 'problems with self-care' look more significant.

Ethnicity

Some ethnic minority groups have a markedly higher infant mortality rate.

Age

The old are more likely to report illness to a doctor.

Region

There are marked differences in mortality, broadly indicating a North–South divide in Britain, with the higher rates occurring in the North.

FACTFILE

- In 1997 life expectancy at birth for males was 74 years, and 79 years for females.
- In 1995 Department of Health statistics reported that life expectancy for those born in social class 1 (Professional) was 7 years more than for those born in social class 5 (manual).
Sources: *Sociology Update* (1999), and *Social Trends* (1999)

Sociological explanations of health differences

Genetic or biological explanations

Differences in health simply reflect natural differences between different sexes, races, or individuals.

The statistical artefact explanation

This view argues that the observed statistical differences in health between different social groups do not reflect real differences; they simply appear to be such, and are the result of the statistical procedures which have 'artificially' grouped certain types of people into the same category. Those favouring the artefactual approach might, for instance, argue that comparing the top and bottom social classes (using any scale) is artificial and exaggerates the differences. Because these class groups are fairly small compared to the other groups, illness and mortality rates within them will appear proportionally greater than in other groups, and may, therefore, give distorted results when compared.

Natural or social selection

The idea of social selection suggests that those in the population with good health will undergo upward social mobility, and those with poor health will experience downward social mobility. Thus, the higher social classes are healthier only because they are composed of the healthiest members of other social classes who have, because of their good health, undergone upward mobility. Equally, the lower social classes have poorer health, not because of environmental factors for instance, but because the least healthy members of the population are downwardly mobile into these classes. In effect, this explanation argues that good or bad health is not caused by a person's class position; on the contrary, the state of their health determines their chances of success in life (lifechances).

Material–Structural explanation

This view argues that the differences between class, gender, ethnic, and age groups, and between regions are the result of the relative socio-economic position of the various groupings. For instance, the higher social classes have more income and wealth, and it is argued that this structural advantage provides access to resources which lead to better health, e.g. better diet, housing, easier working conditions, longer holidays, the ability to buy private medical care. Similar points can be made with regard to gender, ethnicity, region, and even age, since the elderly are disproportionately likely to be in poverty.

Health

Culture or behavioural explanations

This explanation sees differences in health as the result of the ways of life of different social groups. For example, it could be argued that the health of the working class is worse than that of the professional classes because working-class culture and lifestyle is an unhealthy one, involving too much smoking and eating too many fatty foods. This sort of explanation could be applied to ethnic minorities, arguing that higher rate of heart disease amongst Asian groups is due to the use of ghee (a sort of clarified butter) in their diet. Additionally, it might be suggested that some ethnic minorities have a higher infant mortality rate because they are unwilling to accept the advice of 'white' doctors. These are all cultural explanations.

Access to healthcare

Sociologists have noted that social classes do not have equal access to healthcare. Those in the higher social classes have greater ability to buy private healthcare, but even when the National Health Service is considered, various studies have demonstrated that it is the middle classes who benefit most from state provision. Tudor-Hart's 'inverse care law' (1974) argued that more prosperous areas have greater access to the NHS, a finding supported by Whitehead (1994).

Racism and sexism

Racism

In the case of ethnicity, various studies support the idea that medical professionals may apply racist stereotypes to ethnic minority patients. Some sociologists would argue that the NHS and, indeed, private health services reflect institutionalised racism through systematic differential treatment of ethnic minority patients.

Skellington and Morris (1992) point out that those of African and Caribbean descent are more likely to be admitted to psychiatric wards. Bowler (1993) provides evidence that nurses and medical staff can act upon the basis of racist stereotypes. Ahmad (1992) argues that sociological research and the medical establishment is ethnocentrically biased, taking a negative view of non-western approaches to medicine, assuming that all 'Asians' use such approaches and, thus, tending to see this 'group' as 'primitive'.

Sexism

Feminist-influenced sociologists have made similar points regarding the health and treatment of women. Brown and Harris (1978) showed that women were more likely to suffer from depression and stress. This is explained in structural terms, as a result of women's isolation in the home and exclusion from work, as argued in Gavron's study *The Captive Wife*. Abbott and Wallace (1992), in a review of literature, show that the most common contraceptive methods have been designed for women rather than men, and have been a good example of iatrogenic medicine. The term iatrogenesis refers to illness that is caused by treatment provided by the medical profession. Other examples of iatrogenesis would be the side effects of drug treatment, the ill effects of errors in surgery, or patients who become addicted to drugs prescribed by their doctor.

Oakley (1993) has argued that the process of childbirth has been medicalised and, thus, made almost akin to an illness. The medical profession dominates the control of childbirth, and births at home are no longer common. Macfarlane (1990), however, introduces a note of caution. She argues that, while statistics demonstrate women have greater life expectancy, they also show women as having higher rates of morbidity. This is paradoxical. Macfarlane argues that, if women's visits to the doctor relating to pregnancy and menstruation were excluded, men made more visits. This suggests that it is perhaps men who suffer worse health, not women.

> ### Summary
> 1. There are many ways of explaining health differences.
> 2. **It can be argued that it is hard to provide general explanations of such differences and that, in different cases, there will be different explanations.**
> 3. **Nevertheless, sociological explanations have tended to argue that health differences are the result of socially constructed inequalities, although this need not contradict the view that some differences are the result of the broad category of 'natural' differences.**
> 4. Sociological researchers tend to see material–structural and access factors, and the existence of discrimination in the wider society, as of greater importance than the other factors discussed.

Healthcare services

The National Health Service was created in 1948 by the National Health Act. This service provided free medical care for all. In setting up the NHS, the aim was to provide a universal welfare benefit, available to all regardless of means. However, the establishment of the NHS did not mean that private medical care was abolished, and private sector medical care continues to thrive.

This system has continued, albeit with some reforms, up until the present day. However, in 1990 the Health and Community Care Act made major changes to the management of the NHS. This Act led to the creation of the so-called 'internal market', whereby hospitals and General Practitioners were forced to adopt more competitive practices in an attempt to increase the efficiency and accountability of the NHS.

Hospitals are now termed 'independent trusts' and receive funding directly from central government. General Practitioners work as 'fundholders' and are able, in theory, to choose which hospitals they refer patients to on the basis of the quality of service and care. Critics of this system would argue that both hospitals and General Practitioners, thus, have to make decisions about treatment of patients, not just on medical grounds, but on economic grounds in an attempt to improve efficiency.

The changes to the health service during the 1990s reflect the political dominance of the New Right. The New Right believed that society was best organised on the basis of free markets, and thought that this would promote freedom of choice for service users as well as increasing the efficiency of public services.

FACTFILE

- By 1997 about 6 million people were members of private health schemes.
- In 1996–97 only about 7% of skilled manual and 5% of semi- and unskilled workers were members of private health schemes.
  Source: *Social Trends* (1999)

Mental health

Mental health has been studied frequently by focusing on the 'abnormal' individual, but sociological perspectives have been keen to point to the social basis of many views and judgements about mental health.

Goffman's study, *Asylums*, shows how total institutions lead to the creation of a stigmatised identity, and the process which he calls the 'moritification of the self'. This analysis can be interpreted as implying that, to some extent at least, mental illness is socially constructed.

The psychiatrist Ronald Laing, in his work on the family and schizophrenia, argued that mental illness could be caused by the pattern of personal relationships and interactions within the family.

Thomas Szasz (1973) argued that mental illness was a myth, and that it was broadly used as a label to control non-conformity.

It has been argued that some of these sociological views are exaggerated, and that current medical research is better able to demonstrate the physiological causes of some forms of mental illness. However, sociology is still able to make a valid contribution to the study of mental illness, since how people define and respond to mental illness is a social process. Indeed, these issues have become increasingly important following the introduction of the policy of 'community care'.

Care in the Community

Community care was introduced as the result of the 1990 Health and Community Care Act. The Act promotes the treatment of many categories of mental illness by integrating sufferers into the community, rather than treating them in specialist institutions. There are arguments both for and against community care. It could be argued that Care in the Community is a better way of dealing with the mentally ill, precisely because it will lead to de-institutionalisation. It should also reduce the labelling and stigma which Goffman, for instance, has showed occurs in 'total institutions'. Critics on the other hand, might argue that the policy was introduced by the New Right, largely because it offered a way of reducing the costs of mental health care, since specialist institutions could be closed. Care could be pushed onto either families or over-stretched social services departments which could do the work more cheaply.

FACTFILE

- *Social Trends* (1999) reports that between 1992 and 1996, men (aged 15–44) in England and Wales were four times more likely to commit suicide than women in the same age group.
- O'Donnell (1997) claims that women are 50% more likely to be diagnosed as having a mental disorder than men.

Health

Sample questions and answer advice

'Health and illness are defined by the powerful.' Assess the arguments and evidence for and against this view.

(AEB, 1999)

Support for the view that health and illness are defined by the powerful can come from a range of theories, including Marxism, social constructionist views (Foucault, Illich), feminism, and even labelling theory. It would be sensible to focus on a couple of these; Marxism, Foucault and Illich could be particularly useful here. Discussion could evaluate the use of concepts such as commodification, iatrogenesis, and Foucault's notion of discourse as applied to the medical profession. These views can be contrasted with the functionalist perspective. Useful evidence for the argument would be statistics on health inequalities, e.g. the Black Report, and inequalities on the basis of gender and ethnicity should be mentioned, even if briefly. The answer should also involve consideration or evaluation of the role of the health services provided by the welfare state.

'The artefact view of health inequalities asserts that the apparent differences between social groups are simply the result of the inability to measure a complex phenomenon such as health.' Critically examine the sociological arguments for and against this view.

(AEB, 1995)

Arguments for the artefactual view centre around criticism of the validity of occupation classifications and the operationalisation of both class and health.

However, there is persistent evidence of health inequalities on the basis of class (and gender and ethnicity), e.g. the Black Report, and different methods of measurement do at least agree in showing a consistent class gradient. Therefore, despite the undoubted difficulties, sociologists can measure and identify health inequalities between different social groups and attempt to explain them. Answers should also evaluate the artefact view by contrasting with alternative explanations, such as social selection, structural–material, cultural, and biological explanations, drawing on relevant evidence from studies and reaching a logical conclusion. One such conclusion might be that the most important determinant of health differences between social groups are structural–material factors.

TEST YOURSELF

T	I	N	V	E	R	S	E	C	A	R	E	L	A	W	C
U	M	Q	W	S	T	R	U	C	T	U	R	A	L	L	O
D	E	O	R	T	Y	U	I	T	O	P	L	K	H	L	M
O	X	A	R	T	E	F	A	C	T	Z	C	B	N	E	M
R	U	O	D	T	I	P	X	Z	C	V	B	N	M	N	O
H	T	R	I	E	A	E	W	Q	L	J	H	G	F	N	D
A	L	Z	S	X	C	L	V	B	M	A	S	D	D	E	I
R	K	J	C	H	G	S	I	C	K	R	O	L	E	P	F
T	F	D	O	T	S	A	Q	T	E	R	T	Y	U	D	I
F	G	H	U	L	M	P	K	L	Y	P	O	U	I	N	C
G	N	Y	R	U	Y	A	R	V	K	R	U	G	F	A	A
O	A	L	S	A	U	R	U	J	K	W	A	R	V	L	T
U	M	E	E	C	I	S	S	H	R	M	X	T	C	A	I
G	F	K	G	U	O	O	W	E	P	O	I	E	E	Y	O
H	F	A	Y	O	P	N	V	N	Y	T	E	R	A	O	N
Z	O	O	B	F	K	S	V	B	N	T	Y	U	D	D	H
C	G	G	R	E	B	E	C	I	S	S	E	N	L	L	I

Solution on page 126

Summary

1. Definitions of health and illness are contested. Views of what is meant by being healthy or being ill vary between different cultures and times and, even within a society, people do not agree on how to define health and illness. Sociologists conclude that dominant views and definitions of health and illness are largely imposed by those with power.

2. Sociological research has identified clear class differences and inequalities in health and health care, but it is harder to identify and explain social differences on the basis of gender and ethnicity.

3. Statistical data on health inequalities and illness has to be interpreted with great care, since the validity of such data can be questioned. Wadsworth has used the term 'illness iceberg' to refer to the idea that much illness may not be reported, in the same way that there is a dark figure of unreported crime.

4. There is a range of sociological perspectives which can be applied to the study of health and illness, and there are competing sociological explanations for inequalities in health. As with other topics, students should not feel that they have to choose only one theory. Theories can be combined to explain different aspects of health and illness and, as Senior and Viveash (1998) point out, different theories are not necessarily mutually exclusive.

Chapter 12: Stratification and differentiation

PREVIEW

You need to know:
- theories and definitions of stratification and differentiation
- how sociologists measure social class
- how gender and ethnicity influence employment prospects and lifechances
- recent debates about changes in the class structure
- social mobility.

Theories and definitions of stratification and differentiation

Definitions

Differentiation

This is a general term referring to the differences that are associated with social groups or categories, such as gender, age, class, and ethnicity.

Stratification

This term refers more specifically to the hierarchical organisation of social groups. This may occur on the basis of wealth, or status, or some other principle.

Class

This is a particular form of stratification based upon the varying economic resources and economic relationships of different social groups.

Key theories of stratification

Functionalist theory

Functionalists see stratification as an aspect of modern industrial society that is necessary and inevitable. Stratification, and the hierarchy which comes with it, enables a complex industrial society to recruit the most able individuals to the functionally most important positions.

Functionalists see stratification in modern society as being meritocratic, or fair. The education system, which is open to all, enables free and fair competition to gain academic qualifications, which then enables the successful to apply for good careers and the most prestigious positions.

High rewards are gained by those who are successful; but functionalists see this as both fair, and an essential incentive if the best individuals are to be recruited to the functionally most important positions.

TEST YOURSELF

Changes in social class in the UK, 1984–97

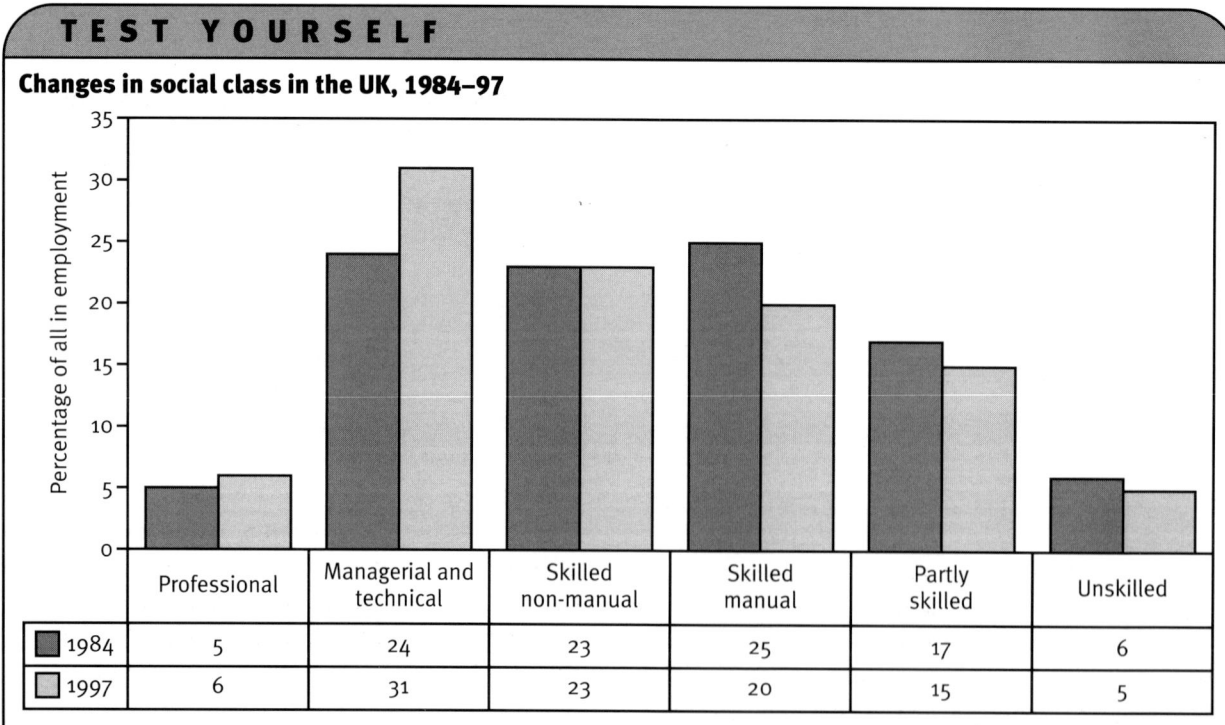

	Professional	Managerial and technical	Skilled non-manual	Skilled manual	Partly skilled	Unskilled
1984	5	24	23	25	17	6
1997	6	31	23	20	15	5

1. Which social class declined most between 1984 and 1997?
2. Which social class has shown the greatest increase between 1984 and 1997?
3. Does the data in the table provide any evidence of embourgeoisement?

Stratification and differentiation

> **Answers**
>
> 1. The skilled manual working class declined most, falling from 25% of the workforce to 20%.
> 2. The managerial and technical class (Class 2) increased most, rising 7% from 24% to 31%.
> 3. The data does not provide any evidence of embourgeoisement. The embourgeoisement theory suggested that the working classes were becoming increasingly middle class, not just in terms of income, but in terms of values and attitudes, particularly in relation to work and politics. The data here simply show how the shape of the class structure has changed. On this basis it does seem that British society has become 'more middle class' in the sense that the middle class has expanded and the working class has declined. This data, though, can be interpreted in the light of various sociological perspectives.

Marxist theory

The underlying view of stratification within Marxist theory is that all societies are divided into two groups on the basis of class. Class is defined quite strictly in terms of ownership; between those who own what Marxists term the means of production, and those who do not. The term 'means of production' refers to any equipment or resources that enable the owner to create wealth, e.g. a factory. The owners are termed the bourgeoisie (capitalists, owners, ruling class), and those who do not own the means of production are referred to as the proletariat (working class).

This means that in the Marxist view there are two main classes in capitalist society. These two classes inevitably have a conflictual relationship, since they have different and irreconcilable economic interests. Marx believed that as capitalist society developed, the condition of these two classes would change: the capitalists becoming increasingly rich; the working class becoming increasingly poor. It was this polarisation of the classes that Marx believed would eventually lead to revolution.

Weberian theory

The German sociologist Max Weber (1864–1920) was critical of Marx's theory of class, and modified it in various ways. Weber argued that class was not defined simply by relationship to the means of production (i.e. ownership or non-onwership). Weber argued that there were many differences between those whom the Marxist theory would term as working class, for example, doctors and factory operatives.

The concept of market situation refers to the fact that there are income differences between doctors and factory operatives, neither of whom in Marxist terms are owners of the means of production. Weber explains these differences in terms of supply and demand. There are fewer doctors than there are factory workers and, therefore, they can demand higher rewards. Thus, although neither are owners of the means of production, Weber argues that they must be seen as belonging to different classes.

Using this theory, Weber argues that there are four main classes; a property-owning upper class, white-collar workers (including professionals), the petty bourgeoisie and the manual working class. Weber also distinguished between class, status, and party, which were seen as different aspects of stratification.

More recent theories

Feminism

Feminist theories have agreed that women are neglected in stratification and class theory. Feminists have seen the main theories of class and stratification as reflecting a patriarchal bias (malestream). Empirical studies of class structure have been based on the occupational background of men, and women's employment has been ignored.

As women's involvement in paid work has increased through the twentieth century, with many households now having two incomes, identifying the class position of women and assessing the difference which this can make to the lifechances of a household has become an important sociological issue.

Feminist sociologists have proposed alternative concepts for analysing the class structure which take note of women's employment, and studies have focused on women's movement in the class structure (social mobility).

New Right

The views of the New Right can be readily applied to stratification. In the view of this perspective, inequalities are the result of market forces and class differences reflect the meritocracy of the market place. In this sense, the New Right shares the outlook of functionalism. Class differences and inequalities are seen as natural and inevitable and, indeed, as beneficial, since they create incentives and rewards for the most able. Sociologists associated with the New Right have typically seen the creation of an 'underclass' as the result of the culture of dependency created by the welfare state.

Postmodernism

Postmodernist theories have argued that structures such as class, gender and ethnicity are no longer so

Stratification and differentiation

CHECKLIST

- ✓ Marxist theories of class and stratification can be criticised for being oversimplified. By reducing all class differences to those between owners and workers, Weberian-influenced critics of Marxism have argued that the Marxist perspective neglects the important and considerable differences in income and lifechances between, for example, a senior manager and an unskilled factory operative.
- ✓ Functionalist theories of stratification can be criticised for the assumption that differences in the division of labour and in the reward structure are based on a consensus about the relative importance of different jobs. Marxists would argue that the differential rewards simply reflect differences in power.
- ✓ Weberian theories can be criticised from a Marxist perspective for neglecting the central importance of the relationship to the means of production. For the Marxist, the Weberian analysis fails to grasp the nature of the structure of classes and class conflict in capitalist society.
- ✓ Feminists have pointed to the malestream bias of many sociological theories of stratification, though sociologists have found it difficult to find a classification system which satisfactorily includes women's position in the social structure. Postmodernists' criticisms of the importance of stratification, while treated sceptically by many sociologists, have led to an increased acceptance that sociology has to examine gender and ethnicity, and class, as well as examining the interrelations between all forms of stratification (e.g. Bradley, 1996).

FACTFILE

- Fulcher and Scott (1999) point out that class divisions are less clear in contemporary British society, although class differences still persist and, in some cases, have increased.
- The class structure can, therefore, be seen as a fragmented structure. People are less likely to think of themselves in terms of a class identity, and their attitudes and values tend to be less reflective of class situation.
- Self-identity is more likely to be defined in terms of non-traditional status (e.g. consumption) or in terms of gender or ethnicity.

important in determining identity, although they offer little empirical evidence in support of this claim. Theoretically, though, postmodernism has been important, suggesting that it is relations of consumption which are now more important than relations of production.

How sociologists measure social class

Operationalisation

Before researching into class structure, sociologists have to operationalise the concept of class. Since class is an abstract concept which cannot be easily observed, sociologists have to pick an indicator of class. Most sociologists use an individual's occupational title to do this, and occupational titles are then placed in class categories.

However, there are a number of occupational classification schemes available for use, and all have various advantages and disadvantages. This issue is a common area for exam questions, since there are debates about which are the best classification schemes and which provide the most valid and reliable guide to the class structure.

Occupational classification schemes

Some of the most well-known classification schemes include: the Hall-Jones scale, Registrar General's Scale, the Hope-Goldthorpe Scale, the Standard Occupational Classification scheme (SOC), the Surrey Occupational Class Scheme and, most recently, the National Statistics Socio-Economic Classification (SEC). The large number of schemes available reflects disagreements amongst sociologists as to the best way of classifying occupations, as well as changes in the economy as new occupations are devised, old jobs die out, and as the incomes and benefits linked to certain jobs change.

There are several advantages for sociologists in using occupational scales and occupation as an indicator of class:

- They are convenient. Information is fairly easy to obtain.
- Most people gain their income from employment and, therefore, it seems reasonable to assume that occupation will be a good indicator of lifechances in general.

Stratification and differentiation

Criticisms of occupational classification schemes

Goldthorpe operationalised class through two sets of differences: work situation and market situation. The first refers to the amount of authority and discretion which different workers have in their workplace; there are for instance big differences between factory workers, supervisors, and junior managers. Goldthorpe used occupation as an indicator of class. Many other researchers also use occupation as an indicator of class.

Marxist-influenced sociologists are critical of Goldthorpe's classification, arguing that it obscures the capitalist class by placing them in Class 1 which includes higher grade professionals (e.g. senior doctors, barristers) and excludes the unemployed and those without an occupational title.

Feminists and others have also criticised Goldthorpe's classification system for excluding women's occupations from analysis, arguing that this is important when more women work and many households, thus, have a dual income.

FACTFILE

- Researchers have responded to the fragmentation of the class structure by devising new classification schemes, which aim to capture the new realities of class with greater accuracy.
- On the launch of the Government's new occupational classification, the National Statistics Socio-Economic Classification, a speaker for the Office of National Statistics claimed that distinctions between manual and non-manual workers were no longer relevant in a service-based economy.
- An Economic and Social Research Council representative commented 'A manual/non-manual divide is simply not a meaningful distinction given the nature of work and occupations in late twentieth-century market economies'.
Source: Adapted from *Sociology Update* (1999)

Gender, ethnicity, employment and lifechances

Sociologists have gathered a great deal of evidence that demonstrates a strong relationship between social class and lifechances. The term 'lifechances' derives from Weber and refers to an individual's chance of doing well in life. An individual with good lifechances will, for instance, benefit educationally, have better chances of good health, gain employment and good quality housing, and be highly unlikely to be imprisoned. As one moves down the class scale, the likelihood of gaining the benefits recedes and the likelihood of being disadvantaged increases.

However, gender and ethnicity are also important forms of stratification in British society, and sociologists have been interested in examining how these forms of stratification can influence lifechances. There has been a particular interest in how gender and ethnicity affect individuals in terms of their job prospects. This is an issue of interest to sociologists, and a frequent area of questioning concerns examination of sociological explanations of the ways in which employment opportunities vary on the basis of gender and ethnicity.

Explaining inequality in the labour market

There are a number of theoretical explanations for the inequalities in the labour market that have been identified. They can be applied in a similar way, whether questions focus upon gender, ethnicity, or even age.

Functionalist or liberal explanations

This form of explanation may often be termed 'liberal', but it is very similar to a functionalist view; textbooks may use either term. A liberal view sees society as meritocratic, and the disadvantage of a social group is the result of a temporary lack of skill or qualifications. Alternatively, liberals may take the view that state intervention is required to remove barriers to equality, by for instance, creating equal opportunities legislation.

A liberal explanation of ethnic or gender inequality would explain it as the inevitable consequence of a lack of skill. In the case of ethnic minorities, this would be due to a lack of technological development in their country of origin, while in the case of women it could be down to the long period of time spent out of the labour force, due to home and family commitments.

The liberal perspective suggests that given time, inequalities on the basis of gender or ethnicity will gradually decline, as both groups' skills improve and, in the case of ethnic minorities, integrate into the wider society.

Marxist explanations

The Marxist perspective sees inequalities on the basis of gender or ethnicity mainly as the result of class exploitation in a capitalist division of labour. Once the

Stratification and differentiation

capitalist system is removed, the Marxist logic argues, so too will discrimination against women and ethnic minorities.

Capitalists divide the working class against itself, thereby preventing recognition of a common class position. Thus, the presence of a potential labour force of women and ethnic minorities enable the capitalist to keep the wages of the (white male) working classes low. Should the working class grow dissatisfied and threaten to claim higher wages, the presence of a reserve work force of women and ethnic minorities, who are in effect cheap labour, can be used by capitalists to enforce acceptance of the capitalist order. Ethnic minorities and women act as what Marxists term a 'reserve army of labour.'

Weberian explanations

The Weberian perspective explains inequalities by drawing on the idea of the market situation of an occupation. According to this perspective, it is the supply and demand for particular jobs which determines the level of reward (pay or wages). Neo-Weberians have argued that this leads to a dual labour market; a situation where there are two levels of job, those which are vital to business enterprises, the core, and those which are less essential, the periphery. This means that the core jobs form a primary labour market, and they have the best rates of pay and the best conditions. The secondary labour market is then made of peripheral jobs, which are not so highly skilled, and which are the first to be cut back when times are hard. This perspective, thus, sees women and ethnic minorities as constituting the labour force for the peripheral jobs.

Changes in the class structure

There are many competing theories which claim to give an accurate account of how the class structure has changed in recent years. Exam questions may often ask candidates to evaluate these competing theories. Even if this issue is not required, a knowledge and understanding of this issue will be invaluable, enabling candidates to provide good answers to other questions on the topic, e.g. on meritocracy or social mobility.

Embourgeoisement

A popular theory in the 1960s, this suggested that the working classes were being absorbed into the middle classes due to rising wages and improvements in the standard of living. It argued that, as a result of these changes, social differences between middle and working classes would also erode. A key study which aimed to test the embourgeoisement thesis was *The Affluent Worker* study, by a team led by John Goldthorpe. The study concluded that, while wage differences between manual workers and non-manual workers were narrowing, important class differences remained:

- Manual workers still had to work more hours than non-manual workers to gain their inproved wages.
- Socially, they still mixed predominantly with other manual workers.

CHECKLIST

All of these explanations can be criticised on various grounds:

✓ While there is some support for the optimism of the liberal view, it is hard to explain the persistence of considerable levels of inequality, in spite of changes in the law.

✓ The Marxist position has been criticised for neglecting gender and ethnicity, and as seeing these as secondary to class if, indeed, it has seen them at all.

✓ Meanwhile, the Weberian approach fails to explain why it is that women and ethnic minorities are in the secondary labour market in the first place.

✓ An alternative explanation is that gender and ethnic inequality is the result of sexism and racism. Classical theories of stratification have not always been able to explain these differences. When they have, it has been because they have incorporated the insights of other theoretical perspectives, as in the case of Marxist–feminist explanations of gender inequalities.

FACTFILE

- Liberal, Marxist, and Weberian approaches to stratification and inequality in the labour market have all tended to be gender-blind. Feminists have called these malestream theories.

- Similarly, it can be argued that all the above theories have been neglectful of ethnicity. The disadvantage of ethnic minorities has often been seen as a reflection of their lower social class position, rather than as an indication of racism.

Stratification and differentiation

- In terms of norms and values, manual workers showed little sign of having adopted middle-class values, although they had adapted to the demands of a new environment. This was evident, for example, in their privatism – their individualistic lifestyles, reflecting working-class life in a large and fairly new industrial town (Luton), working in modern industries such as chemical processing, a car factory, and an engineering firm.

Proletarianisation

Proletarianisation is a Marxist-based theory, and is associated with the American Marxist sociologist Harry Braverman. The theory argues that, contrary to the claims of the embourgeoisement thesis, class differences are actually being levelled downwards. Braverman argued that the skilled working class are being deskilled: their jobs are gradually becoming simpler as technology becomes more sophisticated, thus doing away with the need for many jobs.

This, however, means that wages fall, since employers will not pay high wages for a lesser degree of skill. The same process, Braverman argues is occuring to many middle-class occupations. Braverman's theory, thus, neatly fits in with Marxist class theory, which argues that the classes (bourgeoisie and proletariat) will polarise.

Fragmentation

There are several theories which argue that particular classes are fragmenting, though some may argue that the whole class structure itself is fragmenting. A common focus is the middle classes. Roberts' study (1977) examined the attitudes and perceptions of class of a group of 243 male white-collar workers. Individuals identified four main groups within the middle class, and Roberts argued that the middle class was fragmenting.

Goldthorpe (1983) distinguishes between what he calls the service class and the intermediate classes. The service class consists of administrators, managers and professionals. Intermediate classes include clerical workers, small proprietors and technicians. Goldthorpe justifies this division on the grounds that the market and work situation of each group are distinct, with the service class having significantly better access to key resources, and better lifechances.

Savage et al. (1992) argue that the middle class consists of three main groups, each identified by distinctive assets; property, organisational, and cultural.

Anthony Giddens argues that it is best to see the middle class as one class, who owe their position to educational or technical qualifications. Obviously some members of this group will be better off than others. However, Giddens argues that, since they do not own the means of production and since they do not have to sell their manual labour to capitalists, they should be seen as a distinct and unified group. They are unified through their possession of qualifications which enable them to sell their mental labour power, which gives them better pay, conditions, and lifechances.

Does class still matter?

A variety of sociologists from different sociological perspectives have recently engaged in debating the issue of whether class is still a useful sociological concept.

Postmodernists are sceptical of concepts such as class. They would suggest that increasing affluence and the importance of lifestyle and consumption choices make the concept rather outdated. Furthermore, it could be argued that class is not a concept which has much influence on people's attitudes, outlooks and action.

Since the late 1970s, other sociologists have identified changes in consumption patterns which indicate a blurring of class divisions. Sociologists such as Ivor Crewe, for instance, have argued that class is no longer a useful indicator of voting behaviour.

Peter Saunders too (often labelled as a New Right sociologist, though he does not accept the label), has argued that a key division now is that between those who rely on the state for their consumption of goods and services, and those who work in the private sector and rely on the market. Such distinctions would cut across class divisions, as for instance in the case of a middle-class and a working-class family, who both use state schools and the NHS.

Ray Pahl, a well known British sociologist, widely identified as broadly neo-Weberian, has also been critical of the usefulness of class analysis (1989), arguing that consumption differences have eroded the influence of class in some respects.

Scott Lash and John Urry (1987) have seen post-Fordism (see Chapter 6) as partly responsible for a changing social structure where class is no longer the dominant source of identity.

The underclass debate

Another debate in recent years has concerned the existence of a so-called underclass. The term originated in the 1980s, and was coined by American sociologists W.J. Wilson and Charles Murray. The

Stratification and differentiation

underclass is seen to consist of a variety of different groups amongst the poor; the old, single-parent mothers, the long-term unemployed, the disabled, and the homeless, for example. This diversity has led some to be critical of the term, while others have been critical of the value judgements which the concept frequently involves.

Murray sees the underclass in cultural terms, and argues that they have become dependent upon welfare. He argues that those who are dependent on welfare have a deviant and harmful counter-culture, which is work-shy, irresponsible and feckless, and frequently criminal. He refers to the underclass as a plague. His solution is to reduce welfare benefits and to make claimants earn their benefits – work fare.

Wilson sees the underclass in structural terms. He argues that the underclass in the USA are a black underclass, characterised by high levels of long-term unemployment. British sociologists W.G. Runciman (1991) and Anthony Giddens (1973) both agree that there is an underclass. For Runicman it consists of the long-term unemployed, while Giddens argues that they may be unemployed, or employed on a part-time basis in the lowest paid jobs. American sociologist Herbert Gans (1990) argues that the term lumps together different groups and categories of people and implies that it is more a political, than a sociological, term.

Lydia Morris (1994) is critical of the concept, but sees it as having some use. Morris argues that in both the USA and the UK there has been a significant increase in male unemployment and, at the same time, an increase in poorly paid part-time work for women. She sees these changes as the result of the globalisation of capitalism and the intensification in competition which has led firms to restructure, thus leading to higher rates of unemployment.

Morris argues that this gives sociologists a problem, since class analysis usually uses occupation as an indicator. There is now a larger and very visible stratum of unemployed and part-time workers, who are difficult to classify using the conventional sociological occupational classification schemes. One of Morris's conclusions is that the concept of underclass is perhaps helpful to indicate the way in which individuals with a certain status are excluded from full membership (or citizenship) of society, are stigmatised and seen as outcasts by the majority.

The changing class structure

Evaluating these competing theories can seem difficult. However, some empirical data enables a clearer picture to emerge. The British class structure has been changing over the course of the twentieth century, and continues to change as technology, the economy, and society changes. In particular, sociologists have noted the importance of change in three areas of the class structure:

1. The manual working class has been in long-term decline. In 1911 manual workers constituted 80% of the workforce. By 1991 this percentage had declined to 46%, some 10.9 million workers.

2. The middle class on the other hand has been increasing. In 1901 the middle classes constituted 25% of the workforce. By the time of the 1991 census this had increased to 51%.

3. The upper-class aristocracy has declined, though as Scott points out, it still makes sense to speak of a capitalist class. Scott argues that this class consists of four elements; entrepreneurial capitalists, rentier capitalists, executive capitalists, and finance capitalists. Together, these groups constitute a capitalist class which composes about 0.1% of the population, or around 43,500 people.

Summary

1. **It can be suggested that the evidence does not support either embourgeoisement, proletarianisation, or fragmentation theories. The class structure has certainly changed as indicated above. Moreover, the inequalities between top and bottom have increased over recent years, and relative mobility chances still vary greatly between different social classes. At the same time, the standard of living has improved and British society is generally affluent, though inequalities remain and are increasing.**

2. **However these diverse findings are resolved, what does seem clear is that there is a great amount of empirical evidence demonstrating the real effect class has upon an individual's lifechances. If people think less in class terms, that is an important aspect of social change, and one which will affect an individual's behaviour. Nevertheless, it does not mean that class has disappeared.**

Stratification and differentiation

> **FACTFILE**
> - Increasingly some sociologists argue that the class structure is more fragmented, and as a result it has become important to study the other bases of stratification.
> - **Harriet Bradley (1996)** is one sociologist who takes this view, arguing that sociologists must examine not just class, but gender, and ethnicity, as well.
> - Moreover, Bradley argues that it is important to study the way in which all three elements of stratification overlap and interrelate.

Social mobility

Social mobility refers to movement up or down the social scale. A truly meritocratic society would have considerable upward and downward movement in equal proportions. Sociologists refer to the degree of openness or closure of a society when discussing the degree of social mobility; the more mobility a society has, the more open it is said to be, and the less mobility, the greater the degree of closure.

There are many terms used in the study of social mobility, but the following are the key terms used by sociologists:

- Intergenerational mobility – this refers to mobility between two generations. It would usually be measured by comparing a father's social class against that of his children, e.g. your father was a manual worker, you work as a solicitor.
- Intragenerational mobility – this refers to the mobility which an individual may experience within their lifetime, e.g. you start working life as a manual worker, but later qualify as a solicitor.
- Absolute mobility – this refers to the total amount of mobility within the class structure of a society.
- Relative mobility – this refers to the relative chances of mobility for members of a particular class in a society, e.g. the relative chances of a person from the working class rising to a service-class position.

Key studies and findings

- The Oxford study found there were high rates of absolute mobility. No social class self-recruited more than 50% of its members.
- There was more upward than downward mobility.
- However, despite these optimistic findings, relative mobility chances vary considerably between different classes.
- Kellner and Wilby have expressed this as the 1:2:4 rule of relative hope: a boy from the service class will have four times the chance of a working-class boy of ending up in the service class, and two times the chances of a boy from the intermediate class.
- Goldthorpe's 1983 study lead to some modification of these findings. There had been an increase in working-class mobility into the service class but, at the same time, an increased likelihood for those in the working class of becoming unemployed.
- The most recent national level survey was the Essex study of 1988. This used the statistical measurement of odds ratios to measure relative mobility and found that men from a service-class family were about seven times more likely to gain a service-class destination than men from a working-class family.

Peter Saunders (1995) is critical of social mobility studies, which he sees as unduly pessimistic. Saunders argues that there is much evidence to support the view that Britain is a meritocracy. Any differences in mobility chances reflect the real abilities of different social groups.

> **Summary**
> 1. Questions on mobility will often centre on the issue of whether or not Britain is an open or meritocratic society.
> 2. Students should ensure that they discuss fully the different measurements of social mobility, the range of research evidence, and the differential mobility rates for men and women.
> 3. Clearly, British society is characterised by considerable social mobility in some ways.
> 4. However, many sociologists have been most struck by the continuity since 1950 and the strong differences in relative mobility chances between different social groups.

Gender and mobility

A study by Heath (1981) found that women from social classes 1 and 2 were more likely to experience

Stratification and differentiation

downward mobility than men. In general, women were more likely to be downwardly mobile than men. The 1988 Essex study broadly confirmed the general trend of these findings. As Marshall *et al.* note, however, the disproportionate number of female employment opportunities concentrated in social class 3 (routine non-manual, e.g. clerical and secretarial work) affects women's mobility patterns. A recent survey of research literature by Pamela Abbott and Claire Wallace (1997) confirms and quantifies these findings, noting that 21% of men in Class 1 or 2 occupations are from working-class origins, but that the corresponding figure for women is 15%.

Sample questions and answer advice

How far does sociological evidence support the idea that Britain is a 'meritocratic' society?
(AEB, 1993)

This question can be interpreted as being largely concerned with social mobility. It is possible to contrast functionalist and New Right approaches, which emphasise the freedom of individuals to achieve according to their abilities, with Marxist-influenced and neo-Weberian influenced studies which are more sceptical in assessing mobility in Britain. Answers should explain the different types of mobility, and refer to concepts of openness and closure. Relevant studies include those of John Scott on the upper classes, as well as the main studies of social mobility, such as Goldthorpe and the 1988 Essex study. Other studies relevant to discussion on this topic are Kellner and Wilby, and their 1:2:4 rule of relative hope. It is also relevant to mention gender and ethnicity and the inequalities of opportunity which persist for these social groups. The idea of underclass could also be mentioned here. Discussion of the Essex study should include consideration of the strength of statistical evidence (odds ratios), and the criticisms from sociologists who believe that Britain is meritocratic, such as Saunders.

How far does sociological evidence support the idea that an 'underclass' has emerged in Britain?
(AEB, 1996)

Answers to this question need to tackle the issue of definition from the outset. One key criticism is that the term 'underclass' is used morally and politically, and means different things to different people. Sociologists also vary in their definitions and the term may include; those living on welfare, the old, the unemployed, single parents, the homeless, ethnic minorities, drug addicts, the disabled, and pensioners. Answers can, therefore, discuss the differences between Murray, Marsland, Giddens, Runciman, Wilson, and Morris. The discussion can usefully apply theoretical views on the definition and operationalisation of class, and link the topic to consideration of theories of class fragmentation. In conclusion, recent evidence certainly supports the view that class differences have widened; whether those at the bottom of the class structure are seen as an underclass, will depend upon how class is defined.

Stratification and differentiation

TEST YOURSELF

T	Q	W	E	P	Y	M	R	A	E	V	R	E	S	E	R
C	P	T	P	O	S	T	F	O	R	D	I	S	M	O	E
I	Y	P	A	T	R	I	A	R	C	H	Y	U	O	I	M
L	L	T	R	I	E	W	Q	Z	X	M	N	B	W	V	B
F	I	J	H	G	R	U	I	O	W	Q	Z	X	N	C	O
N	F	Q	S	W	M	A	R	X	E	U	I	O	E	P	U
O	E	R	U	G	C	Z	T	Z	U	B	E	T	R	M	R
C	C	E	T	N	R	H	H	E	S	V	T	I	S	N	G
S	H	T	A	B	W	U	Y	B	L	M	H	U	H	V	E
S	A	Y	T	B	O	U	R	G	E	O	I	S	I	E	O
A	N	Q	S	P	I	O	T	M	D	B	R	K	P	C	I
L	C	F	G	H	J	K	L	L	H	I	G	P	O	X	S
C	E	W	E	B	E	R	A	K	J	L	B	K	I	Z	E
S	S	A	L	C	R	E	D	N	U	I	F	G	U	A	M
N	O	I	T	A	P	U	C	C	O	T	D	B	R	S	E
J	M	H	N	B	V	G	E	J	J	Y	W	C	E	D	N
R	C	X	C	I	T	A	R	C	O	T	I	R	E	M	T

Solution on page 126

Summary

1. Sociologists who are influenced by different theoretical perspectives will define class in different ways. This will influence the way in which class is operationalised and measured, and this is why sociologists frequently disagree in their analysis of the class structure.

2. Until recently, the key area of study in stratification was indisputably class. However, this is now disputed, with many sociologists accepting the view that class is experienced in a more fragmented way due to changes in the organisation of work. This does not mean accepting the view of Saunders and others, that 'class is dead'.

3. Sociologists such as Bradley argue that it is now important to study how other aspects of stratification, such as gender, ethnicity, and age, interact with class.

4. While class is seen by some to have fragmented and to be less of an important influence on self-identity, class inequalities persist, as evidence of inequalities of income and wealth and mobility rates indicate. Equally, sociological studies of gender and mobility indicate considerable differences between men and women.

Chapter 13: Theory and methods

> **PREVIEW**
>
> You need to know:
> - the range of different theoretical approaches which sociologists adopt
> - the relationship between theory and method
> - sources of data and research methods
> - research practice and ethics
> - is sociology a science?
> - sociology, values and social policy.

Key sociological perspectives

Functionalism

Functionalism is a structural theory. Society must be seen as an interrelated system – each part plays a vital role in the success of the whole. This is often referred to as the organic analogy – society can be understood as broadly comparable to an organism. The system has certain essential needs – functional prerequisites – which must be met if the system is to survive. The basic functional prerequisites identified by Parsons are; adaptation, goal attainment, integration, and pattern maintenance.

Society depends on shared norms and values. There is value consensus. Society must maintain harmony and equilibrium, and shared norms and values allow this by integrating members of society around these shared norms. Social control is achieved through sanctions. Durkheim argues that socialisation teaches acceptance of society's moral order, such that people want to obey. Thus, force is not usually necessary.

Societies change in an evolutionary way. Parsons argued that societies would change from simple to more complex systems as they developed, improving their technology and control over their environment. As the social system changes, so the parts must also adapt to fit the needs of the system. Thus, the nuclear family, according to Parsons, best fits the needs of modern industrial society, as does a meritocratic educational system, which allows individuals to reach their maximum potential regardless of class, gender or ethnicity.

Robert Merton developed functionalism arguing that not all parts of the system may be functional – some may be dysfunctional, that is adverse in their effects upon the social system.

Functionalism's heyday was during the 1960s. More recently, sociologists such as Jeffrey Alexander and Niklas Luhmann have attempted to modify the theory. Alexander argues that it is still a useful theory, if it is used as a way of describing (not explaining) relations between social institutions and society. This may be achieved by using concepts of functional needs, but rejecting the notion that such needs will always be met.

Marxism

Marxism, like functionalism is a structural theory, but the key difference is that unlike functionalism, Marxism sees society as based on conflict rather than consensus. Marxists consider that society is best thought of as a system or structure. Marxists see society in terms of the base–superstructure model. The base is essentially the economic system of society – the means by which a society makes, provides, and distributes its goods necessary for survival. Marxists see the base as consisting of the means of production – the equipment used in economic production, and the relations of production. Relations of production refer to the social relationships between different groups of people that arise from the process of production. For example, capitalist production leads to relations of production between workers and employers, or the two classes which Marx terms proletariat and bourgeoisie.

Society is best understood as being formed on the basis of conflict, and particularly the conflict which arises from the ownership of private property. Marxists argue that all conflict is class conflict and reflects the basic clash of interests between bourgeoisie and proletariat, or owners and workers. Owners want to maximise profits; workers want to maximise their wage. In capitalist society, production is organised to maximise profit for capitalists not, as functionalism argues, to fulfil the needs of society.

Marxists see society as held together through coercion rather than consensus. Social control is exerted through ideology – the ideas of the dominant social classes (or ruling class). This is achieved through the superstructure, which consists of institutions such as the government, the education system, the media, religion, and the family. Marxists see the superstructure as inevitably reflecting the base of society. Thus, if the base of society is organised on a class basis, these divisions will be reflected throughout the rest of the structure.

Since the superstructure reflects the base, the system is continually reproduced. Key institutions such as the family, education, the media, and the family, function in such a way as to reproduce the class system. Social change arises when there are changes in the base which lead to contradictions in the system. Thus, feudalism declined as trade and commerce developed, leading to new relations of productions and new social groups (merchants and artisans). Feudal landowners and the system which went with them were no longer compatible with the newly developing system.

Interactionism

Interactionist theories focus on action rather than structure. There are a variety of interactionist theories including symbolic interactionism, ethnomethodology, and social action theory. Interactionist theories are micro-theories, studying social behaviour at the level of interactions between individuals, rather than structures.

Interactionists, such as Cooley, argued that the self-concept was a key influence in explaining human behaviour. A person's self-concept is influenced by the way others respond to them. The concepts of labelling and the self-fulfiling prophecy suggest that this influence can have very important consequences.

The symbolic interactionist Harold Blumer argued that people act on the basis of meanings, rather than structures. The task of sociology is, therefore, to research and understand the meanings which actors attach to their behaviour. Meanings are the product of social interaction between people, but they are continually being modified and vary depending upon the social context and, therefore, require interpretation.

Social order is the end product of shared meanings, and is not imposed by social structures. Social order is more flexible than structural views suggest and is the result of continual interpretation and negotiation.

Postmodernism

Postmodernism is a new theory. It is critical of 'grand theories' (or metanarratives), such as Marxism, functionalism, and feminism (modernist theories), seeing them as mistakenly claiming to be objective.

Postmodernist theory argues that modern society has undergone tremendous political, economic, social, and cultural change. One of the key effects of such change is that it is no longer possible for sociologists to use the key sociological category of class, since society is no longer organised around production. Society has changed from a modern society, characterised by modern insitutions such as the nation-state, to a postmodern society, where such institutions and the social structures which went with it (class, gender, and ethnicity) are fragmenting.

Of greater importance in contemporary society, where there are high levels of affluence, is consumption. Consumer culture is mostly influenced by the mass media and it is this that creates the most important social divisions in society today. It is also argued that there is increasing diversity and pluralism within the broad categories of gender and ethnicity.

The structure–action debate

Sociologists disagree as to whether structure is more important than action or vice versa. Anthony Giddens has argued that sociology requires a synthesis of structure and action. His theory of structuration is an attempt to provide such a synthesis. Giddens argues that people create structures through their everyday actions but that, once created, these structures constrain our individual lives, and may influence our action in unexpected ways.

CHECKLIST

- ✓ **Sociologists disagree over key issues, such as whether society is best seen in terms of conflict or consensus, structure or action. Sociological theories reflect these differences.**
- ✓ **Structural theories, such as Marxism or functionalism, are commonly criticised for being deterministic and neglecting to take seriously the view that people reflect and have reasons for acting as they do.**
- ✓ **Theories which focus on action, such as interactionism, are commonly criticised for voluntarism – the view that people can act freely and relatively unhindered by structural forces.**
- ✓ **Giddens' theory of structuration has been criticised (e.g. Craib, Layder) for being more biased towards action theory, and thus tending to voluntarism.**
- ✓ **Postmodernism offers a criticism of all sociological perspectives, but it too can be criticised. Postmodernists are critical of all 'grand theories', but postmodernism can also be seen as a grand theory and so, in this sense, it is contradictory. Sociologists are also critical of the relativism of postmodernism, which claims that since there can be no truth, there are no grounds for preferring any one theory over others.**

Theory and methods

> **FACTFILE**
> - Marxism and functionalism are structural theories, while interactionism (in its various forms) is an action theory.
> - Structural theories share the view that society can be seen as a structure, and the structure is seen as determining or shaping the way in which individuals act.
> - Action theories, in contrast, focus on the fact that people's actions are meaningful. Action theory attempts to uncover these meanings in order to explain social life.
> - Giddens' structuration theory suggests that *both* structure and action are needed to explain social phenomena adequately.

The relationship between theory and methods

Sociologists have a wide range of methods available to them, but the basic choice is between quantitative methods and qualitative methods:

- Quantitative methods tend to reflect a more scientific approach to sociology and will present tables and charts with statistical data as evidence of a piece of research.
- Qualitative methods tend to focus on the feelings and explanations which people offer for their behaviour.

Which method most appeals to a sociologist, tends to depend on their basic theoretical outlook. Structural sociologists tend to prefer quantitative methods, and interactionist sociologists to prefer qualitative methods. This, in turn, reflects a division between positivists and anti-positivists. Anti-positivists may also be referrred to as phenomenologists, or interpretivists. Positivists take the view that human actions are determined by external structural forces, and the task of sociology is to reveal these structures. This can be done using the rigorous and objective methods used in the natural sciences. Anti-positivists believe that the methods used in natural science are not appropriate for studying human social behaviour. People think and reflect upon their actions, and this means that qualitative methods which probe the reasons and motivations behind individuals' actions are more appropriate.

> **FACTFILE**
> - Positivist sociologists argue that sociology can aim to apply the methods of science to the study of society. Positivists, therefore, prefer quantitative methods, which enable rigorous testing and checking of findings.
> - Anti-positivists (also referred to as interpretivists or phenomenologists) argue that people are very different to objects in the natural world, since they have consciousness and they always act in certain ways for certain reasons. Anti-positivists, therefore, advocate qualitative methods, which enable sociologists to gain data that is valid and meaningful.

Sources of data and research methods

Primary and secondary data

Sociologists may use primary sources or secondary sources of data.

- Primary sources are those which have been collated by the researcher; they are first-hand evidence.
- Secondary sources are those which have not been produced by the researcher. They may include sources of information which were not created with the intention of providing evidence for research, e.g. letters or diaries.

Examples of primary sources

- surveys
- questionnaires
- content analysis
- longitudinal studies
- structured interviews
- panel studies
- experiments
- observation
- participant observation (P.O.)
- non-participant observation
- semi-structured interviews.

Examples of secondary sources

- official statistics
- diaries
- biographies
- autobiographies

- novels
- letters
- birth and marriage certificates
- photographs
- newspapers
- television and radio broadcasts
- government reports
- maps
- parish records.

Obtaining a sample

Sociologists using quantitative methods usually wish to obtain a statistically representative sample so that, when the results of the research are analysed, researchers can make valid generalisations to the wider population. The most frequently used terms and methods of sampling are:

- random
- systematic sampling
- quota sampling
- multistage sampling
- non-random sampling
- snowball sampling.

Random sampling

Random sampling has a specific technical meaning in sociological research. It means that each person or household (or some other relevant unit) in the sampling frame has an equal chance of being selected for the sample group. The sampling frame is a list of the relevant population from which a sample group will be taken. Researchers might use a variety of documents as a sampling frame, such as a school register, a doctor's list of patients, or other official documents, such as the electoral roll or the census. It would even be possible to use the telephone directory as a sampling frame.

In sociological research, the term 'population' refers to the group being studied and from which the sample is selected. For example, in a survey of sixth-form colleges in one town, the survey population would be all the pupils named in the registers of the colleges. From these, a target population would be selected.

To gain a random sample, the researcher would use a computer to pick out at random one-tenth (for example) of the names. Alternatively, to gain a systematic random sample from the sampling frame, the researcher could pick, for example, every tenth name. This would provide a sample a tenth of the magnitude of the sample frame.

Key methodological concepts

To ensure that sociological research is systematic and rigorous, sociologists use the key concepts of validity, reliability and representativeness. Any piece of research may be analysed in terms of these three key concepts, although sociologists may often disagree in their interpretation and evaluation of research findings for a variety of reasons. The terms may be defined as set out below.

Validity

Validity refers to whether research provides a true picture of social reality. Another way of expressing this is to say that research is valid if it measures what it is intended to measure. This points to the difficulty with ensuring validity; sociologists must take care to define (operationalise) what it is that they wish to study. There are many good examples of this issue; e.g. studies of the family must take care not to confuse the family with the household. Questions of validity are also raised by studies using official statistics, such as Durkheim's study of suicide, or crime statistics.

Reliability

Reliability refers to whether a piece of research may be repeated and the same results gathered. Many other studies may be able to repeat Durkheim's findings on suicide, but this does not mean that Durkheim's explanation is correct. Studies may be valid, but hard to replicate. Equally, they may be invalid and easily repeated.

Representativeness

This term refers to whether the findings of a sociological study are representative of the whole population or society. Sociologists wish to generalise from their findings and to be able to make valid statements about a society.

Hawthorne effect or interviewer effect

This is the term given to the way in which respondents' behaviour changes as a direct result of being observed or interviewed. Respondents, aware that they are being watched, depart from their usual behaviour.

Triangulation

Sociologist Ray Pawson argues that textbooks can sometimes suggest that something close to a state of 'methodological warfare' exists between sociological

Theory and methods

FACTFILE

- Sociology has now moved on from the debates between positivists and interpretivists.
- Postmodernists currently claim that truth is not attainable, while realists argue that sociology can systematically produce real knowledge about the social structures which influence our lives.

Science, values and social policy

Sociology emerged as an academic discipline in the nineteenth century. The founders of the subject believed that the scientific study of society would lead to improvements in society, enabling social problems such as poverty and crime to be reduced or even eliminated. This view of sociology suggests that sociology can be objective and scientific, and that the values of individual sociologists do not necessarily bias the results of research. It can also suggest that sociological research may lead to 'social engineering'; designing social policies in order to create a desired outcome, e.g. reducing crime, or reducing the number of single-parent families.

Classical Sociologists such as Marx and Durkheim clearly had strong values which fostered their interest in society and, indeed, directed them to focus on particular issues and questions, while neglecting others. Max Weber argued that while sociologists' choice of research topics and questions will always be influenced by values, it is possible for the researcher, having acknowledged this, to investigate in an objective manner.

In recent years, some sociologists have become more sceptical of the idea of objective sociological research with the implication that it can then be used to 'solve' social problems. Zygmunt Bauman suggests that, whereas sociologists used to be seen as 'legislators' or law-makers who had discovered the truth and could thus fix the parts of society which did not work properly, sociologists now ought to be seen as 'interpreters'. Interpreters offer different analyses of the nature of society and social problems, but they cannot make valid claims to have objective and absolute truth.

This reflects the idea that experts frequently disagree amongst themselves and, thus, the role of sociology is not to lay down laws, but rather to inform debate. Bauman sees this as more democratic, since it potentially allows the public to participate in debates about the nature of society, and the form of social policies required for particular social problems.

Sample question and answer

Evaluate the arguments for and against the view that sociology can be scientific.
(Adapted from AEB, 1999)

Arguments as to whether sociology can be scientific or not can be traced back to the discipline's origins in the nineteenth century and continue to the present day. Positivists take the view that sociology can be scientific, while interpretivists and phenomenologists (or anti-positivists) believe that the methods of the natural sciences are not appropriate to the study of human societies.

Positivists, such as Comte and Durkheim, argued that societies were governed by 'laws', in the same way that the natural world was governed by the laws of nature. They, thus, argued that sociology should aim to identify the causes and effects of social behaviour, and that it should do this by adopting the methods of the natural sciences. Positivists, thus, wish to see sociology adopt the hypothetico-deductive method, whereby theories are constructed and then experiments and tests are carried out to see whether the evidence gathered supports the hypothesis devised by the researcher.

Positivists would argue that such methods are sound and valid, since they provide rigorous testing procedures that are reliable and valid. Given such procedures, and providing that researchers ensure that they use representative samples, sociology can provide valid data and social scientists can make valid generalisations about the subject matter. For Positivists, scientific method (hypothesis testing) means that sociological research produces objective and rational knowledge, which is not influenced by the subjective opinions or values of researchers. Indeed, positivists argue that scientific knowledge represents the highest and most rational form of knowledge and that it is a universal form of knowledge, since it is not tied to any particular social interests. In other words, scientific knowledge is neutral and objective.

An example of positivist sociology would be Durkheim's study of suicide (although some would argue that Durkheim was a realist). Durkheim's study involved devising a hypothesis, operationalising his concepts by choosing appropriate indicators, and then gathering data. Durkheim argued that his results, which were quantified and therefore easy to check and re-test (reliable), supported his hypothesis. The philosopher Karl Popper argues that the deductive form of science is a very robust method of research, since scientists should attempt not to prove that their theories or hypotheses are correct, but rather to try and falsify (or disprove) them. If findings cannot be falsified, they can be taken as correct.

Despite these strong claims, interpretivists are highly critical of the positivist approach. They argue that the scientific method is

Theory and methods

Sample question and answer – *cont*

not appropriate to the study of humans and human society, since people, unlike for instance chemicals or matter, have consciousness and have reasons for acting as they do. This makes human beings much more complex to study in a systematic way, and indeed, they are liable to act differently in an 'unnatural situation' – such as when being interviewed or when answering a questionnaire.

In addition, interpretivists argue that positivists do not accurately portray the true character of scientific method. Far from being a neutral and objective method, scientists may be motivated by all sorts of interests in their research, such as the desire for professional glory, financial reward, or because of political beliefs and values. Scientists may claim that they can separate their personal values, but interpretivists would be sceptical of this claim, perhaps arguing that even the choice of what to research is motivated by values and interests. The philosopher Thomas Kuhn has argued that science is never neutral, and always reflects the norms and values of the society and the time which produces it. Kuhn argues that what he calls 'normal science' creates a paradigm or framework of assumptions, and that these constrain the development of science. Science changes when some key discovery forces the paradigm to be changed.

Positivists and interpretivists give opposing views to the question of whether sociology can be a science. However, the realists argue that both sides of this argument make useful points. Realists, such as Sayer and Bhaskar, argue that both sociology and science are concerned with the study of unobservable entities (e.g. class, sub-atomic particles, black holes) and both are concerned with explaining the causes of events. Sociology also aims to develop models of the underlying structures and processes which cause events in society, and to modify these models in the light of empirical research. In this sense, though, it can be argued that sociology is little different from science. Moreover, realists can concede that positivists exaggerate the objectivity and precision of 'science'. Science and sociology aim to be systematic and neither are capable of making entirely accurate predictions. As Sayer acknowledges, people are simply more difficult to study, since society can be seen as an open system, that is as something which is much harder for the researcher to gain control over.

In conclusion, it can be argued along realist lines that the differences between science and sociology are often exaggerated. Both science and sociology can be systematic and empirical, and in this sense they both have much in common.

TEST YOURSELF

Across
1. Research which measures what it is supposed to measure (8)
5. The key feminist concept (10)
6. Research findings which can be achieved repeatedly (11)
9. Functionalists say that society is based on this (9)
11. Marxist term for the working class (11)
13. Interactionists say that roles are the result of this (11)
14. Functionalists use this analogy (7)
16. Interactionists say that structural theories neglect this aspect of social behaviour (7)
17. Marxism and functionalism are criticised for this (11)
18. Marxist theory is often criticised for this (8, 12)
20. A way of combining different methods (13)
21. A theory which focuses on nature rather than nurture (12)

Down
2. Interactionist theory stresses the importance of this (6)
3. Marxist and functionalist theory both focus on this (9)
4. Marx argues that people are thrown into relations of ... (10)
7. Marxist term for capitalists (11)
8. Feminists say that mainstream theory should be renamed like this ... (10)
10. A form of interactionist theory which examines the methods people use to make sense of society (16)
12. Using a good sample will ensure that your study is ... (14)
15. Something which critics say interactionism neglects (5)
19. Theory based on class conflict (7)

Solution on page 125

Theory and methods

CHECKLIST

✓ Methodological concepts should also be used frequently and should be relevant to many answers. Make sure that you use terms accurately, e.g. do not confuse validity and reliability.

✓ Apply contemporary theories and concepts such as postmodernism and globalisation to your answers, although be sure to be relevant. Postmodernist ideas can be a useful way to round off an answer, since they give a perspective from which to criticise other sociological perspectives and bring the topic up to date.

✓ These theories can be evaluated by contrasting and comparing them to each other. You can improve your evaluation by trying not to make theories sound too simple when criticising them. It is a good strategy in evaluating to try and find positive and negative points in theories or concepts, whether you are generally in favour of them or not.

Summary

1. Sociological theories can be categorised in various ways. Marxism and functionalism are structural theories, whereas interactionism is an action theory. One can also distinguish between conflict (Marxism) and consensus (functionalism) theories. More recently, postmodernists have made a distinction between modernist theories (Marxism, functionalism, interactionism) and postmodernist theory.

2. A key debate in sociology is that between structure and action theories. Anthony Giddens' structuration theory suggests that this debate can be resolved by seeing structure and action as two sides of the same coin. Comments on the structure–action debate can be a good way to introduce or conclude your essays, and provide a strong theoretical framework to base your answers around.

3. Structural theories tend to be inclined towards positivism and, therefore, use quantitative methods, while action theories are usually associated with interpretivism (anti-positivism) and, therefore, with qualitative methods. However, students will be rewarded if they can show that this separation can oversimplify. Many sociologists now triangulate, recognising advantages and disadvantages of both methodologies, and many would be critical of an over-simplistic portrayal of two methodologies.

4. Positivists have seen sociology as a science, while interpretivists have argued that the study of sociology cannot be scientific. More recent views, however, such as those of realists and postmodernists are also important in this debate, and students will benefit if they can demonstrate a knowledge and understanding of these theories, and show how they have contributed to this old debate.

Solutions to crosswords and wordhunts

Crosswords

Chapter 1

Chapter 8

Chapter 3

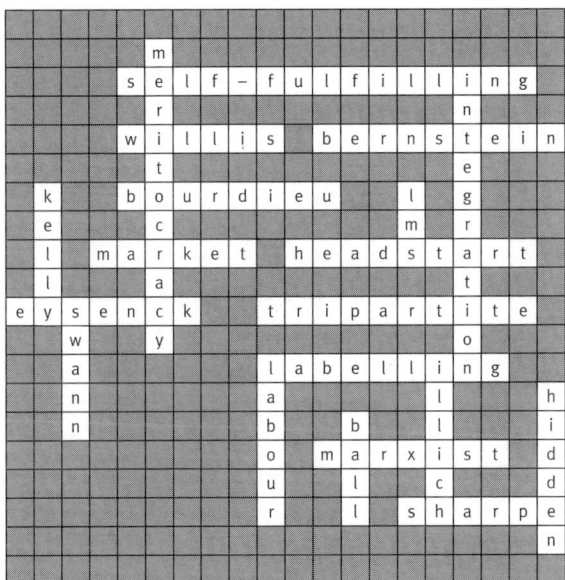

Chapter 10

Chapter 5

Chapter 13

Solutions to crosswords and wordhunts

Wordhunts

Words may be concealed diagonally, vertically, horizontally, or printed in reverse.

Chapter 2: cultural capital, folk, subculture, Frankfurt School, Baudrillard, Mort, Nixon, CCCS, cultural deprivation, globalisation, hybridity, consumerism, labelling, commodification, Hall.

Chapter 4: Townsend, relative, absolute, Piachaud, income, poverty line, universal, underclass, Beveridge, means test, Murray, index, dependency, targetting, social fund.

Chapter 6: alienation, deskilling, informal economy, anomie, rationalisation, Hakim, Taylorism, human relations, Braverman, post-Fordism, Fordism, flexibility, Blauner, leisure, extension pattern, kaizen.

Chapter 7: dealignment, partisanship, zero sum, power, pluralism, psephology, deferential, volatility, Lukes, state, totalitarian, democracy, hegemony, Poulantzas, elites, NSMs, pressure groups, globalisation.

Chapter 9: bilateral aid, GNP, Brandt Commission, Tiger economies, Rostow, dependency theory, satellite, metropolis, Wallerstein, core, periphery, globalisation, TNCs, SAPs, debt boomerang, monoculture, Illich, Freire.

Chapter 11: mortality rate, sick role, commodification, Oakely, artefact, structural, discourse, Foucault, Tudor-Hart, inverse care law, Goffman, Parsons, Gough, Doyal and Pennell, illness iceberg.

Chapter 12: meritocratic, class conflict, Weber, patriarchy, reserve army, Marx, status, bourgeoisie, proletariat, ownership, occupation, lifechances, embourgeoisement, underclass, post-Fordism, mobility.

Index

absolute mobility 113
absolute poverty 34
action theories *see* interactionism
active audience theories of the media 46
advertising, portrayal of women in 18
affluent worker study 15, 54, 57, 110
age, social construction of 8
Anderson, Michael 5
anti-positivists 118, 121, 124

Bauman, Zygmunt 122
Becker, Howard 89, 94, 95, 96
Beveridge Report/Plan 8, 36
bilateral aid 81
biological perspectives
  on crime 89
  on health differences 101
Bourdieu, Pierre 17
bureaucracy, Weber's theory of 53

Chester, Robert 5
Child Support Agency (CSA) 8
childbirth, medicalisation of 100, 102
childhood, construction of 8
Church of England, membership and clerics 73
Clark, David 3
class
  changes in the class structure 106, 110–12
  and crime 90, 94, 95
  and culture 15, 16–17, 20
  defining 106
  and educational attainment 17, 22, 24–5, 26
  and families 5
  and health differences 101, 102, 104, 105
  and infant mortality rates 101
  and life expectancy 101
  and the mass media 41, 42, 49
  measuring social class 108–9
  and new social movements 65
  and stress 97, 98
  underclass 33, 34, 111–12, 114
  and voting behaviour 61, 62, 66–7, 68, 69
  and the welfare state 38–9
  see also working class
colonialism 80, 84, 87
'community care' policies 36, 103
comprehensive education 28
conjugal roles in families 7
constant sum view of power 62
consumer voting theories 66
consumption 117
  and class 111
  and culture 13–15, 17
  household 11
control theory of crime 92
Cooper, David 3
crime
  defining 88, 89
  and ethical issues in research 121

and ethnicity 93–4, 96
explanations of 89–92, 94–5
and gender 88, 89, 92–3, 96
self-report studies of 91
statistics 88, 91, 96
victim studies of 91
see also deviance
critical views of the family 3
cults 73
cultural effects theory of the media 46, 47
culture 11–20
  and class 15, 16–17, 20
  defining 11, 12
  and ethnicity 18
  and gender 17–18
  and health differences 102
  and news values 44
  production and consumption of 13–15
  theories of identity and 12–13
  types of 11–12
  see also subcultures
culture of poverty 32–3, 34
curriculum 26, 28
cyclical unemployment 58

decision-making 62, 64–5
deindustrialisation 56
democracy 63
denominations 72–3
dependency culture 33, 34, 64, 111
dependency theory of underdevelopment 80–1, 81, 84, 85, 87
deskilling 56
development
  aid and strategies for 81–2
  defining 79–80
  and education 85
  and gender 85
  and health 84–5
  industrialisation and urbanisation 83–4
  theories of 80–1
deviance
  explanations of 89–91
  societal and situational 88–9
  see also crime
deviance amplification 48
differentiation 106
direct democracy 63
division of labour, international 81, 86
divorce 6–7
dual sector economies 84
Durkheim, E. 12, 21, 53, 63, 89, 116, 122
  and religion 70, 71, 76, 78

Earth Summit (1992) 82
education 21–30
  banding in schools 22–3, 25
  and development 85
  differences in attainment 24–8

and class 22, 24–5, 26
and ethnicity 27, 28
and gender 26–7, 28
school factors 25–6, 27, 28
exclusions from schools 29
policies 28–9
sociological perspectives on 21–4
and stratification 106
Education Act (1944) 28
Education Reform Act (1988) 28
elite pluralism 63, 64
embourgeoisement 110, 112
emotion work 8
Engels, Friedrich 2
Esping-Andersen, Gosta 38, 40
ethical issues in research 121
ethnicity
  and crime 93–4, 96
  and culture 18
  and educational attainment 27, 28
  and the family 5, 6
  and health differences 102
  and the media 49
  and stratification 108, 109–10
  and wealth 31
export-orientated industrialisation (EOI) 83
extended families 1, 5

families 1–10
  changing gender roles and power relationships 7–8, 9
  and class 5
  defining 1
  diversity of 2, 5, 6
  and divorce 6–7
  ethnic minority 5, 6
  and households 1–2
  and industrialisation 4–5
  single-parent 5–6, 32
  and social policy 8
  theories of 2–4
  typical neo-conventional 5
feminism
  and crime 90
  and culture 13, 16, 17
  and the distribution of wealth 32
  and domestic labour 52
  and education 23, 26
  and the family 3, 4
  and health and illness 99–100, 102
  Marxist-feminism 3, 6–7
  and the mass media 42
  and poverty 33, 34, 38
  and stratification 107, 108, 110
  and the welfare state 38
  and work 53, 54
  and leisure 59
fertility rates 79
folk culture 12
Foucault, Michel 72, 100, 104
Frank, André 80–1
frictional unemployment 58
functionalist theory 116, 117, 118, 124

Index

and crime 89, 90, 91, 93, 94–5
and culture 12, 14, 16, 17
and the distribution of wealth 31–2
and education 21, 22, 23
and the family 2, 3, 4
and health and illness 98–9, 100
and the mass media 41
and power 62, 63
and religion 70–1, 72, 73, 74, 76
and stratification 106, 108
  inequalities in the labour market 109
and the welfare state 37
and work 53, 55

gender
  changing gender relations in families 7–8
  and crime 88, 89, 92–3, 96
  and culture 17–18
  and development 85
  and educational attainment 26–7, 28
  and health and illness 101, 102
  and mental illness 103
  and mobility 113
  and occupation 52, 53
  and stratification 108, 109–10
  and stress 97, 98
  and voting behaviour 61, 62
  see also men; women
General Agreement on Tariffs and Trade (GATT) 82
genetic explanations of health differences 101
Giddens, Anthony 6, 7–8, 9, 70, 74, 111, 112, 117, 124
Gilroy, Paul 94
globalisation
  and culture 18, 20
  decision-making and the nation-state 65
  and development 81, 84
  and the mass media 51
  and religion 72
  of work 54, 55
Gramsci, Antonio 42, 50
gross national product (GNP) 79

Hall, Stuart 85
  Policing the Crisis 48, 49, 93–4
Hawthorne effect 119
health 97–105
  defining 97–8
  and development 84–5
  indicators of 98
  social differences in 101–2
  and social policy 97
  theoretical approaches to 98–101
  see also illness
hidden curriculum 26
high culture 11, 13, 15
households
  with consumer durables 11

defining 1–2
size of 1, 2, 6
human relations theory 54, 55
hypodermic ('magic bullet') model of the media 42, 45, 47

identity
  defining 11
  theories of culture and 12–13
illness
  defining 97–8
  'iceberg' 98, 105
  mental illness 3, 99, 103–4
  theoretical approaches to 98–101
  see also health
import-substitution industrialisation (ISI) 83
industrial sabotage 56
industrialisation
  in developing countries 83
  and the family 4–5
  and functionalist theories of work 53
infant mortality rates (IMRs) 79, 85, 98, 101, 102
information technology 57
interactionism 117, 118, 124
  and crime 90, 95
  and educational attainment 22, 23, 30
  and the family 3, 4
  and health and illness 99, 100
intergenerational mobility 113
international division of labour 81, 86
International Monetary Fund (IMF) 82
interpretivism 118, 121, 122–3, 124
intragenerational mobility 113
IQ, and educational attainment 24

Laing, Ronald 3, 103
Laslett, Peter 5
legal–rational authority 61
leisure, work and 58–9
liberal view, of inequalities in the labour market 109, 110
life expectancy 79, 101
literacy, and development 85
low culture 11–12
Luhmann, Niklas 116

marriage 3, 6–7
Marx, Karl 122
Marxist theory 116–17, 118, 124
  and crime 89–90, 91, 93, 95
  and culture 12–13, 13–14, 15, 17, 19
    youth subcultures 16
  and development 80
  and the distribution of wealth 32
  and divorce 6
  and education 22, 23
  and the family 2–3, 4
  and health and illness 99, 100, 104
  and international aid 82
  and leisure 59

and the mass media 41–2, 42–3, 45, 50, 68
  instrumentalism 41, 42–3, 50
  structuralism 42, 50
and poverty 33–4
and power 63, 64
and religion 71, 72, 74
and stratification 107, 108, 111
  inequalities in the labour market 109, 110
and unemployment 58
and the welfare state 37
and work 53, 55
Marxist-feminism 3, 6–7
mass culture 12
mass media 41–51, 117
  and crime 93–4
  influence of the 45–7
  manufacture and presentation of news 44–5, 51
  ownership and control 42–3, 50
  politics and voting behaviour 67–8, 69
  stereotyping 48–9, 93–4
  theories of the 41–2, 51
  and violence 47–8, 51
Mayo, Elton 54
media see mass media
men
  and masculinity 15, 17–18, 20
  and mobility 113
mental illness 3, 99, 103–4
Merton, Robert 89, 90, 94, 116
middle class, and changes in the class structure 110, 111, 112
modernisation theory 80, 81, 87
moral panics 48, 94
morbidity rates 98, 102
mortality rates 98
multilateral aid 81
Murdock, George 1, 2, 43, 50
Murray, Charles 92, 111–12

National Curriculum 28
National Health Service (NHS) 99, 102–3
nationalism 70, 71, 78
neo-Fordism 56
neo-Marxism, and dependency theory 80–1
New Labour, education policies 29
New Left realism, and crime 92, 94, 95
new religious movements (NRMs) 73, 74–5, 76
New Right views
  on crime 92
  on the distribution of wealth 32
  on education 24
  on health and illness 100, 103
  on international aid 82
  on poverty 33
  on the role of the state 64
  on stratification 107
  on unemployment 58
  and the welfare state 37–8

Index

new social movements 64, 65, 69
New Vocationalism 28
newly industrialised countries (NICs) 83
nuclear families 1, 2, 4–5, 8

Oakley, Ann 7, 9, 100, 102
occupational classification schemes 108–9
oligarchy 63

Parsons, Talcott 2, 5, 12, 21, 37, 62, 116
  and religion 71, 73, 76
  and the sick role 98–9
phenomenology 118
  approach to religion 71–2
pluralism
  and cultural production 14
  and the mass media 41, 43, 50
  and power 62–3, 63–4, 68
  and work 55
politics
  and decision-making 62, 64–5
  and the mass media 67–8, 69
  and political systems 63
  see also power; voting behaviour
popular culture 12, 13, 15
population 79, 83–4
positivism 118, 121, 122, 123, 124
post-Fordism 56, 111
postmodernism 117, 121, 122, 124
  and crime 92
  and culture 13, 14, 15, 18, 20
    youth subcultures 16
  and education 24
  and the family 4, 9
  and health and illness 100
  and the mass media 42, 51, 68
  and religion 72
  and stratification 107–8, 111
  and work and leisure 59
poverty 34–40
  defining and measuring 34–6
  feminisation of 38
  sociological explanations of 32–3
  and taxation 39
  welfare and social policy 36–9
power 61–5
  defining 61–2
  in family relationships 7
  and health and illness 100, 104
  and the role of the state 63–4, 68
  sociological theories of 62–3
  see also politics
pressure groups 65
primary data 118
proletarianisation 110–11, 112
psychological perspectives on crime 89, 90

qualitative sociological methods 118, 120
quantitative sociological methods 118, 120, 124

racism 18, 27, 28, 101, 102
radical psychiatrists and the family 3, 4
random sampling 119
rational choice theory 66
realism 121, 122, 123
reconstituted families 1
relative mobility 113
relative poverty 34, 35
religion 70–8
  and church membership 70, 71, 75, 76
  churches and ecclesia 72
  defining 70, 78
  organisation of 72–3
  and secularisation 70, 74–7, 78
  and social change 73–4
  theories of 70–2
representative democracy 63
research
  ethical issues 121
  methodology 118–20
  practical problems 120–1
  validity, reliability and representativeness 119, 120
Rostow, W.W. 80
Rowntree surveys on poverty 35

sampling methods 119
satellite television 59
science
  sociology as a 121–2, 122–3, 124
  values and social policy 122
scientific management 54, 55
secondary data 118–19
sects 73
secularisation 70, 74–7, 78
semiology 46
single-parent families 5–6, 32
single-person households 2, 6
situational constraints, and poverty 33, 34
social action theory 13, 53–4, 71, 72
social class see class
social democracy 23, 33, 38
social mobility 113, 114
socialisation, and class cultures 17
sociobiology 12
statistics
  evaluating official 120
  and health differences 101
stratification 106–15
  defining 106
  and social mobility 113, 114
  theories of 106–8
  see also class
stress 97, 98, 102
Structural Adjustment Plans (SAPs) 82
structural theories see functionalist theory; Marxist theory
structural unemployment 58
structure–action debate 117–18, 124
subcultural theories of crime 90, 91, 93, 95

subcultures
  school 23
  youth 8, 15–16, 48
suicide, and gender 103

Taylor, F.W. 54
technical change, effects on work 56–7
television 42, 59
Tiger economies of South-East Asia 80
totalitarianism 63
Townsend, Peter 35, 38
training, and New Vocationalism 28
trans-national corporations (TNCs) 65, 81, 84, 85
triangulation 119–20, 124
two-step flow model of the media 46, 47

underclass 33, 34, 111–12, 114
underdevelopment 79–80, 80–1
  see also development
unemployment 7, 57–8, 112
United Nations (UN) 81, 82
urbanisation in developing countries 83–4
uses and gratifications model of the media 46, 47

variable sum view of power 62
Veblen, Thorstein 15
violence, media effects and 47–8, 51
voting behaviour 61, 62, 66–7, 68, 69
  and the mass media 41–2

Wallerstein, Immanuel 81
wealth
  defining 31
  distribution of 31–2
  and ethnicity 31
Weber, Max 122
  The Protestant Ethic and the Spirit of Capitalism 74
Weberian theory
  and the distribution of wealth 32
  and poverty 33
  and power 61
  and religion 71, 74
  and stratification 107, 108, 110
  and work 53–4
welfare state 33, 36–9, 40, 64
women
  in advertisements 18
  and crime 88, 92–3
  and cultural identity 17, 20
  in developing countries 85
  and divorce 6
  employment of 5, 107
  and the family 7, 8, 9
  and health and illness 102
  in the mass media 42, 48–9
  and mobility 113
  and poverty 33
  see also feminism; gender

Index

work 52–7
    conflict and co-operation at 55–6
    defining 52
    and domestic labour 52
    flexible working 59
    gender and occupation 52, 53
    inequalities in the labour market 109–10
    and leisure 58–9
    and occupational classification schemes 108–9
    and technical change 56–7
    theories of 52–5
working class
    affluent worker study 15, 54, 57, 110
    and changes in the class structure 110–11, 112
    and educational attainment 17, 25
    mobility 113
World Bank 82
world systems theory 81

young offenders, and media violence 47
Young and Willmott 5, 7, 9
youth cultures/subcultures 8, 15–16, 48

Notes

Notes